THE IROQUOIS AND THE FOUNDING
OF THE AMERICAN NATION

THE IROQUOIS
AND THE FOUNDING
OF THE AMERICAN NATION

Donald A. Grinde, Jr.

Illustrations by Peter Jemison

III

CONTENTS

THE AUTHOR

Dr. Donald Andrew Grinde, Jr. received his Bachelor's degree in history at Georgia Southern College; his Master's degree in history at the University of Delaware; and his Doctoral degree in history at the University of Delaware in 1973, graduating with honors in English and history (Magna Cum Laude)

His areas of specialization include American economic and technological history, history of the American Indian, and archives and museology.

Born in 1946 in Savannah, Georgia, Dr. Grinde is of Yamasee descent. This tribe was historically one of the foremost groupings in the southeastern area in the Colonial period. Their territory lay in what is now coastal and southeastern Georgia.

He was an assistant professor of history and museology at State University of New York, College at Buffalo, from 1973 to 1977. His articles have appeared in such scholarly publications as the *Western Pennsylvania Historical Magazine*, the *Journal of Erie Studies*, *Pennsylvania History*, and *The Indian Historian*.

ACKNOWLEDGEMENTS

THERE ARE MANY TO WHOM I OWE a debt of gratitude as a result of my research for this book. The work of William N. Fenton, William T. Hagan, Anthony F. C. Wallace, Barbara Graymont and Wilbur R. Jacobs gave me guidance. But I am particuarly indebted to my many Iroquois friends for their patience in helping me gain an understanding of the League of the Iroquois. I can only hope that I have done justice to the history of this remarkable people in this work.

In writing such a book, one is fully aware that translating the oral traditions and customs of a tribal society into the written word is, at best, an imperfect exercise. But the author felt that such an attempt was worth risking to correct the misconceptions about the founding of the American Nation.

To those who gave help, patience, and understanding, my heartfelt thanks. To name only a few such people: Professors Eric Brunger and John Aiken of the State University of New York, College at Buffalo, gave me help when needed. James Reilly, attorney for the Seneca Nation's claims case, offered the fruit of his legal research. The Seneca Claims Commission Papers in the E. H. Butler Library at the State University of New York, College at Buffalo, is perhaps the most comprehensive collection of Iroquois documents in the country. For more than twenty years, James Reilly and others collected data on the Iroquois from every foreign, federal, state and private source available to them. Virtually every treaty, diary, memoir and treatise on the Iroquois exists in duplicate form in the Seneca Nation Claims Papers. I have had a rare opportunity, in the past few years, to discuss this material with the many Iroquois people who have used it. Their help has given me the insight for understanding this unique people.

I owe a great deal to my family and colleagues for their patience and understanding. Sister Martin Joseph Jones, archivist at the Butler Library, graciously allowed me to freely examine their collection. E. A. Renning, assistant professor of geography at the State University of New York, College at Buffalo, produced the maps for this book. My typist, Patricia Bourassa Morin, was most helpful. Several library staffs were liberal with their time and patience, especially the Buffalo and Erie County Historical Society and the Lockwood Library at the State University of New York at Buffalo. Peter Jemison, the artist, has my thanks for his translation of Iroquois symbols into graphic form.

Donald A. Grinde, Jr.
Dewey Beach, Delaware
April 2, 1977

PREFACE

THERE IS AN INCREASING CONSCIOUSNESS IN AMERICAN society of the need to examine the history of American Indians. This interest is a product of the realization that Native Americans played a crucial and sustained role in the history of the United States. However, most of the current research has had implied negative connotations, if not outright misrepresentations. Frontier history, military history, and ethnohistory have generally stressed the "white man's burden" in fighting or civilizing Indian people (although the first step to civilization was either enslavement or extermination). Studies of Indian-white relations chronicle the treaty and landgrabbing era, with little sensitivity to the subtleties of Native American culture. The reader gains little or no appreciation for the Indian point of view or the rationale for his policies and behavior.

The very nature of the sources often prejudices such works from the start. Generally, white accounts of Indians were a mixture of bewilderment, curiosity, and ignorance. Implicit in these sources is the assumption that Indians were an impediment to the progress and development of the American Nation. The result has been a gross misperception of the Native American, his culture, and his positive contributions to the development of American society.

When Europeans first met the civilizations of the American Indian, it was at once a freeing but a perplexing experience. Montesquieu, Locke and Rousseau wrote about the noble savage (or "natural man") in glowing terms. Paradoxically, the whites who came to America sought to subdue, enslave, or exterminate this free and natural society, primarily for economic gain. Religious conversion and education were secondary motives in Indian-white relations, but these

IX

policies still sought to change the Indian into the spiritual and intellectual reflection of European values. The result was alienation, conflict, and war between the two cultures. These actions were in themselves a process of education for both American Indians and whites.

Most scholars have assumed that the educational process was lopsided in favor of the technologically advanced society of Europe. But is a society with superior tools for productive as well as destructive ends necessarily better in the spiritual, social and economic realms? The author thinks not.

Material satisfaction has not spawned any significant and sustained religion, but has chosen to buttress and refine a religion originally from the Middle East—Christianity. Political freedom has been a matter of convenience in the history of Western civilization, as well as in the limited experience of the Twentieth Century. The economy of the West has fueled the remarkable material progress of European culture, but until only a few years ago this progress has been accompanied by mindless disregard of its ravages upon the earth. Essentially, the experience of Western civilization has been as checkered with the good and the bad as that of any other society.

All this is not to say that European society is worthless, nor can one assert that Native American society is without its problems. Basically, the author is trying to cast off the arrogance of Western civilization in order to eliminate the idea of a superior culture. Once this superiority is repudiated, perhaps serious studies of societies and cultures in conflict can be done on the relative merits of each case.

The most notable attempt to study the American frontier and evaluate the impact of Indian-white interaction was done by Frederick Jackson Turner. Although Turner made some salutary observations about the influence of Indian people upon the American frontiersmen, his analysis tended to be environmental rather than philosophical as to Indian contributions. Turner admitted that:

> The wilderness masters the colonist. It finds him a European in dress, industries, tools, and modes of travel, and thought. It takes him from railroad car and puts him in the birch canoe. It strips off the garments of civilization and arrays him in the hunting shirt and the moccasins. It puts him in the log cabin of the Cherokee and the Iroquois and runs an Indian palisade around him. Before long he has gone to planting Indian corn and plowing with a sharp stick . . . In short, at the frontier the environment is at first too strong for the man. He must accept the conditions which it furnishes, or perish, and so fits himself into the Indian clearings and follows the Indian trails. Little by little he transforms the wilderness, but the outcome is not the

old Europe . . . The fact is, that here is a new product that is America.[1]

Eyewitness accounts substantiate and broaden this view. A traveler of the times said:

> The Swedes themselves were accused of being already half Indians when the English arrived in the year 1682. And we still see that the French, English, Germans, Dutch, and other Europeans, who have lived for several years in distant provinces, near and among the Indians, grow so like them in their behaviour and thought that they can only be distinguished by the difference in their color.[2]

In many ways the early accounts of Indian-white interaction stress Indian modes of thought and behavior among Europeans as well as their adoption of Native American material culture. Too often, these psychological observations become obscured in the analysis of Indian agricultural and medicinal contributions. The realm of Indian ideas and their influence upon Europeans may be an elusive topic, but the evidence demands that the historian study it carefully.

However, American historians such as Turner have tended to overlook Indian intellectual contributions; they viewed the frontier as the triumphant evolution of a superior white society over the inferior Indian society.[3] This assumption has racist overtones, because it assumes that the expansion of the white frontier is a positive act and ignores the Indian side of the story. Turner was a child of his times, and he inherited certain cultural values. Another, perhaps greater problem, involves methodology. Can a scholar study the development of the American continent without examining circumstances on both sides of the frontier? Common sense, justice, and the historical method demand that both sides of the story be told. However, textbooks and scholarly works on the frontier still deal with the Indian viewpoint in miniscule or condescending terms. There has been no balance, or semblance of impartiality, in studying the American frontier. The ghost of Turner returns to haunt us when one hears such statements as "Indian history is an unorthodox or esoteric subject." The incongruities of these assumptions need to be pointed out.

This study of the Iroquois in the formation of the United States seeks to strike a more equitable balance in the analysis of two cultures interacting on various levels. The American colonists had deep roots in the European cultures they had left in the Old World. The English Parliament served as a beacon of political freedom and representative government for the colonists and those subjected to the domination of the more autocratic regimes of the Continent. Most of the colonial governments were reflections, to a greater or lesser degree, of the parliamentary system. But the white colonists rebelled against the imperfections and inequities in that system as it was applied to America.

The period dating from the Albany Congress in 1754, to the year 1775, is one in which the critique of the colonial system, by widely different classes and colonies, intensified. Men like Benjamin Franklin and Thomas Jefferson began to look about for ways to change the structure of the colonies, and to unite them. These men turned not only to Plato, Locke and Rousseau, but also to the Iroquois and other Indian peoples, for aid and encouragement in the political, military, and economic spheres of human endeavor.

This work is an attempt to chronicle the role of the Iroquois in forming a part of the political basis for the new American nation. The Iroquois Confederacy, based in New York State, was the most powerful Indian group in Eastern North America. From the earliest colonial contacts, the Iroquois were a force that could not be ignored by any white government, Dutch, French, or English. The Confederacy provided security for the Iroquois within its own boundaries; and outside their land base they constituted a formidable adversary. By the early Eighteenth Century, the Iroquois had strengthened themselves by bringing in the Tuscarora from the Carolinas. Moreoever, their strategic geographic location on important water routes northward and westward further strengthened their military position.

The basis for Iroquois strength lay in the cultural foundations of the people. The Longhouse, with its conception of the kinship state, was the spiritual core of the Confederacy's secular aspects. This legacy of Confederation and the way it functioned had a profound effect upon the minds of many Americans. To uncover the degree of impact and the extent of influence of these Iroquois concepts upon the American people two hundred years ago is the theme of this book.

Such a voyage into uncharted waters is fraught with pitfalls as well as new insights. Few Indians in the Colonial and Revolutionary periods were literate in the English or other European tongues. Mary Brant, Joseph Brant, David Hill and John Deserontyon were Iroquois figures of note who did carry on correspondence. Blacksnake and Cornplanter collaborated with whites to compile brief memoirs. Wampum belts form a large reservoir of evidence concerning the political and religious ideas of the Iroquois. These belts, when interpreted by one steeped in Iroquois tradition, can clarify some of the ambiguities in Iroquois traditions and their relationship with the Europeans. They are historic documents in their own right.

Since the Indians had a society based on oral records, one should also bear in mind that the majority of American colonists could not read or write. One might then ask how the vast number of illiterate colonists knew of democracy since they had no exposure to Plato, Aristotle or John Locke. Perhaps these unread people drew their values in considerable part from the Indian people whom they saw functioning around them. Certainly the white colonists readily used the crops, clothing, and language of the American Indian to cope with the environment. One has the right to believe that they observed the freedom and democracy existing in Indian society as well.

REFERENCES

1. Frederick Jackson Turner, *The Frontier in American History* (New York, 1958), p. 4.

2. Adolph Benson, ed., *Peter Kalms Travels in North America* (New York, 1938), I, 226.

3. Turner, *Frontier,* pp. 14-15.

SYMBOLISM
OF THE IROQUOIS
The Illustrations

THE COVER: EAGLE AND HIAWATHA BELT. The eagle is a vigilant friend of the Longhouse people when it is perched atop the Great Tree of Peace. The Hiawatha Belt reminds the Iroquois of the Great Peace which united the Confederacy.

CHAPTER ONE: TURTLE ISLAND. In the beginning, there was turtle island (the Iroquois term for America), the Sun, and vegetables like corn, beans and squash. The elm bark longhouse symbolizes kinship and the Confederacy.

CHAPTER TWO: GUS-TO-WEH. The traditional headdress. The deer antlers symbolize a chief. The rattle is to indicate the beginning of trade with the Europeans since it is made from the horn of a cow.

CHAPTER THREE: BEAR COMB AND TREE OF PEACE. The Iroquois and the colonists were rivals from the beginning of contact. The Great Tree of Peace, with the buried war club, symbolizes the generally peaceful attitude of the Confederacy in spite of the rivalry.

CHAPTER FOUR: GUS-TO-WEH WITH BROKEN ANTLER. The broken antler represents the loss of certain Iroquois chiefs because they chose the path of war for personal gain.

CHAPTER FIVE: WAMPUM, CROSS, GUS-TO-WEH WITH ANTLER AND MUSKET. This array of objects symbolizes the tension and conflict that came with the arrival of Christianity and European technology. Ultimately, these factors would weaken the effectiveness of Iroquois unity during the American Revolution.

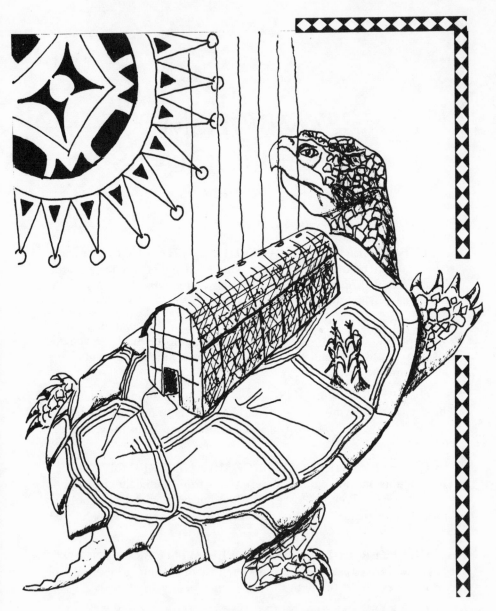

TURTLE ISLAND. In the beginning, there was turtle island (the Iroquois term for America), the Sun, and vegetables like corn, beans and squash. The elm bark longhouse symbolizes kinship and the Confederacy.

Chapter One

THE BACKGROUND
The Iroquois United Nations

THE GANONSYONI, OR PEOPLE OF THE LONGHOUSE, are of the Iroquoian linguistic grouping. The Five Nations (Mohawk, Oneida, Onondaga, Cayuga, and Seneca) formed a Confederacy whose antecedents are shrouded in the mists of prehistory. In the early Eighteenth Century, these nations were joined by a sixth brother to the south, the Tuscarora, who came to live in New York after being forced out of North Carolina through settler pressure and war. Thus, the Five Nations of the Confederacy became the Six Nations, around 1735.[1]

The Iroquois Confederacy was basically a kinship state. It was, and is, a collection of Indian nations bound together by a clan and chieftain system buttressed by a similar linguistic base. But there is much more that strengthens the League of the Iroquois. In their political life, women played a special and profound role. The structure of the Confederacy originated in the "hearth," which consisted of a mother and all her children. Each hearth was part of a wider group called an otiianer.* Two or more otiianers constituted a clan. This matrilineal system was headed by a "mother." All the sons and daughters of a particular clan were connected by uterine families that often lived far apart. Thus, a husband went to live with his wife's family, and his children became members of the mother's clan by right of birth.[2] By uniting all the descendants in the female line of a particular woman, the Iroquois formed cohesive political groups that had little to do with where people lived or what village the hearths originated from.

The oldest daughter of the head of an otiianer usually succeeded her mother at her death. All authority sprang from the otiianers and the various clans making up a nation. The women who headed these groups appointed the male delegates and deputies who spoke for the otiianers and clans at tribal councils. In consultation with other women within these groups, the women formulated issues and questions to be debated and acted upon in the councils.[3] These women recommended to their male spokesmen what view to express and advocate.

The philosophy of the Iroquois was based on the concept that all life is unified spiritually with the natural environment and other forces surrounding the people. These forces had both good and bad aspects, and could be intangible such as hunger, illness, and the dangers of war.[4] The power to deal with these forces came from an inner spiritual force existing in every person. The spiritual power of only one individual was limited, but when combined with the other individuals of the hearth, otiianer, or clan, the spiritual power became strong. Similarly, whenever a person died either by disease or force, through murder or war, the "public" power was reduced. To maintain the strength of the group, the dead were replaced either by natural increase or, in the event of war, by adopting captives of war. This practice of keeping the clans at full strength through natural increase or adoption insured the power and durability of the matrilineal system as well as the kinship state.

The Iroquois believed in the Master of Life, the first being on earth, who directed men to live in peace and love. He was opposed, however, by an evil brother who influenced people to stray from this ideal. The Master, Teharonhiawagon, promised to send an ambassador to help fight evil when the need arose. Before the coming of Hiawatha, the Iroquois were constantly warring over hunting and fishing rights, as well as over tribal territories. Even among the Five Nations, there was petty conflict. Blood revenge, the killing of a man who had slain a relative, caused strife. Disunity among the tribes resulted. In this era of self-destruction, the leaders remembered the teachings of the Master of Life and wondered how to persuade the people to return to his teachings. Many looked for a messenger from Teharonhiawagon. Another group proposed a council be called, of all leaders, to find a way that would end the constant internal strife, and Hiawatha was one of those who pressed for such a council.[5] By most accounts, he was living among the Onondagas and was respected for his oratory and magical powers.

But Hiawatha was pitted against a diabolical Onondaga chief called Atotarho, the symbolic figure of evil, of ferocious appearance, who used all forms of chicanery such as witchcraft and wizardry, to defeat the plans of Hiawatha and his followers. Some say that Atotarho was the Master of Life's evil brother. Still others say he was the half-brother of Hiawatha, and had set up a tyrannical regime with assassins and spies serving his evil purposes. He is described in the most hideous terms. His body is said to have had seven crooks; his hands were like those of the turtle; and his hair was a mass of serpents.[6]

Each time Hiawatha sought to form a peace council, Atotarho's spies would appear to foil the efforts of the peaceful chiefs. From the start, Atotarho viewed Hiawatha as leader of the peace chiefs and began to kill Hiawatha's daughters through magic, one by one. Finally, when Hiawatha had one daughter left alive, he made a last attempt to hold a council. As the chiefs assembled in the woods and built temporary lodges, they learned that Atotarho had heard of the council, and was already among them. The peaceful group became fearful as they awaited Hiawatha. But one day, as Hiawatha's last daughter, who was pregnant, was gathering firewood, Atotarho sprang up and pointed to a large and beautiful creature flying through the sky towards the daughter. Filled with curiosity, the people went headlong to the spot, trampling the woman to death. Atotarho had won again, and the grieving Hiawatha acknowledged defeat, abandoned the Onondagas, and carried the word of peace to other Iroquois tribes.[7]

He traveled among the Iroquois villages talking to the Mohawks, Oneidas, and Cayugas, attempting to convince them to renounce war and internal strife. He spoke of the restoration of peace and brotherhood among the Iroquois. At every village he was given lodging and an audience. However, people were slow to embrace his ideas. They could not forget the old animosities and suspicions. Tradition has it that the Oneidas agreed to accept his teachings if the Mohawks would also consent.[8] Subsequently, the Mohawks and the Cayugas embraced Hiawatha's teachings, with the proviso that he persuade the formidable Atotarho to end his rule of terror and bring the Onondagas into the covenant of peace. An impossible goal, it was thought.

Hiawatha, it was feared, was defeated. But Deganawidah entered his life and changed the nature of things through his philosophy of peace and his visionary powers. Deganawidah's words and purpose made him, in some ways, a greater figure than Hiawatha in Iroquois traditional beliefs. Although Deganawidah has been portrayed as more legendary than real man, he probably was an Indian prophet who appeared at a crucial moment in Iroquois history, to instruct Hiawatha.[9]

Little is known about Deganawidah's early life except that he was a Huron from eastern Ontario. Roughly translated, the name means "man, the thinker." He was raised by his mother, who taught him to understand humankind, and filled him with a philosophy of love. She also caused him to be conscious of the fact that he had a divine purpose in the world. Paradoxically, the Indian prophet was destined to cause

3

the downfall of the Hurons, indirectly, through his message to the Iroquois.[10]

Deganawidah was not without human frailties. Some accounts say he stammered so much, he could scarcely talk. But his handsome face was said to have reflected the soul of a mystic. Like most prophets, he had experienced a powerful vision which transformed him. In his vision, he saw a giant evergreen, reaching to the sky and gaining strength from three counter-balancing principles of life. These principles were a stable mind and a healthy body in balance, with peace between individuals as well as groups. He saw that humane conduct, thought, and speech was a prerequisite for equity and justice among peoples. Finally, he envisioned a society in which physical strength and civil authority would reinforce the power of the clan system. The tree had four roots which stretched out to the four directions of the earth. From the base of the tree a snow-white carpet covered the surrounding countryside. This white carpet protected the lands of the people who adopted the three double principles. At the crest of the evergreen, an eagle was perched. Deganawidah recognized the tree as humanity, living within his principles governing relations among human beings. The eagle was humanity's lookout against enemies who might disturb the peace.[11] Ideally, the protective carpet could be extended to the four corners of the earth to provide a shelter of peace and brotherhood for all mankind.

Deganawidah perceived the vision as a message to him from the Master of Life to bring harmony into the human condition and unite all peoples into a single family guided by the three double principles. However, his work could not begin with the Hurons because he was fatherless, an outcast with no standing. So he bid farewell to his mother and left Huron country to carry his ideas to the other Iroquois nations. Since he was a man without a tribal bond, he moved freely from one nation to another.[12] However, his words, uttered in a stammering manner, were not well received.

Events transpired in such a way that Deganawidah, in the course of his wanderings, finally met Hiawatha. Some versions of this history say that Deganawidah united all the tribes except the Onondagas, and that he persuaded the discouraged Hiawatha to attempt the conversion of the evil Atotarho. But the two men did meet, decided to work together, and complemented each other in their common cause to end the bitter strife in Iroquois country. Deganawidah gave substance to Hiawatha's vague appeals to unity, offering a practical plan of government based on specific principles. Because Deganawidah was a poor speaker, Hiawatha became his messenger to the Iroquois nations, finally gaining acceptance of the message of The Great Peace.[13] The

Mohawks, Cayugas, and Oneidas agreed to the Great Peace, but the Onondagas, led by Atotarho, still held out.

With Deganawidah's help, Hiawatha was now able to convert the intransigent wizard. According to one account, Deganawidah held a council of all the chiefs who had agreed to the Great Peace, including Hiawatha. They decided to go to Atotarho together. To aid in straightening out his twisted body and mind, the council members made thirteen strings of wampum and chanted the Six Songs. These were part of the Dead Feast. When two spies who were sent to find Atotarho returned, telling horrible stories about his physical features, Deganawidah told the wavering chiefs that it was their duty to remake the evil wizard's mind. So the chiefs proceeded to Atotarho's village, singing. When they reached the village, the council was ushered into Atotarho's presence. Although the dreadful shape of the evil one horrified them, they unwrapped the thirteen strings of wampum and began singing the Six Songs. This soothed Atotarho. Deganawidah then said to him, "We will straighten out your mind now." As the chiefs continued singing, they handed Atotarho a string of wampum. Deganawidah told the wizard that the song belonged to him alone, and it was called "I use it to beautify the earth." Noting that Atotarho's mind was becoming transformed, Deganawidah passed his hands over the evil one's feet, changing them from their tortoise shape with claws like a bear's, to the normal feet of a man. After the prophet had restored Atotarho's distorted hands, he brushed the hissing snakes from the wizard's hair. Next, he decreed that the wizard's head should become human. Last, Deganawidah straightened the twisted body of Atotarho and pronounced him to be redeemed; the evil one was now reborn and charged with implementing the message of peace that Deganawidah spoke of.[14]

There are other versions of this redemption, in which Hiawatha combed the serpents of evil thoughts from Atotarho's hair. In fact, loosely translated, the name Hiawatha means "He, the comber." The transformed tyrant now became the Onondaga chief, the "firekeeper," the most important member of the new Confederacy.[15] To this day, the Great Council Fire of the Confederacy is kept in the land of the Onondagas. Regardless of the interpretations, Atotarho became benign and agreed to join the League, provided only that the Senecas be included. This was done soon after Atotarho's transformation. The Iroquois were now well on the road to peace and confederation.

Under the aegis of Hiawatha and Deganawidah, the clan leaders of the five tribes gathered around the council fires to fashion the laws and government of the Confederacy. Joined by the leaders of the League, Deganawidah planted a Great Tree of Peace called the Great

White Pine (Tsioneratasekowa) in the land of the Onondagas. Under the shade of the tree, the down of the Globe Thistle was spread for Atotarho and his cousins in the Confederacy to sit upon. There the leaders were to guard the fire of the League. Before this body, all affairs of the Confederacy were to be conducted, according to Deganawidah. Great White Roots spread out from the Tree of Peace, even unto the four directions. The nature of these Great White Roots was and is, strength. Anyone outside of the Five Nations who obeys the laws of the Great Peace (Kaianarekowa), and makes this known to the statesmen of the League, may trace back the roots to the tree. If the mind is obedient and promise is made to obey the wishes of the Council of the League, they were welcome to take shelter beneath the Great Tree. The eagle was also placed atop the tree, to be eternally vigilant against any impending danger.[16] Thus was the vision of Deganawidah coming to pass.

Since the fire was to be maintained by Atotarho, the League was to meet always at Onondaga. When the League was not in session, and a meeting was desired by any council members, a messenger was to be sent to the firekeepers of the Onondagas with a complete explanation of the issue to be discussed. Atotarho would then call his Onondaga chiefs together and determine whether the issue was of sufficient importance to call to the attention of the Council.[17] If the business proposed for discussion was determined to merit such consideration, Atotarho sent runners to summon all the chiefs to sit beneath the Great Tree of Peace.

Deganawidah gave strict instructions governing the conduct of the League and its deliberations. Some of these may be described:

When the Council is assembled, the Council Fire should be kindled (not with chestnut wood) and Atotarho should then open the meeting formally. Atotarho and the other Onondaga chiefs will then announce the purpose of the meeting and what is to be discussed.[18] The rising smoke of the Council Fire piercing the sky is a signal to the Iroquois allies that the Council is in session.

During the course of deliberations, Atotarho and the thirteen other chiefs of the Onondagas shall keep the area around the fire clean, using the wing of a seagull (Tsiowatstekawe Onerahonstsha). Should a crawling creature come near the Council Fire, a staff presented to the leaders of the Onondagas should be used to turn it away.[19] If the Onondaga chiefs are unable to do this, they may enlist the aid of the remaining members of the Council.

The Mohawk council members are divided into three groups: Tehanakarine, Ostawenserentha and Soskoharowane being the first. Tekarohoken, Ayonwatha and Satekariwate are the second.

Sarenhowane, Teyonkekwen and Orerekowa are the third. The first group listens only to the discussion of the second and third segments, to insure that no errors are made. If an error occurs, the first group should call attention to it. When the dispute is settled between the second and the third groups the decision should be referred to the Seneca statesmen for their approval, in accord with the Mohawk chiefs.[20] Subsequently, the question is to be thrown across the fire to the Cayuga and Oneida chiefs on the opposite side of the council house.

Deganawidah's instructions were precise in every way, all designed to create a form of government guided by traditions of peace and understanding.

According to his great design, the Council is to be composed of fifty sachems. They are obliged to meet every five years, and more frequently if necessary. The chiefs are appointed by the female leaders of the tribal otiianers. Although the sachems served for life, they could be removed by the female leaders for misconduct, sickness, or other reasons causing them to be ineffective.

The Onondagas sent fourteen delegates to the Council. The Cayugas were permitted to send ten. The Mohawks and Oneidas had nine delegates each, and the Senecas eight. None of the sachems could be warriors. The reasoning for this was sound: they might adopt warlike positions and attempt to promote warlike policies. None of the positions were hereditary. Upon the death of a chief, the leader of his otiianer appointed a new man, who adopted the name and functions of the man he succeeded. So the names and duties of the first council were made permanent. An Onondaga named Atotarho was always firekeeper and moderator. The places of Hiawatha and Deganawidah were the only ones not reappointed. After their death, their seats remained empty, since they were to be present in the spirit.[21] Hiawatha and Deganawidah had founded a lasting confederacy that functions even today.

Thus it was, that the conduct and structure of the Council demonstrates the unity and completeness of man and the environment. Whenever a council is held, the Onondaga statesmen greet the other members and express their gratitude to the earth, the streams, the lakes and pools; to the corn and fruits, to the medicinal herbs and trees, to the trees of the forest for their usefulness, and to the animals who provide clothing and food. Thanks was given to the great winds and the lesser winds; to the Moon, the Sun, the Thunderers and the mighty warriors, and to the messengers of the Creator who expressed his wishes. Also, gratitude is expressed to the Great Creator who dwells in the skies above, who gives all things useful to mankind, who is the ruler

7

and source of health and life. After this thanksgiving, the Onondaga leaders declare the Council open, but it cannot be in session after dark.[22]

The laws of the confederacy are based on the teachings of Deganawidah, to insure the Great Peace and protect the lives and liberty of the participants. Individual rights, safety and justice were assured. The blood feud, a terrible and divisive force, was outlawed. Under the new law, when an Indian killed another person, the grieving family no longer had the right to avenge the killing by taking the life of the murderer. Instead, the bereaved family was obliged to accept twenty strings of wampum from the slayer's family (ten for the dead man and ten for the life of the murderer himself). If a woman was killed, the price was thirty wampum strings.[23]

Wampum played several major roles in the life of the Iroquois. Hiawatha introduced the custom of using wampum at the founding of the League. He decreed and regulated its use. Wampum was designed to bring peace and unity among the Five Nations and take the place of blood. He first used wampum with the Mohawks. After telling the Council of its use, Deganawidah used wampum to console or wipe away the tears of Hiawatha, whose heart was grieved through the loss of his daughters. This was the first Condolence Ceremony. It exists today without change. The first wampum used by Hiawatha was probably made of fresh water shells. Earlier forms for decorative and communication purposes may have been wooden, or constructed from porcupine quills.[24]

As the Iroquois began to trade with the New England tribes, especially the Narragansetts, wampum became more plentiful, since the Atlantic coast is a great source of purple and white quahog shells. Gradually, wampum assumed sacred connotations. It became a medium of communication as well. Wampum strings served as credentials and symbols of authority. No Iroquois chief would listen to a messenger or pay attention to a report until he had received official information through a runner who possessed the proper belt or string of wampum. Thus, wampum certified a messenger or a promise. Treaties were not recognized unless they were accompanied by wampum. Belts were exchanged at treaty ceremonies as symbols of friendship and promises made. Often as many as forty belts would be exchanged at such a ceremony. To break a treaty under these conditions was a sacrilege. Also, all laws passed by the League were recorded with a certain string or belt of wampum. The treaty or law that was placed on wampum was memorized by trained and delegated individuals. Hence, wampum was the record keeping function of the confederacy.[25] It dictated credentials, protocol, and was the record of enacted laws.

Through the establishment of the new laws and the Council Fire of the League, Deganawidah had realized his vision of universal peace and brotherhood. While the new consciousness with its guarantees of an end to blood feuds applied only to the five tribes, the Great Peacemaker believed that the protective carpet of white eventually would spread to all peoples of the world. He visualized a Council Fire for all nations spreading towards the rising and setting sun, all over the earth. In turn, the newly converted people would teach their neighbors the message of peace and brotherhood. He did not doubt that his message would in time be embraced by all mankind.

One day, according to Iroquois tradition, he called the people together and spoke to them. He declared he would be seen by men no longer. Then he embarked in a white canoe on Lake Onondaga and disappeared into the setting sun.[26]

Hiawatha remained, to carry the word of peace to other Iroquoian tribes. Initially, the Hurons, Eriez and Neutrals accepted the message, tentatively. Then Hiawatha and his messengers journeyed further, throughout the Northeast and the Midwest. He is said to have traveled as far as Lake Superior and the waters of the Mississippi. When he returned to the five tribes, he brought back strings of wampum, attesting to these distant tribes' adherence to his creed.[27] These journeys increased the stature of Hiawatha among his people, and the Iroquois viewed him as capable of bringing all nations on earth to the Great Peace.

Some say that Hiawatha spent his last days among the Mohawks as an elder statesman. Another tradition tells of his following Deganawidah into the mists of Lake Champlain in a white bark canoe. When Hiawatha died, the Iroquois viewed him as being very close to the Master of Life. Both he and Deganawidah were rapidly cloaked in mystery and legend at their death.[28]

Hiawatha's initial efforts among other tribes proved to be somewhat short of success. Few outside nations fully understood the new message that had been kindled at the Council Fire of the Onondagas. Failing to cooperate with the League after three warnings, the League's constitution stated that the war chief should let a string of white lake shells fall from his outstretched hands.[29] This indicated that force must be used against the transgressor to bring that tribe to the white carpet of peace.

Crusading parties struck out in all directions to carry the word of the League and Deganawidah's principles. When the French came to North America, the Iroquois were waging such a crusade against the Hurons of the St. Lawrence River. The French did not understand the nature of the conflict and viewed it as a war without purpose.[30]

The introduction of the fur trade and the contact with the European technology added an economic motive to the religious crusades of the Iroquois. Because the Iroquois could muster more than a thousand men for a campaign, neighboring tribes were subdued. These included: the Eriez, Susquehannocks, Tobacco People, Hurons and Neutrals. Gradually, the Iroquois extended their message through military might as far as the Tennessee River to the south, and Lake Superior to the west, and into New England and Canada. As was their custom, adopted prisoners brought into the clans maintained the Iroquois strength.[31]

Throughout the crusades and military forays into the lands of neighboring tribes, the message of the Great Tree of Peace was ever the purpose and aim of the Confederacy. They became benign supervisors of the dependent tribes. Internal discord was discouraged. But the Indian nations brought under the Confederacy could expect the moral and military support of the Iroquois in time of need. Troubled nations were often sent a delegation of chiefs to restore tranquility, and were advised as to how to cope with difficulties.[32]

As the whites overran the lands of surrounding tribes, several tribes sought refuge and sanctuary among the Iroquois. Many Delawares from Eastern Pennsylvania and New Jersey sought the shelter and protection of Deganawidah's Confederacy. In the same way, the Piscataways from the Potomac River Valley, the Nanticokes from the Delmarva Peninsula, the Saponis and Tutelos from Virginia, and the Tuscarora from North Carolina came to sit under the Great Tree of Peace. The Iroquoian Tuscaroras were invited by the Oneidas to become the sixth member of the Confederacy in the early Eighteenth Century.[33]

Throughout the time of intense settler pressure, and wars with other native peoples, as well as with European powers, the Confederacy maintained its power and strength. Reasons for the endurance of such a confederation are many, but perhaps the idea of expanding the Longhouse is most important. This principle gave everyone under the Tree of Peace a ready analogy to everyday life in the understanding of the government. The physical environment and family relations had a direct bearing on the functioning of the League.

The Longhouse was more than just a shelter. It was the basic unit upon which the entire society was constructed. Certain physical factors in the Iroquois lifestyle reinforced the concepts of the Longhouse, as we shall see.

The People of the Longhouse lived in stockaded villages in elevated areas which were easy to defend and more often were located near a water supply. Fifteen to twenty-foot long palisades surrounded and protected a group of Longhouses. A ditch was dug around palisaded walls. Bark platforms at the top supplied with stones, served the Iroquois' needs during attacks.[34] The palisades acted as a defensive wall and also helped to keep forest animals from foraging within the village.

Longhouses were the typical dwelling unit within the stockade. The use of the Longhouse as a dwelling, however, extended from New England to the Savannah River and westward into the Great Lakes region. A number of families were housed within each Longhouse. The size of a village might vary from four or five bark lodges to more than a hundred. The Longhouse varied in size from twenty feet by sixteen feet and fifteen feet high, to huge multiple family dwellings sixty feet by eighteen feet and eighteen feet high. In some instances, Longhouses have been known to be more than three hundred feet long, in the more populous villages.[35]

In building the Longhouse, a row of forked poles were placed in the ground, between four and five feet apart. Cross poles were lashed to the forked uprights to form an arched roof. Slender poles or rafters were then secured to the roof frame, and traverse poles were added to further strengthen the overhead structure. Large pieces of bark were then tied to the frame. The bark was obtained in the spring, by stripping the trees when the sap began to flow. Elm, ash, cedar, fir, spruce, or basswood were the usual sources of bark. An outer set of poles kept the bark in place on the sides and roof. Smoke holes were built into the roof at about twenty-foot intervals. These holes would usually be covered with a piece of bark.[36] The hearth beneath the smoke hole was shared by two families.

Doors were built at each end of the Longhouse. Animal hide or hinged bark was used, and this covering could be lifted up. Along the inside wall, bunks were constructed which served as beds at night and benches in the day. Corn, dried fish, and other foods hung from overhead. The dwelling was compartmentalized to accommodate each family. Storage space was available in the corners and in closets between the compartments. At the front of the Longhouse, over the door, pictures of clan symbols were placed to represent the families living in that Longhouse.[37]

By the end of the Eighteenth Century, bark structures gave way to hewn log buildings. Wood frame houses began to appear. However, the bark houses were built and used well into the mid-Nineteenth Century.

Agriculture was reserved for the women, although the men helped in clearing the fields and other heavy work. But the actual planting and harvesting was the domain of the women. The Three Sisters (corn, beans, and squash), were the traditional crops grown. Stone and wooden implements were used to till the soil. Corn was the most important crop. It could be eaten immediately, or dried and stored for the winter. Iroquois cornfields were large, and planted in "hills." Beans could be dried for future use. Squash or pumpkins were stored in a cool place or cut into strips and dried.[38]

The women also gathered nuts, roots, wild berries, and fruits. Sassafras roots, birch bark, hemlock twigs, and spicewood were steeped in boiling water to serve as beverages. Maple syrup or maple sugar was used as a sweetener. Also, sunflowers were raised and pressed, to extract the oil for cooking and hair dressing. They were also used in various religious rites.

Tobacco was grown and much prized, not only for smoking but also for religious purposes. Masks used in ceremonials were consecrated by attaching bags of tobacco to them. Tobacco was also burned as an incense. The rising smoke was a visible prayer to the Creator. Tobacco also warded off evil. In many ways, this plant had deep spiritual meaning for the Iroquois, and was widely used in religious observances and rituals.

The men were the hunters, although the wives often accompanied their husbands on hunting parties. On such occasions, they took charge of the camps. The hunting season began in the fall and continued until midwinter. Another hunt took place in the early spring. These expeditions frequently took the men away from the village for long periods of time. Moose, deer, beaver, bear, and elk were the animals sought. Bows and arrows, tomahawks, snares, and traps were utilized. Large deer drives were common and small animals were taken with snares or the bow and arrow.

Spring, summer and fall was also the fishing season. Lines, nets, harpoons, or weirs were used. Usually the fish were dried. Mussels were also sought and were a mainstay in the diet of the people.[39]

As with most peoples, the relationship of man to the universe was explained through a creation story. There were two major forces in the Iroquois conception of the universe. These were the Twin Boys. Creator, or Upholder of the Skies, was the good twin. He was responsible for cultivated plants, animals, rivers, and man. Among the whites he was often referred to as the Great Spirit. The Bad Twin, Flint, created monstrous animals, poisonous plants and other evils on earth.[40]

Most of the winter festivals centered around the agricultural cycle, except for midwinter, which concluded the fall hunting expedition. From the time the maple sap started to flow in the early spring, to the fall harvest, the Iroquois had ceremonies expressing gratitude for the gifts of the Creator. Such festivals conveyed a feeling of oneness with nature. For instance, when the corn and other garden crops had ripened, the people called a meeting to give thanks with dances for the green corn. People and corn were considered sisters, and "they whispered to a person in the fields," it was said.[41] Animate and inanimate were united as one, under the auspices of the Creator.

Natural forces were described in kinship terms. The thunder that brought rain was a grandparent. The moon was a grandmother who helped people in the dark and measured time. The sun was an elder brother who warmed the earth and provided daylight. The life supporters, corn, beans, and squash, known as The Three Sisters, strengthened and sustained the Iroquois. All these things came from the Great Creator, and the Iroquois gave thanks for the gifts.[42] Not only were the people linked to the state by kinship ties, but also to the environment and all living things. Since all Iroquois society was divided into clans named after certain animals, the People of the Longhouse also had a close relationship in symbolic form with the animal kingdom.

The clan was headed by a woman. This clan mother was the head of the household, and the stewardess of the affairs of the earth, such as planting and harvesting. All things were symbolically related. This produced unity and strength.[43] Unity, not only in a political sense, but also in a spiritual and environmental sense, was the binding force in Iroquois life.

Thus, the League of Deganawidah and Hiawatha was an extension of the kinship principle. It was a symbolic as well as a physical household. Roughly translated, the League of the Ganonsyoni means, "a lodge spread out far." All individuals and all tribes were considered as one family living together. Moreover, the spiritual values and sense of unity with the environment served to strengthen this analogy, since man was interpreted as being related to all things.

The symbolism existing in Iroquois societal structure, in secular government, and political union, and in religious practice as well, was deeply understood by all. Thus were seated the nations of the Confederacy in the Longhouse:

The Mohawks were Keepers of the Eastern Door of the Lodge; the Senecas were the Keepers of the Western Door. In the center, the Onondagas were named the Firekeepers and Wampum Keepers. The Mohawks, Onondagas, and Senecas were the Elder Brothers. The Oneidas and Cayugas, the Younger Brothers. The younger and elder brothers sat on opposite sides of the symbolic lodge with the Onondagas seated in the center to provide a balance between the two sides.[44]

Although the League was intended to be a coalition of united nations acting with one mind, the vicissitudes of local politics often hampered its operation. Kinship concepts strengthened the League, while local autonomy often made it impotent. (Federalism is always plagued with problems of states' rights but perhaps this problem is more tolerable than a centralized tyranny. The cost of freedom is always dear.)

Military power and the exercise of it was the most impressive aspect of Iroquois culture to an outsider. Before white contact, the Iroquois used wooden armor. This proved ineffective when firearms and metal points for arrows and spears were introduced. The Iroquois also developed sophisticated military tactics. They would often feign retreat and draw an enemy into a trap, then rush to the foe before he could discharge his weapons. Guerrilla tactics were used to destroy an enemy as an additional strategy of war. As the Iroquois obtained more and more firearms, guerrilla tactics became more and more prevalent.[45]

Contrary to the usual textbook interpretation, Iroquois "war" activities were not adventuristic, chance events. There were reasons for the use of force. Protection of the homeland and family, defense of the tribe's boundaries, and economic necessity such as guarding planted fields, usually brought the so-called "war parties" into action.

Iroquois men could achieve prominence by ability in war, other than through the hereditary clan system. Although the title of sachem, the peace chief, was hereditary within the lineages of a clan, ordinary men could rise to fame through military expeditions or religious crusades. Once war had been declared, anyone could form a war party. An aspiring war chief or one who was already famous would often go through the village sounding the war cry. Upon striking his hatchet into the war pole, the leader would relate his courageous deeds and begin a war dance. Men who wished to follow him joined in the dance. A feast followed.[46]

But the women had a significant influence on the warriors, and frequently could either prevent or encourage a war party by their approval or disapproval. If the women refused to give the warriors moccasins and charred corn pounded into a meal sweetend with maple sugar, they were effectively saying "No" to the proposed military venture.[47]

The culture and historical background of the League of the Iroquois is rich in ideals that unify people in spite of their differences. The Confederacy exemplified these concepts.

The clan system, with its ability to adopt persons in order to maintain the strength of the clan and the nation is a good example of this effort. The words of peace from Hiawatha and Deganawidah helped to forge an alliance of tribes that survives even today despite many weaknesses. The creation story and the thanksgiving festivals all play a part in bolstering this cohesion. Wampum provided the necessary mode of communication, and all these factors made the League a strong and durable coalition.

In spite of settler pressure, the Iroquois ability to resist intrusion remained strong throughout the colonial period. On several occasions the Iroquois suggested to the colonists that they would do well to follow their principles of confederation. These admonitions did not go unheeded. Throughout the Eighteenth Century, the democratic principles of the Iroquois League were discussed by Enlightenment scholars attempting to build a more humane, just form of government. The American people were at this time also struggling with these ideas, in their own pragmatic way. All the while, however, there was a functioning democracy at their very doorstep. Due to cultural differences, and different ways of perceiving the world, the direct influence of the Confederacy on the formation of the United States is not always apparent. Nevertheless, this native government of balance and compromise, with its concepts of federalism, has distinct similarities to the early instruments of government adopted by the American people. Quite frequently, practical minded Americans scoff at the idealistic systems of European Enlightenment philosophers, but the American colonist could not deny the effectiveness and durability of the Iroquois Confederacy. This legacy of freedom, exemplified by the Confederacy, is even today only dimly perceived by the American people. But it was a profound factor in the founding of the American nation.

---

*Note: The word "otiianer" refers to the women heirs to the chieftainship titles of the League, the 48 authorized names for the chiefs of the Iroquois, passed through the female side of the otiianer. The otiianer women selected one of the males within their group to fill a vacated seat in the League. Two or more otiianers usually comprised a clan.

REFERENCES CHAPTER ONE

1. Clark Wissler, *Indians of the United States*. (Garden City, New York, 1967), pp. 128-129.

2. Hazel W. Hertzberg, *The Great Tree and the Longhouse: The Culture of the Iroquois*. (New York, 1966), pp. 55-60.

3. Henry R. Schoolcraft, *Notes on the Iroquois*. (Millwood, New York, 1975), p. 80.

4. See William W. Canfield, *The Legends of the Iroquois: Told by "The Cornplanter."* (Port Washington, New York, 1902), passim; and Frank H. Severance, ed., *Publications of the Buffalo Historical Society* (Buffalo, 1903), VI, pp. 415-416.

5. Schoolcraft, *Iroquois*, pp. 76-79; and Paul A. W. Wallace, *The White Roots of Peace* (Port Washington, New York, 1946), pp. 12-13.

6. Wallace, *White Roots*, pp. 16-17; and Hertzberg, *Great Tree*, pp. 88-89.

7. Wallace, *White Roots*, p. 20; and Harriet Maxwell Converse, *Myths and Legends of the New York State Iroquois* (Albany, 1908), pp. 117-118.

8. Canfield, *Legends of the Iroquois*, pp. 137-148.

9. Wallace, *White Roots*, p. 5.

10. *Ibid*, p. 4.

11. Tehanetorens, *Wampum Belts* (Onchiota, New York, n.d.) pp. 6-7.

12. Wallace, *White Roots*, p. 7.

13. Tehanetorens, *Wampum Belts*, pp. 6-7; and Wilbur R. Jacobs, "Wampum, the Protocol of Indian Diplomacy," *William and Mary Quarterly*, Third Series, IV (October 1949), pp. 596-604.

14. Edmund Wilson, *Apologies to the Iroquois*, (New York, 1960); and Alvin Josephy, *The Patriot Chiefs* (New York, 1972), pp. 21-22.

15. Tehanetorens, *Wampum Belts*, p. 7, and Josephy, *Patriot Chiefs*, p. 22.

16. *The Great Law of Peace of the Longhouse People* (Akwesasne, 1971).

17. *Ibid*.

18. *Ibid*.

19. J.N.B. Hewitt, "Review of Parker's Constitution of the Five Nations," *American Anthropologist*, XIX, 3 (July-September 1917) 432-433; and Lewis Henry Morgan, *League of the Ho-De-No-Sau-Nee or Iroquois* (New York, 1901), I, 5-6.

20. See *Peace of the Longhouse*.

21. See Morgan, *League of the Iroquois*, passim.

22. See *Peace of the Longhouse*.

23. Hertzberg, *Great Tree*, pp. 104-105.

24. Tehanetorens, *Wampum Belts*, pp. 5-6; and "The Founding of the League of the Iroquois," *The Conservationist*, XXX, 4, (January-February 1976).

25. *Ibid*.

26. Canfield, *Legends of the Iroquois*, pp. 137-148.

27. Josephy, *Patriot Chiefs*, p. 26.

28. Wallace, *White Roots*, pp. 4-5.

29. Arthur C. Parker, *The Constitution of the Five Nations*, (Albany, 1916), pp. 52-55.

30. Hertzberg, *Great Tree*, p. 111.
31. Donald A. Grinde, Jr., "A Historical Sketch of the Eriez Indians," *Journal of Erie Studies*, II, 2 (Fall 1973), 25-27.
32. Josephy, *Patriot Chiefs*, p. 28.
33. J.N.B. Hewitt, "Hiawatha," *Handbook of American Indians North of Mexico*, ed. by F.W. Hodge, BAE Bulletin 30 (Washington, D.C., 1907), I, 546; Hewitt, "Deganawidah," *Ibid.*, pp. 383-84.
34. James A. Tuck, "The Howlett Hill Site: An Early Iroquois Village in Central New York," in *Iroquois Culture, History and Prehistory* (Albany, New York, 1967), ed. by Elisabeth Tooker, p. 78.
35. *Ibid.*
36. Barbara Graymont, *The Iroquois in the American Revolution* (Syracuse, New York, 1972), p. 10.
37. Elisabeth Tooker, *An Ethnography of the Huron Indians, 1615-1619*, BAE Bulletin 190.(Washington, D.C., 1964), p. 13.
38. Graymont, *Iroquois*, pp. 10-11.
39. *Ibid.*
40. William N. Fenton, "This Island, the World of the Turtle's Back," *Journal of American Folklore*, LXXV, 298 (October-December 1962), 283-300.
41. Graymont, *Iroquois*, pp. 11-12.
42. Morgan, *League of the Iroqois*, I, 141-216.
43. Wissler, *Indians*, pp. 136-137.
44. See *Peace of the Longhouse*.
45. Josephy, *Patriot Chiefs*, p. 27.
46. Graymont, *Iroquois*, p. 20.
47. *Ibid.*, p. 21.

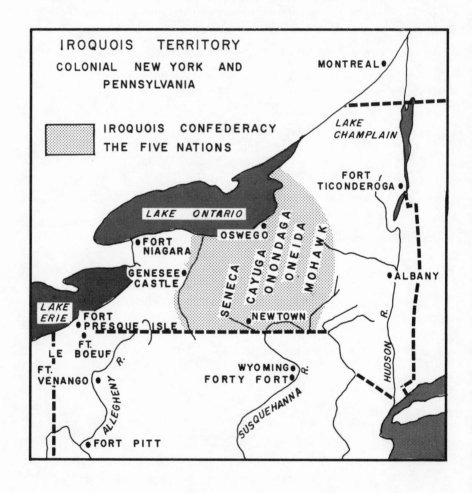

IROQUOIS TERRITORY
COLONIAL NEW YORK AND PENNSYLVANIA

IROQUOIS CONFEDERACY
THE FIVE NATIONS

MONTREAL

LAKE CHAMPLAIN

FORT TICONDEROGA

LAKE ONTARIO

OSWEGO

FORT NIAGARA

GENESEE CASTLE

SENECA CAYUGA ONONDAGA ONEIDA MOHAWK

ALBANY

LAKE ERIE

FORT PRESQUE ISLE

FT. LE BOEUF

NEWTOWN

HUDSON R.

FT. VENANGO

ALLEGHENY R.

WYOMING FORTY FORT

SUSQUEHANNA

FORT PITT

Chapter Two

IROQUOIS
AND COLONISTS

THE ENTRY OF THE EUROPEANS INTO THE New World, and their subsequent interaction with Native Americans, triggered changes in both white and Red cultures. Although a sizeable amount of scholarship points out the impact of European ideas and material culture on Indians, little has been done to analyze the contributions of Indian cultures in changing the white man, and more specifically the American colonist. John Locke's interest in freedom, and the formation of British colonial governments, is no casual association.

The Lockean concept that men in their natural condition are in a state of freedom to order their actions, comes from a study of aboriginal societies. Since Locke asserts that mankind is in a state of natural equality, the logical conclusion is that no man has more power and rights than another. Natural law teaches that people are equal and independent and that no one ought to harm another in his life, liberty and possessions. This concept is strikingly similar to the teachings of Deganawidah. Furthermore, the basis for Locke's philosophy parallels Iroquois beliefs in that the British philosopher believes that everyone is bound to protect himself and protect the rest of mankind when his own preservation is not endangered. In a state of nature, man has the power to punish transgressions of the laws of nature, to protect the innocent, to restrain offenders, and to receive reparations for injuries done to him. All offenses should be punished according to the degree of its severity, so that such offenses are a poor bargain for the offender, thus

19

giving the transgressor cause to repent, and to deter others from doing the same. This is a message of peace, goodwill and brotherhood. It was also, in Locke's time, a protest against the autocratic monarchies of England and the rest of Europe.[1]

John Locke is pointing out the imperfections in his own native land (particularly the "divine right" arguments of James II) and seeking a new vision of society in his reflections on man's natural state. Locke also asserts that while the natural state of man is peace, goodwill and mutual assistance, convenience and God made man inclined to gather into groups. Language and understanding facilitate this process. The missing component in nature for man is an established, settled, known law, enforced impartially by properly delegated authorities. Man formulates a political or civil society whenever a number of people unite in one society (each person relinquishes his executive power under the law of nature) to form one people, one body politic under one supreme government. Essentially, Locke subscribes to a form of contract theory of the origin of society.[2] The experiential process seen in the formation of the Iroquois Confederacy and the words of Deganawidah express the same ideas as those of John Locke, with at least one critical distinction. Locke's ideas were not accepted in Europe in the late 1600s, while the Iroquois had lived in such a democratic state for centuries.

According to Locke's perception of the social contract, absolute monarchy is inconsistent with civil society. If the prince holds legislative and executive powers, there is no impartial judge and no appeals process. In such absolute monarchies of the "civilized" world, the subject is the slave of one man. But no man should be subjected to the political power of another without his consent. When man forms a society by consent of the individuals within it, he enters into an agreement to follow the dictates of the majority. After all, there is no real contract if one is left free and under no ties except those that bind him in nature. Although unanimity is nearly impossible, a measure of it can be obtained through debate and a balancing of opinions. Locke states that all governments of the world that had their beginnings in times of peace were established by consent of the people.[3]

Man gives up his unlimited freedom and power, because the enjoyment of it is very uncertain, according to Locke. If it were not for the corruption and viciousness of degenerate men, there would be no need for any society but that derived from the state of nature. The great and main end of man's uniting into groups is the mutual preservation of their lives, liberties and *estates* (property).[4] Here is a major concept where the Great Peace differs from Locke, since property held by individuals is of little concern to the Iroquois. Perhaps this is the tragic flaw in the Lockean system.

Locke's primary natural law, which is to govern the legislative authority itself, is the preservation of society for the public good of every person in it. Next, the first and fundamental law of the commonwealth is the establishing of legislative power. According to Lockean theory, the power is not only supreme but also sacred and unalterable when placed in the hands of the legislative body by the people. But the legislative power does not have absolute authority and control over the lives of the people; it is limited to that which promotes the public good. Moreover, the British philosopher believed that the laws of nature do not cease to operate in society, but stand as eternal rules for all men, legislators as well as others. Therefore, the legislative power has no right to enslave, destroy, or impoverish its subjects. The government cannot rule by arbitrary decree and edict. Standing laws are needed. Locke also enjoins the legislature against taking property without a subject's consent. Taxes can only be levied by consent of the majority. Finally, the legislative or supreme governmental body cannot delegate the powers of lawmaking to other hands. The legislative body and not the prince is the soul of the commonwealth. The legislative power represents the people, and the people are the sole judge as to the ability of a government to act in society's interests.[5]

Locke's political philosophy was not without practical implementation. In 1669, he incorporated some of his equalitarian ideals in the first constitution for the Carolinas. King Charles II had granted the Carolinas to a number of British nobles. One of the grantees was the Earl of Shaftesbury, Locke's patron.[6] However, in many respects, the document does not have as democratic a spirit as some of Locke's other writings.

Plainly, the old world was struggling intellectually and politically to throw off the tyrannical trappings of absolute monarchy and its consequent abuses. The tribesmen of America seemed, to many Europeans, to be free of such abuses. The Iroquois not only had this freedom but also possessed a kinship state that insured the consent of the governed. There were many colonists who came to America who were imbued with libertarian views and probably recognized that the government of England was at best only an imperfect reflection of these views. Many came to the American colonies for economic reasons as well, of course, but the spirit of freedom and the ideal of natural man had been kindled. In America, the colonists saw this freedom widely exercised by American Indians. Even the cultural arrogance and racism of the English colonists could not fully disguise their astonishment at finding Native Americans in such a free and peaceful state. This recognition, while it was not widespread, was held by many influential colonial leaders. However, it did not deter others from considering the Indians to be unregenerate, savage, and a barrier to be removed in the onward march of the Europeans to the west, to land, and to the protection of their own liberties.

The Eighteenth Century Enlightenment glorified knowledge, the sciences and the arts, civilization and progress. It boasted of the achievements of man. But this smugness was shaken by Jean Jacques Rousseau. The French philosopher believed that the sciences and arts were the fruits of indolence and luxury as well as the sources of moral decay. According to Rousseau, man is by nature good and innocent. Morality is not a product of reasoned thinking but of natural feeling. Consequently, the worth of man depends not on his intellect, but on his moral nature. The essence of this nature is feeling. Goodwill alone has absolute value. Rousseau stresses the importance of sentiments in mental life; he also denies that the development of reason brings about the perfection of man. If men are equal by nature, then society, through the institution of property, has made them unequal. Society now has masters and slaves, cultured and uncultured, rich and poor, as a by-product of reasoned thinking. Therefore, civilization as western man knows it, has corrupted man's natural inclinations. The result is the slavish and lordly vices: envy and hatred on the one hand; contempt, cruelty and arrogance on the other. These vices make society and life itself artificial and mechanical. Since the origin of virtues and vices are to be sought in social and political institutions, the only hope for the improvement of mankind lies in the bettering of society.[7]

Rousseau's concept of the "noble savage" is more of a hypothesis than a reality. His portrayals of man in the original state of nature stemmed from accounts he had read of aboriginal tribes around the world. But the "noble savage" is a social and political fiction, to enable people to understand one aspect of human nature that is operative at all times. Thus, he departs from human nature as it is now constituted and eliminates the influence of social intercourse and institutions such as education, and seeks to isolate the essential and instinctive nature of man. This essential nature is immediate feeling, and the role it plays in binding all people together. It is feeling that man shares in common, beneath the intellectual activity, science, art and other artificialities of so-called civilization.[8] Long ago, Deganawidah and Hiawatha realized the need to share this concept in the kinship state and the Condolence Ceremony.

One should not mistake Rousseau's "return to nature" as a demand to go back to nature in all its simplicity and naivete. Rather, the French philosopher was trying to reawaken, within the framework of society, the feelings and sentiments that promote equality and social justice. Essentially, Rousseau's appeal is to humanize the institutions and governments of man to form a just and democratic society.[9] Again, the Iroquois Confederacy had realized these needs through strife and grief, and finally through the Great Peace.

Rousseau differs from Locke in that he substitutes direct government for representative government. The Frenchman demands political rights and liberty of thought for all men. He took the Lockean ideal of democracy seriously. If all men are created free and equal, he reasons, with the same natural rights and capacities, then there is no reason for rule or inheritance by the privileged classes. This injunction holds for the aristocracy as well as for the industrial bourgeoisie. Education is the key to the creation of a more natural society. If the "noble savage" surrenders his freedom, he does so through a social contract in which he surrenders freedom for the liberty of citizenship. Freedom is complying with a self imposed law. Education is also a largely negative process, according to Rousseau. One must remove unfavorable conditions, so that the child will learn to distinguish between good and evil.[10] In essence, the social environment and education become the tools for improving man.

Parallels about the ways people live in groups are always easy to make, since man has developed many institutions that are similar throughout the world, such as religion, education, and the family. However, the men who came to North America (particularly the French and English) were struggling with the old political, economic, and social perceptions of their society. The French and English found a strong confederacy in the northeastern part of North America which they grew to respect. The ideas of the Iroquois were not so different from the liberal ideas of Seventeenth and Eighteenth Century Europe, but in the "New World" they were functioning in an established society rather than an abstract situation. However, the obsession with private property, especially on the part of Locke, proved to be the major point of friction between Indian and white. Thus, the conflict between the two cultures often centered around land and title to it. The debate still goes on today, as to whether real freedom can be attained through other means than communal ownership of property. The fact remains, though, that the Iroquois Confederacy, with its clan system, was a functioning and free tribal democracy at the time of white contact. Most European nations were grappling with these concepts of peace and freedom in theory rather than practice.

Aside from parallels about the concept of freedom and democracy, the Iroquois were economically linked with these two colonial powers during the colonial period. The French were to the north of the Iroquois and the English were to the south. When the English inherited the colony of New Netherlands, they became very close to the Iroquois, since Albany was an important trading center for the Iroquois. The English sought to maintain this friendship through gifts. English goods were of superior quality and cheaper than those of French manufacture.

The Iroquois modes of trade and production were distinctly different than those of white Europeans. The economic system of the Iroquois was largely environmentally determined. Essentially, the kinship system, the state and religious practices were the results of different systems of production, consumption, and distribution. Climatic conditions in New York were conducive to agriculture. Game of all kinds was abundant. The stock of fish was virtually inexhaustible. The Iroquois worked in stone, but more often in wood, since it was more readily available and easier to work.[11, 12] In their agricultural pursuits, the staple grain maize, involved clearing the ground, planting, cultivating, and harvesting. From beginning to end, the process consumed a whole summer filled with work. At the time of white contact, the Iroquois were depending more and more upon agriculture for their economy. Villages with large cornfields were routinely described by early French missionaries.[13]

In this economic system, the whole population had a share in production. Iroquois patterns of hunting, fishing and agriculture did not allow for the permanent appropriation of sources of supply by any group or individual. No one could live exclusively on the product of someone else's labor. The men and women divided their activities fairly evenly in production and distribution of the products of their labor and agricultural pursuits.[14]

Both men and women worked in organized groups. The need for cooperation in agriculture reinforced the family and the clan. The kinship system was linked together by strong ties of economic interest. The women worked the soil collectively, not only to expedite the business of producing crops but also as a social activity, often choosing an older active woman to oversee the labor in the field. Even in the gathering of firewood, the women employed cooperative methods. Other activites, such as fashioning skins and basketry, were carried on within the clan system. Thus, competition based on economic advantage was avoided.

The men worked collectively also. The clan organization was critical for defense. The agricultural settlements worked by the women needed protection from marauders. Cooperative game hunting was more productive than the individualized approach. The men and woman consequently shared a common kinship and economic system.[15]

Thus was the economic democracy of the Iroquois reinforced by their ideas of political democracy. For the Iroquois, they were not separate. One could not exist without the other. Everyone should have free access to the means of production, just as one has free access to the political process. Hence, the Iroquois' collective ownership of the land clashed with the white European's ideas about private property. No wonder land became the central point in Indian-white relations.

Considering this brief overview of economic factors in Iroquois society, one needs to go only a short step further to gain an understanding of what happened when European methods of production, technology, and economic system was brought to bear upon Iroquois life. Hunters who went out for game in order to provide food and clothing, were deployed to hunt for skins in order to supply the French and English merchants. The sharpest of competition developed among the tribes and within the tribes for the lucrative fur trade. White settlers overran the Indian cornfields, causing havoc in many cases, the resulting near-famine producing yet another element in native economy. Corn fields and plantings of other needed foods were also subjected to the same fate. Iroquois society was disrupted politically as well, because with the native economy destroyed, other means of subsistence had to be developed; as a result, the social system itself would undergo change.

The Europeans bargained for Iroquois labor in the hunt through distribution of their superior utensils, made of metal, and transformed native hunting methods through the use of guns and powder. Bows and arrows were not as fast, nor as effective as were the firearms brought by the Europeans. Tribes competed for guns and powder, because once having hunted in this more modern way, the old skills lost their pleasure and their efficiency as well. By withholding guns, powder, utensils, goods for clothing, and even manufactured or bought food, the Europeans could play one tribe against another, and force concessions which normally would not be granted.

In this regard, attention should be directed most particularly to the misnamed "gift" giving of the English and French. This is made to appear a gratuitous bestowal of gifts in order to assuage the feelings of the Iroquois, and as a compliment to some chiefs and sachems. This was true only to a very small extent.

The Iroquois were not dependent upon the Europeans for goods and food in the early days of contact. While wampum was used as a means of exchange, and in place of money in the earliest days of the colonial settlement, very soon money as a commodity held sway. But the Iroquois desperately needed the goods of foreigners. One way to obtain them was through the so-called "gifts," which were actually given in exchange for services, as barter, or as payment for conditions of agreements or treaties. The "gift giving" was an interim step in the total destruction of Iroquois economy. This, to the author's knowledge, is nowhere to be found in the textbooks, nor in the works of scholars on the Iroquois.

Thus was insult added to injury. For the gift giving actually supplied the needs of the Iroquois because the European influx had destroyed their native, environmental-controlled economy. In turn, the action of giving gifts was made to appear as a gratuity to the Indians, and the Iroquois were painted as greedy monsters who wanted only the most for the least given in return.

Such is the nature of the European-Indian interaction, that misconceptions and misunderstandings proliferate, in place of the basic knowledge that should be stimulated by a study of the objective conditions of the people.

In the diplomatic maneuvers during the colonial period, the European powers sought to squeeze a recognition of English sovereignty out of the Iroquois. Several royal governors of New York attempted to use the terminology "father," and "children" in their negotiations with the nations of the Confederacy. Although the Hudson Bay tribes had accepted this phraseology by the 1680s, the Iroquois did not accept such a subordinate status. The Iroquois did not consider themselves to be subjects. They were allies of the British politically and economically, before the revolutionary period. They insisted they were free, and required the New York governors to address them as "brethren."[16] At times, the Iroquois used words to confuse the colonists and preserve their own freedom. Sachems would often open a speech, stating, "Wee have putt our selves under the great Sachim Charles that lives over the great lake," and then conclude with the reminder that "we are a free people uniting ourselves to what sachem we please." Shortly after this declaration of independence to the English in 1684, the Iroquois made the same point to the French. An Iroquois sachem stated, "We are born free, we neither depend on Yonhondio (the governor of New France) nor Corlaer (governor of New York). We may go where we please, and carry with us whom we please and buy and sell what we please."[17] This spirit of freedom both vexed and fascinated the British and French.

The Iroquois were not without a direct involvement with the colonists. However, their policy was not directed by the English or French, nor did the goals of other European powers influence them. They charted their own course and made their own decisions within the League councils at Onondaga. In the last half of the Seventeenth Century, at the seat of the Confederacy, the Five Nations grappled with a problem that called for astute military and diplomatic skill. The Indians wanted to maintain their position as middleman in the lucrative fur trade of North America. Having earlier brought the Hurons to the white carpet of peace, the Confederacy sought to establish direct trade relations with the Ottawa, Nippissings and Sioux. The French, on the other hand, were building forts in the Great Lakes region, to circumvent Iroquois activities.

In 1656, the Confederacy blockaded the rivers leading to Montreal and ambushed tribesmen who attempted to trade with the French. The French were now in a dilemma. Either an alliance with the Five Nations, or extermination of the Indians appeared to them to be the only alternatives. Both actions were attempted. Both failed. The Iroquois continued to maintain their strength through the adoption policy, as described in the Great Law. In the end, the Ottawas became the suppliers and the Iroquois the middlemen, with Albany as the buyers. This was logical, since the English paid higher prices for furs and traded in better quality commodities.

The Ottawa-Iroquois alliance spelled disaster for New France, and the French spent the last third of the Seventeenth Century trying to disrupt this trading partnership. They made periodic attacks on the Iroquois during this period, destroying many villages and food supplies. In 1666, the French were so successful that the Indians sued for peace and invited French missionaries into the towns, to guide them in the "true way." When the time was right, however, the natives would throw the French out. In 1675, the Iroquois defeated the Susquehannocks and incorporated them into their Confederacy. With this added strength, they turned on the French, drove them out of their country, and launched attacks against French bases of power. In 1680, the Iroquois invaded the Illinois country, destroying forts and villages. Attacks were launched again in 1684 and 1689. The last attack was in retaliation for a French offensive into Seneca country in 1689.

The French were occasionally able to enlist the support of the Ottawas and remnants of the Hurons, but these tribes clearly understood that their natural alliance was with the Iroquois, particularly since they paid the best prices for furs. Hence, the support of these two tribes was only salutory. Often giving only the appearance of hostility against the Iroquois, the Ottawas and Hurons would state, "we are all brothers, who ought to form only one body, and possess but one and the same spirit." The covenant of the Confederacy played an important part in this decision. These two tribes also reasoned that the French "invite us to go to war against the Iroquois; they wish to use us in order to make us their slaves. After we have aided in destroying the enemy, the French will do with us what they do with their cattle, which

GUS-TO-WEH. The traditional headdress.
The deer antlers symbolize a chief. The rattle is to indicate the
beginning of trade with the Europeans since it is made from the horn
of a cow.

they put to the plow and make them cultivate the land. Let us leave them to act alone; they will not succeed in defeating the Iroquois; this is the means for being always our own masters."[18]

By 1700, it was apparent that although the English outnumbered the French, they could not defeat them due to their own disunity and the lack of military supplies from the mother country. On the other hand, the French had been unable to destroy the Iroquois and were thus suffering a serious disadvantage in the fur trade. The strategic geographic position of the Iroquois made them the keystone in the fight for the commerce of North America.[19] But it now became clear to the Indians that sustained wars were draining their strength; it was also increasingly clear that they could not expect military assistance from the British.

The Iroquois solution was a stroke of bold diplomacy. In the summer of 1701, they entered into negotiations with the English and French, signing treaties almost simultaneously at Albany and Montreal. To the French, they promised neutrality in any future war between the French and English. (This was a great gain for the French, who had been plagued by Iroquois independence.) To the English, who had lost an ally, the Iroquois ceded their western hunting lands, newly conquered from the Hurons. Through this piece of diplomacy, the Iroquois implied that their primary allegiance was still to the English. Actually, the land cession was merely symbolic, since the English were unable to occupy or control the land. In fact, the lands in question had been recently reconquered by the French and their allies the Wyandots. To complete the settlement, the Iroquois made peace with the tribes to the west of them.[20]

This policy worked well for fifty years. The Five Nations became the Six Nations when the Tuscaroras were brought into the Confederacy, and the Iroquois further increased the power of the Confederacy by absorbing remnants of coastal tribes and elements of western tribes to whom they had brought the message of the Great Law. Thus, they had become the dominant Indian force in the northern woodlands of America and Canada. In the early Eighteenth Century, the Iroquois were about as numerous as the white inhabitants of New York. But they were a force to be reckoned with in trade as well as in military and diplomatic affairs—a power greater than might be expected by virtue of their population in sheer numbers. Writing home in 1711, the governor of Quebec noted this position of power, stating that war with the Iroquois should be avoided at all costs, since the "five Iroquois villages (nations) are more to be feared than the English colonies."[21]

The alliance system established by the Iroquois would be tested during the three intercolonial wars of the Eighteenth Century (Queen

Anne's War, 1701-13; King George's War, 1744-48; and the French and Indian War, 1754-63). The Iroquois tried to maintain a neutral position during all these intercolonial conflicts, but the Confederacy was not able to act with complete unanimity, so they vacillated between the two powers. Only the Mohawks seemed to be thoroughly dependable as British allies, while the Senecas often leaned toward an association with the French.[22]

The first half of the Eighteenth Century was a time when English missionaries came among the Iroquois. In 1704, the Society for the Propagation of the Gospel sent Thoroughgood Moore to them, their first Anglican missionary. He would work mainly with the Mohawks, the most easterly tribe. But the Mohawks delayed giving Moore permission to work in their country for more than a year, so he asked that the Society transfer him to a more promising area.[23] This was the beginning of a continuing effort by the English to convert the Mohawks to the Anglican persuasion.

In 1710, several Indian chiefs visited Queen Anne. Thoyanoguen (Hendrick) was among them. He was one of the most outstanding of the Mohawk leaders. John Brant was also one of the party. He is believed to be the grandfather of Joseph Brant, the Mohawk revolutionary warrior. The Mohawks pledged their support to the English Crown and requested that the Queen send missionaries. The request was approved, and forwarded to the Society. A chapel was built, and a fort constructed for protection near the lower Mohawk castle called Teyawendarokough. William Andrews was their missionary in 1713 and estimated the total population of the Mohawks there to be about 600.[24]

Throughout the early part of the Eighteenth Century, the Iroquois met in frequent council with English and French officials. One of the most perceptive assessments of Indian-white relations during this period comes from Canassateego, Seneca. In 1742, at a council in Lancaster, he spoke on behalf of the Six Nations to the Pennsylvania officials. He spoke of the good relations with the Penn family, and how previous treaties confirmed the "League of Friendship" that existed between the two parties. In return for this good faith, the Iroquois would "preserve the road free from all encumbrances." The Pennsylvanians in return "would enlarge the fire and make it burn brighter . . . and assure to you we shall do the same by adding to it more fuel."[25] The imagery of the League was being used to demonstrate good faith.

Canassateego spoke of deeper bonds between the English and the Iroquois. He stated "we are bound by the strictest leagues to watch for each other's preservation; that we should hear with our ears for you, and you hear with your ears for us. This is equally agreeable to us; and we shall not fail to give you early intelligence, whenever anything of consequence comes to our knowledge." To strengthen this bond the Seneca chief confirmed the words with the presentation of a wampum belt for "the renewal of our amity and the brightening of the chain of friendship."[26] Thus, the diplomacy of the period between Iroquois and white was filled with the League's rich heritage, and an admonition to follow its principles.

At Lancaster in 1744, the great Iroquois chief advised the colonial governors:

> Our Wise forefathers established Union and Amity between the Five Nations. This has made us formidable; this has given us great Weight and Authority with our neighboring Nations. We are a powerful Confederacy; and by *your observing the same methods, our Wise Forefathers have taken, you will acquire such Strength and power. Therefore whatever befalls you, never fall out with one another.*[27] (Emphasis supplied.)

In their attempts to balance the French against the English, the Iroquois were also advising the English on how to strengthen themselves.

The Council at Lancaster reinforced the Iroquois inclination to trade with the British. The Iroquois hunters in the Ohio, known as Mingoes, along with the Delawares and Wyandots, came to Lancaster to form a trading alliance with the British. English trading posts were built on the Miami, Sandusky, and Cuyahoga Rivers with Iroquois consent, as a result of this meeting. The Confederacy formalized its dominance over the Ohio region by appointing "half-kings" and by allotting tracts of land to various dependent tribes.[28] In this way, the Iroquois used the Ohio region as a fulcrum to play the French and the British against each other. It was a sound policy and was used until 1763. The Confederacy had a policy of peace toward the "far Indians;" political manipulation for those nearby, and armed neutrality towards the European powers. Commercial profit and a seizure of the balance of power resulted.

This strategy caused the European powers to alternate between the conviction that the Iroquois were on their side, and the suspicion that they had gone over to the other side. Consequently, the French and English policy toward the Indians was to secure their neutrality by making economic and political concessions to them. The economic crunch as a result of the increased economic dependency upon European goods would come later.

When King George's War heated up in 1746, Indian-white diplomacy became more difficult. William Johnson was appointed commissioner for Indian affairs that year, and began a long career for the Crown. Johnson learned the customs and language of the Mohawks, which proved to be invaluable in later years. He had a number of children by Mohawk women and acknowledged them as such. He had several children by Mary Brant, a Mohawk clan mother and granddaughter of Hendrick.[29]

Johnson knew the ways of the Iroquois, and was well liked, particularly among the Mohawks. Hendrick had a high regard for the Englishman and expressed his regard when he said, ". . .he has Large Ears and heareth a great deal, and what he hears he tells us; he also has Large Eyes'and sees a great way, and conceals nothing from us."[30]

Hendrick himself had learned a great deal about the white man's politics. Thomas Pownall, a shrewd observer of colonial Indian affairs, described him as ". . .a bold artful intriguing Fellow & has learnt no small share of European Politics, (he) obstructs & opposes all (business) where he has not been talked to first . . ."[31] Thus, relations and customs among the English and the Iroquois were blending to accomodate the needs and mores of both cultures.

Throughout the first part of the Eighteenth Century, the English and French clashed along their colonial borders in North America. Although the English outnumbered the French twenty to one, the struggle for white control of North America was a protracted one. The immediate provocation came in western Pennsylvania. The French began to build a chain of fortifications in the Great Lakes and Mississippi Valley region. In western Pennsylvania and Ohio, a group of influential Virginians had banded together to form the Ohio Company. They laid claim to the Western Reserve, hoping to make a great profit. The company had the support of Governor Dinwiddie of Virginia, who had learned of the French designs through George Washington's preliminary expedition into the area in 1753-1754. In the summer of 1754, Dinwiddie sent Washington into the area again. The young major found that the French had built forts at Duquesne, Venango, Le Boeuf and Presque Isle in western Pennsylvania.[32]

The French had begun to move into the Ohio Valley in the late 1740s. The Iroquois became anxious. Half King, their sachem, had sent three messages to the French during this period, ordering them out of the Ohio region. The French replied,

I do not like your selling your lands to the English, they shall draw you into no more foolish Bargains. I will take care of your Lands for you and of you. The English give you no Goods but for your land. We will give you our goods for nothing.[33]

It now became clear that the French were moving to an all-out occupation on the Ohio area, and were hiring Indian hunters to supply their soldiers with meat.[34]

Before Washington's preliminary expedition in 1753, a council was held at Carlisle, Pennsylvania. The Pennsylvania commissioners accepted wampum, shells, calumet pipes and skins from the various tribes assembled to talk about the French advance. In return, the commissioners gave a beautiful wampum belt to the Six Nations delegation. On the belt, six figures were depicted holding hands.[35] The first five figures represented the Iroquois Confederacy; the sixth denoted the Pennsylvania colonial government facilitating a close unity between the Quaker colony and the Iroquois.

After the Indians had received strouds and handkerchiefs to wipe their eyes, and apologies for not having their weapons mended, they began to return to the Ohio region. Horses were provided for the journey.[36] But the French continued their encroachments and Half King was dubbed an "old woman" and was threatened with being put in chains if he did not stop complaining about their military operations.

Thus, in 1753, Governor Dinwiddie decided to probe the situation. Young Washington struck out for western Pennsylvania to warn the French that they were occupying English land. Christopher Gist accompanied the young major on this journey to Venango and Fort Le Boeuf.[37] At Logstown, Washington encountered Monacatoocha and Shingis of the Delawares. Giving a twist of tobacco and a string of wampum to Monacatoocha, he requested that a runner be sent to Half King (who was supposed to be his guide).[38] After Half King and several others had joined the party, they met Chabert Joncaire at Venango in late 1753. The Frenchman immediately began to court the favors of the Indians in Washington's party. Joncaire handed out liquor and presents so liberally that everyone was rendered "incapable of business." This vexed Washington, who feared he was losing the Indians' support, but Gist was able to regain the confidence of the Ohio natives by the time the young major prepared to leave for Le Boeuf.[39] Upon his arrival, the French commander, Legardeur dé St. Pierre politely refused the English request to withdraw from the Ohio region.

Again Half King was plied with presents and liquor by the French. As more of the same followed, Washington wondered whether he would lose his guide, but Half King kept his promise. The young major also warned the Iroquois sachem against the flattering advances of Joncaire. On the return journey, Washington's life was threatened by an Indian who attempted to ambush him. It was believed the ambush was the result of French bribes. But this incident and the entire journey points out the dependence that both the English and French had upon the Iroquois.[40] In 1754, Washington would once again be accompanied by Monacatoocha and Half King.

In May 1754, when Washington was trying to find a small party of French under Jumonville in western Pennsylvania, the Virginia commander was completely dependent upon his Indian guides. Before they reached the Indian encampment, the English party was ". . .frequently tumbling one over another, and so often lost that fifteen or twenty minutes search would not find the path again."[41] But when Half King and Monacatoocha joined the English, Jumonville's hiding place was found in little time. Subsequently, Jumonville was killed and Monsieur La Force was captured. Washington was gratified, since these men had been trying to sway the Ohio Indians to support the French.[42] His gratification was short lived, however, since Louis Coulon de'Villiers avenged the death of his countryman by forcing the major to surrender at Fort Necessity.[43] Hence, the prestige of the English colonies in the eyes of the Iroquois had fallen, when the colonies met at Albany to discuss French encroachments and Indian policy.

The colonial delegates assembled at Albany in the summer of 1754 under the sponsorship of the Crown, to attempt a common peace with all the Indian tribes (especially the Iroquois), and win them over to the English in the impending war with France. The most important result of the conference was the acceptance by the delegates of a plan to unite the colonies. The plan for intercolonial union was drawn up by Benjamin Franklin. The Albany Plan of Union called for a "general Government . . . under which Government each colony may retain its present Constitution."[44]

Franklin met with both the delegates and the Iroquois and hammered out a plan which he acknowledged to be similar to the Iroquois Confederacy. The Iroquois at the Albany Council criticized the delegates for showing weakness in the face of French encroachments. Hendrick referred to the English as "women" and hinted the Iroquois would not ally themselves with the "thirteen fires" until a suitable form of unity was established among them. Although the plan was not approved by the colonial assemblies because of their reluctance to give up any of their powers, the plan itself is evidence that serious thought was even then being given to confederation, reflecting the ideas of the Iroquois Confederacy.

Basically, the plan provided: Parliament was to establish a general government in America, including all the thirteen colonies, each of which was to retain its present constitution except for certain powers that were to be given to the general government. The king was to appoint a president-general for the government. Each colonial assembly would elect representatives to a grand council. The president-general, with the advice of the grand council, would have certain powers, such as handling Indian relations, making treaties, deciding upon peace or war, raising troops, building forts, providing warships, and finally to make such laws and levy such taxes as would be needed for its purposes.[45]

Thus, the roots of intercolonial unity are in the Indian-white relations of the early Eighteenth Century. During this time, men like Franklin saw in the Iroquois Confederacy a model to build upon. Franklin would later expand upon these ideas during the American Revolution, but the origins were at the conference at Albany, and Franklin freely acknowledged this before the Albany Congress:

> It would be a strange thing . . . if Six Nations of ignorant savages should be capable of forming such a union and be able to execute it in such a manner that it has subsisted ages and appears indissoluble, and yet that a like union should be impractical for ten or a dozen English colonies, to whom it is more necessary and must be more advantageous, and who cannot be supposed to want an equal understanding of their interest.[46]

While this statement was only a grudging acknowledgment of Iroquois influence, it demonstrates the debt that he and other colonists owed the Indians in framing the Albany Plan of Union.

Intercultural relations were not always so fruitful. White accounts of the colonial frontier were not always glowing. Charles Woodmason, an itinerant Anglican minister, painted a lurid picture of the Carolina back country, which the Tuscaroras were also aware of. Woodmason stated, "For thro' want of Ministers to marry and thro' the licentiousness of the People hundreds live in concubinage—swopping their wives as Cattel, and living in a state of nature, more irregularly and unchastely than the Indians . . ." Living conditions were also appalling. "Their cabins (are) quite open and expos'd. Little or no bedding, or anything to cover them—Not a drop of anything, save Cold Water to drink—and all their cloathing a Shirt and Trousers Shift and Petticoat. Some perhaps a Linsey Woolsey. No Shoes or Stockings—Children run half naked. The Indians are better Cloathed and Lodged."[47] After preaching in the Carolina backcountry, Woodmason was appalled at such ". . .a Medley! Such a mixed Multitude of all Classes and Complexions." He was abhorred by their after-service "Revelling Drinking Singing Dancing and Whoring." He also stated that most ". . .of the Company were drunk before I quitted the spot—They were as rude in their Manners as the Common Savages, and hardly a degree removed from them."

Although claiming to close his eyes in horror at this revelry, Woodmason did keep his eyes open long enough to make astute observations about the young ladies. He said these women were "bareheaded, barelegged and barefoot with only a thin Shift and under Petticoat—Yet I cannot break them of this—for the heat of the Weather admits not of any [but] thin Cloathing." With eyes half closed, Woodmason observed that young women "have a most uncommon Practise . . . They draw their Shift as tight as possible to the Body, and pin it close, to shew the roundness of their breasts, and their Petticoat close to their Hips to shew the fineness of their Limbs—so that they might as well be in Puri Naturalibus—Indeed Nakedness is not censurable or indecent here, and they expose themselves often quite Naked, without Ceremony—Rubbing themselves and their Hair with Bears Oil and tying it up behind in a bunch like the Indians—being hardly one degree removed from them."[48] The Reverend Woodmason's accounts may be biased, but one fact emerges: the frontier was a place where customs and institutions of white Europeans underwent changes, both for good and bad.

In the light of frontier animosities, most Indian nations tried to remain neutral during the intercolonial wars of the Eighteenth Century. During the French and Indian War, the Iroquois were reluctant to ally themselves either with the French or the British. Even though they had a lasting friendship with the British, they were not inclined to take up arms against the French. Indeed, the early defeats of British expeditions caused them to be cautious.[49] Eventually, William Johnson would persuade the Iroquois to support him in an expedition to Crown Point on Lake George. The Crown Point expedition began in the summer of 1755. Johnson went up the Hudson River to the great carrying place of Fort Edward with about three thousand seven hundred militiamen, commanded by testy New England officers who disliked Johnson's authority.[50] They were also uneasy with the presence of the three hundred Indian warriors, led by old Hendrick.[51] Many of the Iroquois warriors had followed Indian trails to get to Fort Edward, rather than take the tedious route of the white transports up the Hudson.

In the face of this threat, the French reacted by taking the offensive. Baron Dieskau, the French commander, rushed southward from Quebec with a large force of French, Abenakis and Caughnawagas.[52] But the British were prepared to meet this drive. After a stirring ovation delivered by Hendrick, the Iroquois were also ready for battle. The British were able to keep this force supplied through the use of a new road from the southern end of Lake George to the western bend in the Hudson River.

Dieskau, intent on destroying Johnson's base of supplies, encamped north of Fort Edward early in September. Assuming that he was closing in on the fort, Dieskau came upon the road to Lake George and encountered Johnson's advance Indian scouts. On September 14, 1755, Johnson's militiamen felt the pressure of the more numerous French forces and retreated to join the main contingent.[53] Subsequently, the center of the British forces moved up to engage the advancing French. At this point, Hendrick and his men saved the day by flanking the French on either side and fighting fiercely. This cost the Iroquois many lives, including outstanding leaders such as old Hendrick, who was one of the first to die.[54] His death made the Iroquois more resolute in the battle against the French.

The British won a costly, bloody victory. The determining factor was the ferocity of the Iroquois attacks on the French flanks. Once more the strength and significance of the Indians had been demonstrated to both the French and the English. Johnson reaped a personal glory, but the Iroquois had lost many young men in battle and nothing could bring them back.[55] By eliminating the French from North America, they were forfeiting their position as a balance of power.

However, Johnson's victory did not cause the Iroquois to embrace the English wholeheartedly. In December 1756, an Iroquois delegation (excluding the Mohawks) went to Montreal to reaffirm their relationship with the Governor of Quebec. The French had most success with the Senecas, since the fortified trading post at Niagara distributed a quantity of gifts to them. Many Senecas had even taken up the hatchet against the British by this time. Johnson wrote despairingly of the Seneca situation, "Our ill Success hitherto hath intimidated them . . . In short, without some striking Success on our Side, I believe they will not join us."[56]

During the year 1757, Johnson tried to keep most of the Six Nations neutral in the conflict. Although the Iroquois were willing to join in the war on either side, they wisely wanted all the battles to be fought far from Central and Western New York. The Confederacy was opposed to any expedition through the Iroquois homeland.[57] Johnson did manage to send out some raiding parties to protect frontier settlements and obtain intelligence as to the whereabouts of the French. In 1758, Johnson could bring more than four hundred Iroquois warriors into the field for the attack on Ticonderoga. Johnson stated he was able to gain the support of the Confederacy, since the French had ". . . neither provisions nor Presents to give them."[58] By 1759, the situation had changed for the British. The Iroquois now welcomed an expedition through their homeland to conquer Niagara. The English reduction of Louisbourg, Fort Frontenac, and Fort Duquesne helped the Iroquois to reconsider their earlier position. A French ship laden with trade goods was lost at sea, while Albany still had plenty of goods made available to the Indians. The Iroquois realized that the French were in the twilight of their power in North America. The long standing neutrality of the Confederacy was now changed. After meeting with the Iroquois, Johnson had persuaded the entire Confederacy, ". . . to agree to Join, and go with us against Niagara . . ."[59] He then took five hundred Iroquois with him to Oswego to meet Brigadier General John Prideaux, and together they successfully attacked the fort at Oswego. Prideaux was killed during the battle, so Johnson took command of the British forces. As word of the victory spread, the Indian contingent swelled to nine hundred men.[60]

In June 1760, Johnson called for men to attack Montreal. About six hundred warriors responded. Many of the tribesmen living in the Montreal area also responded to his call. Sir William reported he was sending gifts to "foreign Indians" who were switching their allegiance from the sinking French Empire.[61] By August 5, 1760, the native contingent had reached one thousand three hundred and thirty. Johnson reported to William Pitt, "Thus Sir, we became Masters of the last place in the Enemy's possession in these parts and made those Indians our friends by a peace, who might otherwise have given us much trouble."[62]

The defeat of the French and their departure from Canada at the end of the war upset the balance that the Iroquois had sought to maintain. Reluctantly, they attached themselves to the British, but they could no longer play one European power against another. The English now occupied all the forts surrounding Iroquois country. Gradually the Indians were being encircled, with only Europeans as prospective allies.[63] However, at the end of the French and Indian War, the Confederacy did not perceive this as an immediate threat.

As the war wound down after 1760, the British did not choose to be so liberal in their gifts to their Indian allies, as they had been in their time of need. Sir Jeffrey Amherst, commander-in-chief for North America, had different ideas from Sir William Johnson in the conduct of Indian relations. Amherst thought that Indians should be concerned with bringing in skins or they might become mischievous. Moreover, he directed his officers to hand out powder, arms and clothing sparingly, for hunting purposes only, and to exercise caution in doing so. He also established a trading schedule at Fort Pitt and other posts, increasing the exchange rates for pelts and strouds.[64] For a society whose economy was built upon agriculture, hunting and fishing for food, and dependence upon the fruits of the land, this was but another long step in the development of dependence upon a European economy. The way back was now nearly impossible.

A rising hostility was being shown towards the English, most particularly because of Amherst's frugal policy, which reacted against the western Indians at Detroit and Niagara. This was so clear, that

Johnson felt it necessary to call conferences explaining the new policy. The Indians would not accept the explanations, and antagonism grew, so that Johnson's life was in danger on his journey westward. In Illinois, belts of wampum were already circulating inviting the Indian nations to take up the hatchet against the British. Many tribes had exhausted their stores of powder as a result of war.[65] On September 6, 1761, at Fort Detroit, the Ottawas implored Johnson to consider their need for powder, necessary for hunting, for the fur trade as well as for food. Johnson replied guardedly,

> That he should in due time consider the wants which they had represented and hoped they would for the future by their hunting and by an industrious way of life be enabled to Support their familys without other assistance.[66]

But the Ottawas would be fortunate indeed if they received any powder from the British, since the total expenses allowed for Johnson's journey amounted to only three hundred and five British pounds.[67] Much of this money went to pay assistants and other incidentals of the journey.

In April 1762, Johnson held a congress with the Six Nations. A huge wampum belt was offered to the Iroquois to represent the "Ancient Covenant Chain" between the Six Nations and the British. Johnson also promised that the English would keep the chain intact so long as the Confederacy held fast its promises to be allies of the Crown. In turn, the Senecas promised their allegiance to the English.[68] The other nations of the Confederacy declared they would continue their support of their English brethren.

But Amherst's policy of frugality was beginning to bear a bitter fruit. In May 1762 at Fort Pitt, George Croghan, deputy agent, began to send reports of dissatisfaction among the neighboring tribes. They were beginning to miss the more liberal trade policies of the French and those English officers before Amherst. The Indians asked Croghan for the ". . . Reason why we allways was calling them to Council During Ye War & giveing them presents & now Take no Notice of them. They say ye French was butt a poor peple (sic) butt they allways Cloathed any Indians that was poor or Naked when they Come to see them."[69]

As a result of such policies, war rumors began to circulate and abuses by whites inevitably brought retaliations from the tribesmen. Many of the border conflicts were directly related to the refusal of goods in 1762. George Croghan handed out goods to disgruntled Indians to preserve peace in early 1763.

To Croghan and others, it was painfully obvious that a border war was brewing. Croghan used a whole year's salary to forestall this event, by distributing goods. White settler pressure in western

Pennsylvania also served as an impetus for war.[70] Thus, the continuing decay of Iroquois economy and the lack of goods to supply the Indians with needed commodities, brought distrust on the part of the Indians. Discontent turned to hostility. Seeing evidence of this, the British were in their turn uneasy. On the frontier, both Indian and white would soon be faced with disaster.

The Senecas were the first to act, as a result of the new containment policies. As early as 1761, a group of Senecas including Guyasuta, the maternal uncle of Handsome Lake, carried the red wampum belt from the Onondaga council to Fort Detroit. In the very shadow of British military might, the Senecas asked the Delaware and Shawnee of Ohio, and the Chippewa, Huron, Potawatomi, and Ottawa of Detroit to make common cause with the Six Nations in a simultaneous surprise attack on the British posts at Pittsburgh, Presque Isle, Venango, Niagara, and Detroit. But the Ohio Indians decided not to join in the plan and revealed the preparations to the British. The plan would be revived by Pontiac in the spring of 1763. Two more Seneca war belts were circulated among the Delaware, Shawnee, Miami and other Indians around Detroit.[71]

The Senecas let go of the Covenant Chain the very next year, after it had been secured in Pontiac's rebellion. Pontiac did not follow the Seneca plan in detail, but it was certainly a factor in fostering the surprise frontier assaults in the spring of 1763. Pontiac had not intentionally organized a pan-Indian uprising, but several factors helped to further his cause. The prior circulation of the Seneca plan suggested the method of the campaign. Also, the French were holding out in Louisiana and gave encouragement to the venture. Resentment towards the English for their withholding of goods played an important part in the rebellion. The British failure to open up adequate trade channels was another key reason. Finally, the preachings of a new messiah, the Delaware Prophet swayed many tribes, since he promised a return to an earlier tribal purity if the English were driven out.[72] Pontiac's siege of Fort Detroit probably triggered all these animosities.

Pontiac's rebellion aimed to destroy the British chain of forts, removing the English from Indian land between the Allegheny Mountains and the Mississippi River. The Ottawa, Chippewa, Potawatomi, Huron, Miami, Wea, Delaware, Mingo (Six Nations people living in the Ohio region), Shawnee, and Seneca mounted the assault against the British forts. As the eastern members of the Confederacy treated with Johnson, they attempted to lull him and Amherst into a false sense of security. Meanwhile, the Senecas attacked and destroyed the forts at Venango, Le Boeuf, and Presque Isle.[73] In addition, they nearly annihilated two British detachments at Devil's Hole as they were following the newly cut road along the cliff, above the whirlpool at Niagara Falls. The ambush at Devil's Hole demonstrated the vulnerability of the British. About five hundred Senecas surprised a convoy of twenty-five horse and ox drawn wagons protected by thirty men and an officer. At a narrow place in the road, a volley from the side of the trail stopped the British. While confusion reigned, the Senecas moved in with tomahawks for hand-to-hand combat. The settlers and soldiers, taken completely by surprise, were unable to mount a defense. Teams of stampeding animals plunged over the cliff. Drivers became tangled in harness leather or were trampled by kicking and screaming animals. The soldiers tried to fight hand-to-hand with their backs to the cliffs, but to no avail. Only two men in the party escaped with their lives.[74]

Hearing the shots, two British companies (about eighty men) rushed to help. They were met in a new ambush before they reached Devil's Hole. They too were cut down by an initial volley followed by intense hand-to-hand combat. Within a few minutes, half the relief force was also dead. When the garrison from Fort Niagara arrived on the scene five officers and sixty-seven men lay dead on the trail.[75]

Nevertheless, the scheme to roll back the British to the Allegheny Mountains ended in failure. Fort Detroit, Pitt, and Niagara held out against the combined Indian onslaught. Eventually, the British were able to bring in reinforcements, and Indian food supplies began to dwindle. The Senecas settled their differences with Sir William Johnson in July 1764, receiving sharp rebuke from him during a congress at Niagara. The Senecas gave up the leaders in the rebellion and ceded the portage route at Niagara to the British, who prudently made few reprisals. Moreover, the Proclamation Line of 1763 had set a boundary between Indian and white territory that recognized the Indians as owners of their traditional lands.[76] But the English flag still flew over the garrisons in the heart of Indian country.

During Pontiac's rebellion, it is quite probable that Handsome Lake heard of the Delaware Prophet's message, and he might even have been exposed to his teachings. Although the Prophet made few converts among the Senecas, his message did serve as a spiritual catalyst for the rebellion. The Prophet lived on the banks of the Cuyahoga River near Lake Erie (present day Cleveland). He is said to have had visions in which the Creator spoke to him. While communicating with the Creator, this man received a code of detailed instructions to follow to avoid the perils of worldly misery and damnation confronting the Ohio and Iroquois Indians along the frontier. If the code were followed, the Indians would be able to drive the white men out of their country and return to the simplicity and happiness of their original state. Neolin, "the Enlightened," as he was known, preached of repentence and the proper means of regaining the favor of the Creator.[77]

Neolin told the people that the Great Spirit had ordered them to make sacrifices and renounce the ways of the white man. Indian people would then return to a former and happier state. He talked of giving up alcohol and abstaining from sexual intercourse to rid themselves of sin. He said that fire should not be made by flint and steel, but by rubbing two sticks together. People were to learn to live again without trade with the Europeans. The message was one that stressed the revival of ancient customs, in order to give the people the strength and resolve to resist the encroachments of the white man. He prophesied that, after a period of negotiations with the Europeans, there would be an Indian uprising in 1762.[81]

The Delaware Prophet's message was a mixture of the old and the new. Some of his recommendations were not at all traditional. He asked that people give up "medicine songs" and war rituals. He introduced such European concepts as a high-god for both white and Indian, as well as written prayers and a written "Great Book." These teachings touched off a spiritual revival. The Prophet sold copies of his spiritual chart for one buckskin, or two doeskins apiece. Disciples sprang up throughout the frontier and to the west. People traveled miles to hear him speak. His idea of a boycott was so effective that a Pittsburgh trader said the Delaware ". . .have quit hunting any more than to supply nature in that way." Pontiac became a convert and used the message to fuel his rebellion.[82]

An unnamed Onondaga Prophet also began to preach at the same time. He recounted a vision in which the Great Spirit told him that "when He first made the World, He gave this large Island to the Indians for their Use: at the same time He gave other Parts of the World beyond the great waters to the rest of his creating, and gave them different languages: That he now saw the white People squabbling, and fighting for these Lands which he gave the Indians." Furthermore, the Onondaga Prophet stated that ". . .in every Assembly, the Company of Governors, and Great Men, He heard nothing scarce spoke, or talk'd of, but claiming, and wanting, large Possessions in our country." He asserted that this was not the intent of the Creator and it was to be expected that ". . .when the white People first came, like Children, among Us, that He was quite displeas'd, and would, altho their Numbers were ever so great punish them if They did not desist."[83] Thus, the prophetic vision of the evil of the white man's ways spread, gaining wide acceptance.

In 1766, Pontiac went to Oswego to make peace with the British. Johnson was able to conduct his diplomatic efforts in relative tranquility in the years before the American Revolution. With the French influence liquidated in Canada, the threat of an invasion from the north was removed. All signs pointed to a strong and lasting alliance with the Iroquois.[84] But the introduction of missionaries among them began a new wave of disruption in the Confederacy.

With the coming of missionaries in the 1760s, the tribes of the League were to experience a drifting apart. New England missionaries had begun to labor among the Oneida and Tuscarora in the early 1760s. The Moheconnuck or Stockbridge Indians were granted permission to settle among the Oneidas and have a mission. Onoquaga on the Susquehanna River, New Stockbridge, and later Brothertown were centers of missionary activity. The Brothertown tribes (remnants of six New England and Long Island tribes) were ministered to by Samson Occum, a Mohegan. Indians and whites who had been trained at Eleazar Wheelock's school in Connecticut went among the Iroquois preaching the word of Christ and setting up schools.

Perhaps the most influential of these missionaries was Samuel Kirkland. His influence was both spiritual and political, especially among the Oneidas and Tuscaroras. He was enthusiastically endorsed by William Johnson for work with the Senecas in 1764, but after two years with the Senecas he left them and decided to spend the rest of his life with the Oneidas. Kirkland's work among the Oneidas and their dependents, the Tuscaroras, made him much loved by them. He was also a key figure in thwarting Johnson's diplomatic maneuvers on the eve of the American Revolution. This New England Puritan, with "New Light" principles, was a patriot to the core.[85] Because he was held in such high esteem among many of the Iroquois, he would cause Johnson considerable difficulty as the American Revolution unfolded.

The vision and message is similar to the teachings of Deganawidah and Hiawatha, but the influence of the European and his ways was incorporated into the code. According to tradition, the Delaware Prophet dreamed that he went searching for the Creator and finally found a mountain of glass, where he met a beautiful woman removing a white robe and bathing. Neolin climbed the mountain, using only his left hand and foot and arrived in heaven. There he found a stockaded village with a gate and a handsome guide dressed in white, who took him to the Creator. The Master of Life took Neolin by the hand and sat him on a hat bordered with gold. Hesitantly, the Delaware Prophet listened to the Creator.

The Creator told the Prophet to advise all Indian people to stop excessive drinking, committing adultery, and singing medicine songs. He also told the Prophet that he gave the land to Indian people and no others. He stated that Indians were overly dependent upon the white man's technology. The Creator asked that the Prophet and his people renounce the ways of the white man. In conclusion, the Creator said, "Here is a written paper which I give thee . . . teach it to all the Indians and children . . . . I command thee to repeat morning and evening, the prayer which I have given thee."[78]

In response to these admonitions, Neolin stated that he could not read. However, the Master of Life said that when the Prophet returned to earth he would send a chief to his village, one who could read. Neolin promised obedience and returned to his village, speaking to no one until he had presented to the chief the laws and prayers the Creator had given him. Through another vision, the Prophet drew a pictograph on a deerskin parchment, explaining the soul's progress in this world and the hereafter. This drawing was called the Great Book of Writing. Subsequently, Neolin traveled about preaching, and explaining the map.[79]

Neolin preached that in the beginning the Master of Life had entrusted to the Indians a beautiful country to fish and hunt in (depicted on the outer portion of the deerskin). In the old days, access to heaven was direct and simple, but the coming of the white man complicated the process.

Neolin argued the old way had been lost by "being remiss in the expression of our gratitude to the Great Spirit, for what he has bestowed upon us; by neglecting to make him sufficient sacrifices; by looking upon a people of a different color from our own, who had come across a great lake, as if they were part of ourselves; by suffering them to sit down by our side, and looking at them with indifference, while they were not only taking our country from us, but this (pointing to the spot), this, our own avenue, leading into those beautiful regions which are destined for us." Indians were now forced into finding a new way to heaven, he said, but this new way was more hazardous since the Indian must now face the sins and vices introduced by the whites.[80]

When Kirkland came among the Oneidas, he was supported by David Fowler, a Montauk Indian schoolmaster. Fowler and his wife were Christians and had received their education at Wheelock's school. Fowler acted as interpreter for Kirkland until he learned the Oneida language.

Very soon the missionary began to influence the conduct of the Oneidas. He was concerned about drunkenness and so serious was the problem that he issued an ultimatum only a few months after his arrival, requiring the villagers to forego spirits of any kind. He also proposed that a committee of six to eight men (chiefs) be appointed to assist him in enforcing this rule. These men had the power to seize any liquor within the community and destroy it. Kirkland stated that if the Oneidas would not agree to his request, he would end his missionary relationship with them.[86]

For four days, the Oneidas deliberated over this pronouncement, and then agreed. They unanimously endorsed eight men nominated by the minister, to enforce sobriety. With this committee set up, the Oneidas began to resist the offerings of alcohol by traders. In the face of free liquor, the tribesmen declined, saying: "It is contrary to the minister's word, and our agreement with him." Although there were several lapses, this showed the power Kirkland had over the Oneidas even in the early years of his ministry.[87]

The Tuscaroras and Oneidas were greatly interested in Christianity, and were deeply moved by Kirkland's sermons. People from outlying villages came to hear him preach. His church would be filled, and people stood outdoors in the snow because of the overflowing congregation.[88]

The minister had strict standards about baptism that caused some problems, since many Iroquois had been taught by Anglican and Roman Catholic missionaries that baptism was critical in order to be saved. But Kirkland asserted that only the regenerate, or the children of the regenerate, could be baptized. The Reverend refused to compromise on this point, even when a child was near death. It would cause trouble in later times.[89]

Kirkland often preached three times on Sunday, and he lectured and catechized several times during the week. The sermons were long and tiring. His journal for December 26, 1775, demonstrates his dedication:

> Preached both parts of the day by the desire of some from John 3-19 111.
> I also lectured between meetings. I have had but half an hour retreat from eight in the morning to ten in the Evening—yet I feel as if I had done nothing for God—am not only an unprofitable but an unskillful servant.[90]

These religious meetings would often go on until midnight, and the minister's superiors often admonished him for such excesses. But the Iroquois informed Kirkland that followers of the traditional way spent many hours at their ceremonies, therefore Christians could not do less for their God. The missionary explained to his superiors in this way:

> These nocturnal conferences will undoubtedly be condemned by those who are unacquainted with Indians, and my situation among them. When their minds are more than usually engaged to inquire into any important subject, their feelings would be

very much hurt by my refusing to discuss it with them as long as they desired; and the subject itself perhaps would never after be revived.[91]

Two centuries later, this process would be called brainwashing.

Kirkland's influence among the Iroquois extended to educational and agricultural pursuits as well. One of his assistants, Deacon Thomas, taught school at the Tuscarora town of Kanadesko, as well as catechizing. Parents were eager to have their children taught in their own language, and by 1770 the people of Kanowalohale asked Kirkland for a permanent schoolmaster. The Reverend also obtained farming implements and carpenter's tools to encourage the adoption of such trades among the Oneidas and Tuscaroras, and he saw to it that these tools and implements were used effectively and fully. In fact, he stated that by using the tools in common, more use was obtained from them than he could have done "for a whole year."[92]

The minister was also busy settling quarrels and other personal matters. "Every little petty difference in family or between Relations must be brought to me," he warned. This was a burdensome task, but he was probably sought on these questions because of his impartiality.[93]

Welfare was also an area in which Kirkland exercised influence. He often received appeals for food and clothing for destitute people. Because the principle of hospitality was deeply ingrained in Iroquois character, many Indians were often reduced to poverty. A visitor was invariably offered food, and if he were hungry, he would eat. If not, he would taste the food and then thank his hosts for their hospitality. Failure to perform this ritual would be an extreme discourtesy.[94] But this often caused hardship for some, and Kirkland gave freely. He often borrowed money to provide food and clothing for destitute people. No clearer evidence than this may be found of the dire effects of the imposition of a commodity economy upon the natural economy of the the the Iroquois. The men were now hunting for pelts instead of food. The fields received less attention. And the people grew more and more dependent upon European manufactured goods.

It was through these activities that the minister's influence grew among the Oneidas and Tuscaroras. Though his doctrines were sometimes vexing to the Indians, he was becoming an indispensable part of the community.

In the fall of 1770, Kirkland broke his connections with the Wheelocks and their school and put his work under the direction of the *Boston Board of Commissioners for the London Company for the Propagation of the Gospel in New England and Parts Adjacent in America*. The Corporation of Harvard College provided some support as well. Now the attention of the Oneidas and Tuscaroras was upon Boston, because it was in Boston that the commissioners lived. Support for schools and churches also came from Boston.[95] In the next few years, when revolutionary sentiment would be inflamed, all opponents to the Crown would be called "Bostonians," and most of the Oneidas and Tuscaroras could not be made to believe that Boston was the source of all evil.

New England influence among the Iroquois spelled trouble for Sir William Johnson, and he was aware of it. Although he approved of Wheelock's Indian School and Kirkland's intention to minister to the Iroquois, he also saw the beginnings of revolutionary sentiments as early as 1764. The British colonial tax measures after the French and Indian War, known as the Grenville Plan and the Townshend Acts, cause considerable discontent among the colonies. It appeared to Johnson and others that this rebellious spirit was centered in New England. The Sugar Act of 1764 hit New England hard, causing a stirring emotional reaction in Parliament in response to the problem of taxing the colonies without their representation. In 1765, Boston's opposition to the Stamp Act was also vigorous. Moreover, the formation of the Sons of Liberty in western Connecticut that same year alarmed Johnson. The home of Andrew Oliver, tax stamp collector, was ransacked at this time, and the house of Lieutenant Governor Thomas Hutchinson was destroyed by a Boston mob.[96]

As the question of the right of Parliament to tax the colonies became a burning issue, Johnson realized that such a rebellious attitude would lead to more violence and disrespect for British authority. If such ideas were allowed to prevail, Johnson saw how they would undermine his own authority as Indian superintendent. Indeed, England's whole policy towards the tribes could well become influenced and even controlled by colonial legislatures. He also perceived that the colonial legislatures were more interested in Indian land than in the trading interests of the Imperial administration.

Sir William now viewed the ministry of Samuel Kirkland and Eleazar Wheelock as a danger to his authority. He remembered that the New Englanders were a determined lot. In the 1600s, Massachusetts Bay argued constantly with the British Crown about its charter. He also remembered that the New Haven Colony had given shelter to the regicides of Charles I during their time of need. Johnson would now become more cautious in his dealings with Wheelock and his missionaries.[97] He would also try to blunt Kirkland's influence.

On March 5, 1770, a mob of Bostonians harassed a contingent of British soldiers, who were goaded into firing into the crowd, killing five and wounding six.[98] The "Boston Massacre" alarmed Johnson and his friends. Surely, the presence of New Englanders among the Iroquois was now questionable.

In 1768, at the Treaty of Fort Stanwix, Johnson had also experienced trouble with the New Englanders. Jacob Johnson and David Avery had replaced Kirkland for a few months due to his illness. Both men were at Fort Stanwix and opposed the moving of the boundary line between Indian and white settlements further west, because it interfered with future missionary plans. They criticized Johnson for this action and influenced the Oneidas to disagree with the proposed boundary line. Johnson was furious, and Wheelock apologized to him for this political maneuver. However, distrust intensified, and Sir William proposed that the position of the Anglican Church should be secured in America through an Anglican Episcopate.[99] This would thwart the designs of the Puritan New Englanders.

The idea of an American Episcopate was charged with political animosities by the 1760s. Southern Anglicans were disinterested in the proposal, since the vestries had great power which they did not want to relinquish. But northern Anglicans pressed vigorously for a bishop. This united the New England Congregationalists and the Presbyterians of the Middle Colonies into opposing the proposal. They feared an American Episcopate because they thought an American bishop would exercise powers such as the English bishops had, to restrict the rights of other religious denominations.[100]

In the light of these controversies, Johnson attempted to discourage the construction of a new meeting house under the sponsorship of the Boston commissioners. Although the Oneida's building could hold only half the congregation and was rotting, Johnson did not want the sachems to request the new building from Boston, but rather from the King. In the fall of 1770, the new meeting house was approved by the commissioners, and Kirkland suggested that a sawmill be constructed to help in building the new structure. In early 1771, Johnson visited Oneida country and told the Indians that it was more prudent to request the new church from the King than from the Bostonians. He argued that the people of Boston were rebellious and seditious, enemies of all proper government. Bending history a little, Johnson said that Bostonians had killed their king and fled to Massachusetts for safety. As a result of this slaying, the white people were now divided, he explained. He appealed to the Oneidas to stand behind their covenant with the King and support the established procedures. His words held considerable weight with the Iroquois.

Johnson also explained that Anglican ministers did not insist upon regeneration before baptism, as Kirkland did. He said that the Anglican ministers would be far more flexible in the application of their doctrine. Plainly, he was utilizing both political and religious arguments to persuade the Oneidas to remain in close alliance with the Crown. Religion had always been one of the tools of Indian diplomacy, used by both the British and French. A loyal Anglican minister among the Oneidas would give the tribesmen proper religious instruction, as well as proper political instruction should the need arise. Such a cleric could link the Oneidas as strongly to the Crown as the Mohawks were. Johnson asked the Oneidas to at least consult the King about any actions they were considering.[101]

On February 1, 1771, the Oneida chiefs presented Johnson's proposals to a council. Two days later, an all day council of the people was held to discuss the issue. Kirkland was invited to present his viewpoint. The warrior party supported Kirkland while the chiefs seemed reluctant to take a firm stand. The missionary had converted several prominent warriors; these men became his staunch supporters. In the end, the minister prevailed. He also noted that the Oneida warriors were not easily controlled by the sachems. This rivalry between the warriors and the chiefs became advantageous to Kirkland as the Revolution drew closer.

The tendency of the warriors to override the wishes of the peace chiefs was expressed by a Seneca war chief, as early as 1762 at Johnson Hall. When the superintendent expressed surprise and dismay that few sachems were at the meeting, the Seneca war chief said:

> The Reason that you do not see many of Our Sachems at present here is that the Weather and Roads having been very bad, they were less able than we to travel, & therefore, we the Warriors were made Choice of to Attend you & transact business; and I beg you will consider that we are in fact the People of Consequence for Managing Affairs, Our Sachems being generally a parcell of Old People who say Much, but who mean or Act very little, So that we have both the power & Ability to Settle Matters, & are now determin'd to Answer you honestly, and from our hearts to Declare all Matters fully to you.[102]

The warriors were greatly attached to Kirkland. Their faith in him was unshaken even in the face of Johnson's opposition. Kirkland himself said, "Numbers of them said they would go with me to prison or death—where I followed Christ, they would follow me." Many Oneidas were concerned about the personal and theological laxity of the Anglican ministers whom they had encountered. They thought that baptism should denote a changed life and said that the feasting and drinking at Anglican baptisms was deplorable. The warriors asserted they would have continued along a path of destruction, if they had not had a minister to give them lessons in "Regeneration, Repentence, and Faith."[103]

In their discussions with the sachems, the warriors rejected the comment that the Bostonians had "killed their King," as Johnson had said. Instead, they emphasized the great amount of preparation and prayer that had gone into the decision to petition the Boston commissioners for a new church building. They felt that the Lord's blessing was upon their actions. In one statement, the warriors argued through the Free Church tradition for separation of church and state. "We fully agree with you, that all affairs should be laid before Sr. William. But in church affairs, & even all that immediately respects the Kingdom & government of Jesus Christ, we must go directly to God, by his word & ministers, & we judge it as proper & no less honorable that the House of God should be built by the Ministers of the great King Jesus, as by the King of England himself." In typical fashion, the warriors ended, asking for unity. "Let us all go on with one heart and one mind and then look out for Gods blessing."[104]

In view of these arguments, the sachems agreed. They had no desire to upset the delicate balance between the warriors and themselves for such a controversy. They were diplomats and politicians and realized Kirkland's influence upon the whole community. In fact, one of the sachems told the minister as much on the morning of the people's council meeting.[105]

Finally, the controversy was solved to everyone's satisfaction but Johnson's. In 1773, the Oneidas raised their church with the help of a professional carpenter and two assistants, and thus became the talk of the Confederacy. In 1774, they built a large steeple over the church despite Kirkland's objections, who maintained that "religion loves simplicity." But the Oneidas reasoned that if the white people could have steeples, then so too could they. Indian religion was equal to the white man's and Indians were entitled to worship God in a commodious building.[106] Truly, the Oneidas now had their own meeting house, their own minister, and the religion of their choosing.

There were other events brewing within the Confederacy, events that would be heightened as the Revolution began. One of the land deals in the Treaty of Fort Stanwix was the surrendering of Iroquois land and the land of dependent tribes south of the Ohio and Susquehanna Rivers. The Ohio lands were used by the Mingoes, Shawnees and other subordinate Confederacy tribes. The Iroquois claimed to represent all the occupants and users, so they negotiated the sale, and kept all the proceeds. They believed they were disposing of frontier friction by opening up all of Kentucky and parts of western Pennsylvania and West Virginia to settlement. But they also sold off the land of their allies to the south, the Shawnees.[107] The Shawnees subsequently joined a confederacy of western Indians in order to resist white expansion.

After the Treaty of Fort Stanwix, the Confederacy was confronted with an incredibly difficult diplomatic task. They had to maintain the friendship of the British and the Shawnee. The British felt they had bought the land from the true owners, the Iroquois, and expected the old tenants to be removed, making way for white settlers. The Shawnee pressed the Iroquois to live up to their old commitments involving defense and protection, as prescribed under the Great Tree of Peace. Iroquois influence with the British hinged on their ability to control other tribes, but the means to control them rested on the Iroquois' ability to protect them from British intervention. So the Confederacy went from playing one side against another, the British and French, to being put in a squeeze.[108] They could not join the rebellious Shawnees and yet they could not fault them for fighting the white settlers.

Many Iroquois, especially the Seneca, were sympathetic to the Shawnee cause. The Senecas saw the frontier riff-raff crowding them in, living now under the shadow of British garrisons. Finally in 1774, many Senecas joined the Shawnee, Delaware and Wyandot in Lord Dunmore's War. This was a war that almost provoked the Confederacy to wage a general war all along the English frontier. The conflict demonstrated the deteriorating relations between Indian and white, and the inability of both sides to effectively control their own internal affairs.[109]

The origin of Lord Dunmore's War lies in the activities of a white surveying party in the land south of the Ohio. One day, Michael Cresap and his party of land jobbers missed their horses and blamed the Shawnees. In revenge, the white party slaughtered a peaceful hunting party. Among the dead were some of the relatives of Captain John Logan, a Cayuga, who had taken a Shawnee wife and moved westward. A few days later, a party of white men invited a group of Indians to come to the Virginia side, got them drunk, and killed them. Among those slain were a brother and sister of Logan. The woman was pregnant. Logan was now without any close relatives. Other Indians attempted to cross the river in canoes to rescue them; they were shot in midstream.

Logan was infuriated and stricken with grief. That summer he attacked several families located on Indian land and killed many of them. By late summer, border raids increased and the Ohio frontier was raging in conflict.

The Senecas lost no time in joining the Ohio Indians. They were angry about the gruesome killing of Bald Eagle, who spoke English well and lived among the Delaware. He was a kindly man to all who knew him. In the winter, he had gone after furs down the Monongahela River. As he was returning in the spring, he was shot by a white man and scalped. The killer propped his body upright in the canoe and set it adrift.

Dunmore, the Virginia governor, called out the militia to punish Logan, although he acknowledged the Indian had ample justification. Several thousand Indians and whites met at the Battle of Point Pleasant. The Indians (Shawnee, Mingo, Delaware, Wyandot, Cayuga and Seneca) were outnumbered, and were defeated by the militia. The League at Onondaga refused to sanction the war and chose to ignore the Shawnee who were trying to form their own western confederacy.[110]

The Iroquois still held sway along the northern frontier, as the American Revolution drew still closer. But the price was blood and tortuous diplomatic maneuvers. The white man's consuming passion for land nurtured a growing distrust on the Indian side. Both sides were anxious for freedom and justice. But sharing the land and cooperating peacefully was not acceptable to the Europeans. A love/hate relationship developed among most white frontiersmen. While the whites respected the knowledge and freedom possessed by the Indians, they were unwilling to deal with them honestly, as the "brothers" they so often had professed themselves to be. Both sides operated under declarations of peace, but were unable to settle their differences.

All through the colonial period, the Iroquois pointed out the need for the white colonists to unite. Slowly, the vision of such unity began to take shape in the colonial mind. Statements declaring the need for unity were heard eloquently at the Albany Congress, where the Iroquois addressed the colonial leaders. In spite of the terrible clashes along the frontier, the Iroquois ideas about government and freedom had a profound impact upon the Americans. The example of such an operating Confederacy had greater weight for Americans, certainly, than the words (which they could not read) of a Plato, Aristotle, Locke, Rousseau or Montesquieu. The Americans, although grudgingly, respected the ways and ideas of the Iroquois and adapted many of these ideas in spite of cultural differences and animosities. The words of Benjamin Franklin and the living conditions along the white frontier pointed toward a new and unique concept of democracy. In 1747, Governor George Clinton of New York observed that most American democratic leaders ". . . were ignorant, illiterate people of republican principles who have no knowledge of the English Constitution or love for their country."[111] Obviously, these unread people were gaining a sense of freedom from the American environment and its native peoples long before the outbreak of the American Revolution.

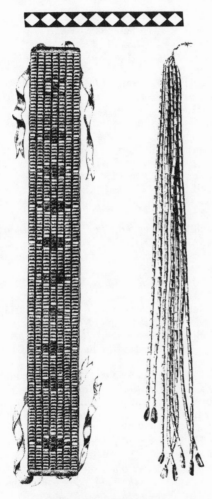

Left: Belt of Wampum.
Right: String of Wampum

REFERENCES CHAPTER TWO

1. John Locke, *Second Treatise on Civil Government*, 1690, Chapter I-V. Reprinted in Charles Sherover, ed., *The Development of the Democratic Idea* (New York, 1974).

2. *Ibid.*, Chapter VI, paragraph 57.

3. *Ibid.*, Chapter VII, paragraphs 87-90.

4. *Ibid.*, Chapter XV, paragraph 173.

5. Benjamin F. Wright, *American Interpretation of Natural Law* (Cambridge, 1931), pp. 64-71.

6. Benjamin P. Poore, comp., *The Federal and State Constitutions, Colonial Charters, and Other Organic Laws of the United States* (Washington, 1878), II, 1389.

7. Charles M. Sherover, ed., *Annotated Edition of the Social Contract* (New York, 1974), Book One, Chapters I and II.

8. *Ibid.*, passim; and see Bernard Sheehan, *Seeds of Extinction: Jeffersonian Philanthropy and the American Indian* (New York, 1973) for an analysis of such themes in the American context.

9. Sherover, ed., *Social Contract*, Book Three, Chapter VII.

10. *Ibid.*, Book One, Chapters III and VI, Book Three, Chapters IV and V.

11. Reuben Gold Thwaites, ed., *The Jesuit Relations and Allied Documents* (Cleveland, 1896-1901), XLII, 71.

12. Sara H. Stites, *Economics of the Iroquois* (Lancaster, Pennsylvania, 1904), p. 21.

13. Thwaites, ed., *Jesuit Relations*, XXXVIII, 255; and XIV, 235.

14. Morgan, *League of the Iroquois*, p. 323.

15. James E. Seaver, *Deh-he-wa-mis*; or, A Narrative of *the Life of Mary Jemison* (Batavia, N.Y. 1842), p. 70-71.

16. E. B. O'Callaghan, *Documents Relative to the Colonial History of New York* (Albany, New York, 1854), Chapters II and III, pp. 535, 557-561, 712-714.

17. *New York Colonial Documents*, III, 417-418; and Cadwallader Colden, *The History of the Five Nations of Canada* (New York, 1922), I, p. 69.

18. See Anthony F. C. Wallace, "The Origins of Iroquois Neutrality: The Grand Settlement of 1701," *Pennsylvania History*, XXIV (July, 1957).

19. Graymont, *Iroquois*, p. 27.

20. Lawrence H. Lederer, ed., *The Livingston Indian Records 1666-1723* (Gettysburg, Pa., 1956), p. 25n; Peter Wraxall, *An Abridgement of the Indian Affairs Contained in Four Folio Volumes, Transacted in the Colony of New York, from the Year 1678 to the Year 1751* (Cambridge, Mass., 1915), pp. 9, 11, 39, 116. See also *New York Colonial Documents*, IV, pp. 889-905, 908-911.

21. William J. Eccles, *The Canadian Frontier, 1534-1760* (New York, 1969), p. 133.

22. Nash, *Red, White and Black* (Englewood Cliffs, N.J., 1974), pp. 247-248.

23. Lawrence H. Lederer, ed., *Livingston Records*, p. 191; and John W. Lydekker, *The Faithful Mohawks* (Cambridge, 1938), p. 13.

24. See Richmond P. Bond, *Queen Anne's American Kings* (Oxford, 1952).

25. From Cadwallader Colden, *History of the Five Nations*, II, pp. 18-24.

26. *Ibid.*

27. See Lucy K. Cohen, ed., *The Legal Conscience: Selected Papers of Felix S. Cohen* (New Haven, 1960), pp. 315-327.

28. Anthony F. C. Wallace, *The Death and Rebirth of the Seneca* (New York, 1972), p. 112.

29. See James Sullivan, *et al.*, eds., *The Papers of Sir William Johnson* (Albany, N.Y., 1921-65), XII, 1062-1075.

30. *Sir William Johnson Papers*, I, pp. 339-344.

31. See Wilbur R. Jacobs, *Wilderness Politics and Indian Gifts* (Lincoln, Nebraska, 1966), p. 77.

32. Wallace, *Seneca*, p. 114.

33. See *Minutes of the Provincial Council of Pennsylvania from the Organization to the Termination of the Proprietary Government* (Philadelphia, 1838-1853), V. p. 667.

34. *Ibid.*, V, p. 623.

35. *New York Colonial Documents*, VII, p. 883.

36. *Pennsylvania Colonial Records*, V, pp. 680-681.

37. Louis K. Koontz, *The Virginia Frontier*, 1754-1763 (Baltimore, 1925) has a good account of the expedition.

38. John C. Fitzpatrick, ed., *The Diaries of George Washington, 1748-1799* (New York, 1925), I, p. 46.

39. *Ibid.*, I, p. 56.

40. *Ibid.*, I, pp. 61-64.

41. R. A. Brock, ed., *The Official Records of Robert Dinwiddie, Lieutenant Governor of Virginia, 1751-1758* in Virginia Historical Society *Collections*, III, p. 179.

42. See *Pennsylvania Colonial Records*, VI, p. 142; and *Dinwiddie Papers*, III, pp. 179-181.

43. *Pennsylvania Colonial Records*, VI, pp. 141-143, 161-163.

44. Leonard W. Labaree and Whitfield J. Bell, Jr., eds., *The Papers of Benjamin Franklin* (New Haven, 1962), V, p. 387.

45. *Ibid.*, V, pp. 387-392.

46. Albert Henry Smythe, ed., *The Writings of Benjamin Franklin*, (New York, 1905-07), III, p. 42.

47. Charles Woodmason, *The Carolina Backcountry on the Eve of the Revolution*, ed., Richard J. Hooker (Chapel Hill, 1953), pp. 15, 33.

48. *Ibid.*, pp. 56, 61.

49. George Croghan to William Johnson, September 10, 1755, *Sir William Johnson Papers*, II, pp. 28-30.

50. *Ibid.*, I, p. 542.

51. William Johnson to the Board of Trade, September 3, 1755, *New York Colonial Documents*, VI, pp. 993-997.

52. "Indian Proceedings," May 28, 1755, *Sir William Johnson Papers*, I, pp. 634-635.

53. *New York Colonial Documents*, VI, pp. 1003-1004.

54. *Ibid.*

55. *Sir William Johnson Papers*, II, pp. 343-350.

56. *Ibid.*, IX, 785; and Lawrence Henry Gipson, *The Victorious Years, 1758-1760*, Volume 7 of *The Great War for Empire* (New York, 1949), pp. 64-66, 73.

57. Gipson, *Victorious Years,* pp. 241-242, 342-343, 349-356.
58. *Sir William Johnson Papers,* III, p. 271.
59. *Ibid.,* III, pp. 27-30, 271.
60. *Ibid.,* III, pp. 122, 271.
61. *New York Colonial Documents,* VII, p. 433.
62. William Johnson to William Pitt, October 24, 1760, *Sir William Johnson Papers,* III, pp. 269-275.
63. Graymont, *Iroquois,* p. 32.
64. *Sir William Johnson Papers,* II, p. 345.
65. *Ibid.,* III, pp. 428-503.
66. *Ibid.,* III, p. 472.
67. *Ibid.,* III, p. 503.
68. *Ibid.,* III, pp. 670-717.
69. George Croghan to William Johnson, May 10, 1762, *Ibid.,* pp. 732-734.
70. George Croghan to William Johnson, March 12, 1763, *Ibid.,* IV, pp. 62-63.
71. Wallace, *Seneca,* pp. 114-115.
72. *Sir William Johnson Papers,* XI, p. 141.
73. Nash, *Red, White and Black,* p. 303.
74. Wallace, *Seneca,* p. 116.
75. *Ibid.*
76. *Sir William Johnson Papers,* XI, p. 141.
77. Nash, *Red, White and Black,* p. 304.
78. Wallace, *Seneca,* pp. 117-119.
79. Nash, *Red, White and Black,* p. 302.
80. Wallace, *Seneca,* p. 119.
81. Nash, *Red, White and Black,* p. 303.
82. See Robert Navarre, *Journal of the Conspiracy of Pontiac,* 1763, translated by R. Clyde Ford (Detroit, 1910).
83. *Sir William Johnson Papers,* X, pp. 505-506.
84. Graymont, *Iroquois,* p. 33.
85. Wallace, *Seneca,* p. 126.
86. Graymont, *Iroquois,* pp. 34-35; and William M. Beauchamp, *History of the New York State Iroquois* (Port Washington, N.Y., 1961), p. 202.
87. Samuel Kirkland Lothrop, *Life of Samuel Kirkland* (Boston, 1847), pp. 205-207.
88. Samuel Kirkland to Eleazar Wheelock, February 15, 1770, *Papers of Samuel Kirkland,* Hamilton College.
89. Samuel Kirkland to Levi Hart, January 17, 1771, *Kirkland Papers,* and Samuel Kirkland to John Thornton, February 6, 1771, *Kirkland Papers,* see also Beauchamp, *New York Iroquois,* pp. 221-222.
90. See Journal of Samuel Kirkland, June 18, 1774-January, 1775, p. 41, *Kirkland Papers.*
91. Lothrop, *Kirkland,* pp. 300-301.
92. See Journal, 1770-1771, pp. 6, 8, 22, *Kirkland Papers.*
93. *Ibid.,* p. 27.
94. Lewis Henry Morgan, *Houses and House Life of the American Aborigines* (Chicago, 1965), p. 45.
95. Graymont, *Iroquois,* p. 39.
96. Lawrence H. Gipson, *The Coming of the Revolution* (New York, 1954), pp. 90-95.

97. See Journal, 1770-1771, pp. 31-32, *Kirkland Papers*.

98. Gipson, *Revolution*, pp. 201-202.

99. *Sir William Johnson Papers*, XII, 748-749, and Wallace, *Seneca*, p. 122.

100. William W. Sweet, *Religion in Colonial America* (New York, 1947), pp. 71-72.

101. Graymont, *Iroquois*, pp. 43-44.

102. *Sir William Johnson Papers*, III, pp. 697-698.

103. See Journal, 1770-1771, pp. 32-33, *Kirkland Papers*.

104. *Ibid.*, pp. 34-37.

105. *Ibid.*, p. 37.

106. See Journal, 1773, 1774-1775, passim, *Kirkland Papers*.

107. Gipson, *Revolution*, p. 140.

108. Wallace, *Seneca*, pp. 122-123.

109. *New York Colonial Documents*, VIII, p. 490.

110. Wallace, *Seneca*, pp. 123-125.

111. *New York Colonial Documents*, VI, pp. 670-671.

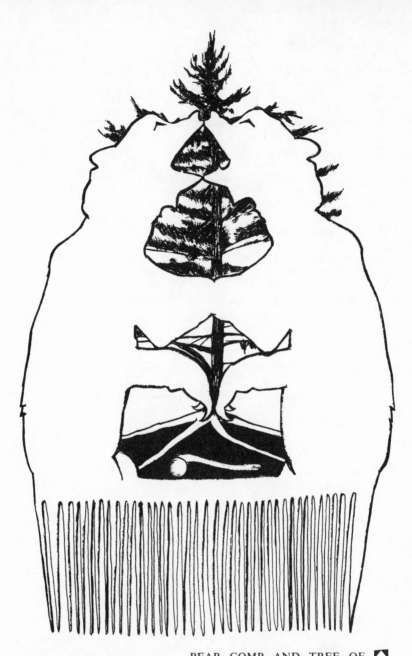

BEAR COMB AND TREE OF PEACE. The Iroquois and the colonists were rivals from the beginning of contact. The Great Tree of Peace, with the buried war club, symbolizes the generally peaceful attitude of the Confederacy in spite of the rivalry.

Chapter Three

THE BEGINNING
OF THE REVOLUTION

O N THE EVE OF THE AMERICAN REVOLUTION, the Iroquois Confederacy functioned much as it had in the past, but the tensions on the
American continent were forcing them into situations they did not
relish. The Johnson family fought hard to keep them on the side of the
Crown, and they respected the Johnsons. There was a long history of
friendship and trust between the British and the Iroquois. However,
the American patriots also represented themselves as friends. The
reaction to such an internecine quarrel was traditional neutrality on the
part of the Iroquois.

The American colonists were resisting new taxes, trade regulations, and military establishments that would hinder the westward
movements of white settlers and impede their economic development.
By 1772, opposition to British measures became more organized.
Committees of Correspondence were formed. Mobs terrorized British
colonial officials attempting to enforce the regulations. In September
1774, the First Continental Congress met to formulate grievances
against British colonial policy. A boycott of British goods was set up.

The first serious skirmishes occurred at Lexington and Concord in
the spring of 1775. The Second Continental Congress met to establish
an army. Now the colonial officials faced armed insurrection. Benjamin Franklin offered a revised version of his Albany Plan of Union to
the Continental Congress, but the Congress shelved it for the more

practical task of waging war. Only towards the end of the Revolution would the American colonists take up the critical matter of establishing a formal structure of government for the new, emerging nation.[1]

As the great experiment in democracy was launched, the author of the Declaration of Independence freely acknowledged his debt to the Indian people. In comparing the freedom of Indian society to the oppression of European society, Thomas Jefferson noted:

> Imperfect as this species of coercion may seem, crimes are very rare among them (Indians); so much that were it made a question, whether no law, as among the savage Americans, or too much law, as among the civilized Europeans, submits man to the greatest evil, one who has seen both conditions of existence would pronounce it to be the last; and that the sheep are happier of themselves, than under the care of wolves. It will be said, that great societies cannot exist without government. The savages therefore, break them into small ones.[2]

The crux of the difference between colonial and European perceptions of government is that Americans desire self-government rather than government by experts. This distrust of governmental power and the strong urge towards local control, (even though it appears to be less efficient) are crucial factors in Indian society, and the colonists saw the wisdom of this view.

When Jefferson discussed the principles of government with the Cherokees, he came to the same conclusion as the tribesmen. In agreement with Indian democratic practices, Jefferson said:

> The fool has as great a right to express his opinion by vote as the wise, because he is equally free and equally master of himself.[3]

This statement would have startled Plato, Aristotle and Machiavelli. However, Indian chiefs would refuse to make decisions without discussing it in council and then gaining approval of most if not all the people. This deliberate and time consuming form of democracy so vexing to white administrators in dealing with tribes is one of the keystones in American democratic thought as well. The source of such sentiment is not in the minds of Europe, as people have so often been led to believe, but in the experience of Europeans encountering the social environment of the democratic Indian societies.

That is the enduring legacy of the Iroquois and other Indian peoples in the formation of the United States. This deference to public opinion has slowly spread to other parts of the world, but its roots are deep in the American soil, whose natives planted the Great Tree of Peace. Quite early, the Congress realized that the role of the Iroquois and other Indian nations played an important part in the war for American independence. Although lamenting his workload in a number of areas, John Adams realized the need to secure Indian allies in the following statement:

> When fifty or sixty men have a Constitution to form for a great Empire, at the same time that they have a country of fifteen hundred miles extent to fortify, millions to arm and train, a naval power to begin, an extensive commerce to regulate, numerous tribes of Indians to negotiate (sic) with, a standing army of twenty-seven thousand men to raise, pay victual, and officer, I really shall pity those fifty or sixty men.[4]

Acting upon one of the most critical of these tasks, the Congress passed an act dividing Indian country into three departments, with three commissioners for the northern department and one each for the remaining departments. Actually, the Congress was following a policy similar to the French in previous years.[5] That is, they attempted to gain the support of Indian nations. Failing that, they sought the neutrality of the Iroquois Confederacy and its affiliates.

With the death of William Johnson in July 1774, the British had an initial disadvantage in foiling American efforts. Before his death, Johnson had been trying to explain why the whites were not adhering to their treaties with the Indians, in preventing settlers from moving west of the 1763 Proclamation Line. This was an embarrassing question for Johnson, but one to which the Iroquois demanded answers and action, not promises. However, the British government, three thousand miles away, found it increasingly difficult to enforce its treaties with the Iroquois and prevent its colonists from advancing along the frontier.[6] It could not even control its own agents in the colonies, as Lord Dunmore's War clearly indicated. Lord Dunmore and others were not opposed to turning a profit on these newly opened lands, even though the methods of acquisition were at least suspect and generally illegal.

Quintock (Kentucky) was filling up with settlers, and the Shawnees as dependents of the Confederacy were appealing to the Grand Council at Onondaga. Harrodsburg and Louisville were already firmly established on the Ohio in 1773. The Iroquois were alarmed, since many of the people from the Six Nations were resettling in the Ohio region. Talk of war grew within the Confederacy, and Johnson sought to soften this injury by promising that the king would punish these lawless individuals. Johnson reminded the Iroquois of their covenant with the Crown and asked that they not engage in reprisals. He knew that if the Iroquois joined the Shawnees in resisting the whites in Kentucky, other western tribes would join the resistance movement, just as they had done during the rebellion of Pontiac. Such a strenuous task proved too taxing for the aging Sir William, and he died at a meeting with the Iroquois while discussing these matters. The assembly of chiefs was stunned by his sudden death, but Guy Johnson, Sir William's nephew and son-in-law, stepped in to fill the breach left by the elder. Guy Johnson was well known within the Confederacy and had served an ample apprenticeship under Sir William. Upon receiving the news of William Johnson's death, General Thomas Gage, the British commander, quickly approved the temporary appointment of Guy Johnson to carry on his uncle's work in the Indian department. In reporting Sir William's death, Gage also stated that he felt Guy Johnson was ". . .fit for employment."[7]

Meanwhile, the colonists were formulating their own policy toward the Iroquois. In 1775, the Continental Indian agents were traveling among the Iroquois and portraying the rebellion as a family affair that the Iroquois had best stay out of. The Mahican or Stockbridge Indians who helped the colonists around Boston in 1775 were moved to Oneida to convince them that the American cause was just and reasonable. The Reverend Samuel Kirkland utilized this move to persuade the Tuscaroras, Oneidas and Stockbridge that neutrality was the best course.[8]

Kirkland also brought pressure on the Mohawks to take a neutral course. In May 1775, patriot delegates told the Mohawks at Albany that they had no quarrel with the Iroquois or with Sir Guy Johnson. After this conference, Johnson left Albany for western New York to inform the Senecas and Cayugas as to the course of events and to advise neutrality. Nevertheless, rumors that he was trying to incite a frontier war were rampant along the frontier.[9]

Guy Johnson stressed the need to strengthen the "Great Old Covenant Chain Belt" which symbolized the friendship between the British and the Six Nations. The large wampum belt was twenty-one rows of beads wide. But this new trouble among the whites was a matter of critical concern and a great council was called at Onondaga to discuss the matter. If such a council were not called, then each nation of the Confederacy might pursue a different course. Kirkland asserted the council would be ". . .one of the most important meetings that the Six Nations have had for many years—and the consequences more extensive."[10] Most people expected that cooler heads would prevail and young warriors anxious to make a name for themselves be curbed. The war chiefs had recently agreed to consult the sachems and be bound by the outcome of such discussions.

Communications between the war chiefs were to be established among the villages and they, in turn, would take the news to the sachems. This procedure was established to prevent warriors from acting independently, and to strengthen traditional controls. But the consent of the governed is often a tenuous relationship, in both Indian and white political structures. This consent was the key to maintaining Iroquois neutrality. When it broke down, the old controls would no longer be operable.[11]

The Grand Council met in late 1774 for nearly a month, to deliberate over these important matters. Joseph Brant (Thayendanega), a brother of Mary Brant, was sent by Guy Johnson to take notes and report back to him. Thayendanega would become a key figure in the military operations of the Iroquois Confederacy, as the war for American Independence dragged on. Brant was not new to wilderness warfare. At the age of thirteen, in 1756, he was with Sir William Johnson at Lake George. Two years later, he was one of the guides who led the Bradstreet Expedition to the French Fort Frontenac on the north shore of Lake Ontario. Two hundred and fifty redcoats went with the Mohawks, and another twenty seven hundred colonial volunteers tagged along. Fort Frontenac fell, and Joseph now had more friendly relations with the American colonials. He began to appear more often at Johnson Hall, and he became interested in education. Subsequently, Sir William sent him to the Moor Charity School for Indians at Lebanon, Connecticut. He was an able student but dropped out after a year. By 1765, Joseph Brant was married and settled in the Mohawk Valley. His wife was the daughter of an Oneida preacher, and he had translated the Gospel according to St. Mark into Mohawk. He also accepted a job as a secretary to Sir William Johnson and acquired farmland, cattle and an interest in a gristmill. On the eve of the American Revolution, Joseph Brant was respected by Indian and white alike.[12]

Brant reported that the Six Nations at the Grand Council wished to remain at peace. The Confederacy wanted the Shawnees to settle their differences with the white Kentuckians. Since a small Cayuga war party had already left for Kentucky, the Grand Council censured them for violating the procedures of the Confederacy, which was acting as a unit and seemed strong in its resolve to remain neutral.[13]

Brant brought this news back to Guy Johnson. The new superintendent was pleased, since this meant that the whole western frontier would not go up in flames. Although the Senecas were not then disposed to accept British influence, they seemed pleased with the decision of neutrality.[14]

With the Grand Council ended, Johnson turned to the vexing problem of dealing with the patriot missionaries among the Tuscarora,

Oneida, and Stockbridge Indians. Kirkland was Johnson's principal adversary. The superintendent well remembered an occasion when the dissenting pastor had bested him in a controversy involving the building of an Oneida church.

In 1775, Johnson received a delegation of Oneidas led by Conoghquieson, an Onondaga sachem. This delegation presented a long list of complaints about Kirkland's activities among them. Although Conoghquieson did not live among the Oneidas, he still bore resentment toward Kirkland for his religious and secular activities. The Onondaga sachem said that many of the people wanted a Catholic or Anglican minister who would baptize their children whether the parents were regenerate or not. This was a legitimate grievance to some Oneidas, since thirty children had died without baptism during Kirkland's tenure among them. According to their previous exposure to Catholicism, baptism was a certain way of receiving salvation. Kirkland's answer to this argument was the typical Puritan one, that baptism did not guarantee salvation.[15]

Conoghquieson also accused Kirkland of running a store for his personal gain (this was untrue), and he stated that Kirkland looked too much to public affairs instead of religion. According to the Onondaga sachem, Kirkland ". . .is always collecting news and telling strange matters of the white people, whilst he endeavours to represent us as a people of no consequence to them." He was referring to Kirkland's interpreting the proceedings of the Continental Congress to the Oneidas (at their own request). The pastor's interpretation was obviously biased towards the patriot side. He was also accused of meddling with ". . .civil affairs, and opposes our methods of government—and the transaction and deliberation of our Cabinet council he transmits to N. York, Boston and England . . ." Kirkland had relayed the news of the Iroquois decision not to join with the Shawnees in resisting the English.[16] Due to these alleged indiscretions, Conoghquieson asked Guy Johnson to remove the Puritan clergyman.

Johnson promised the delegation he would study the accusations. He also gave his interpretation of the quarrel between England and the American colonies in these simplistic terms:

> This dispute was solely occasioned by some people, who notwithstanding a law of the King and his wise Men, would not let some Tea land, but destroyed it, on which he was angry, and sent some Troops with the General, whom you have long known, to see the Laws executed and bring the people to their sences, and as he is proceeding with great wisdom, to shew them their mistake, I expect it will soon be over.[17]

When news reached Kanowalohaie about Conoghquieson's complaints, three headmen, Thomas, young Hendrick, and Gahsaweda, went to Johnson praising Kirkland. This delegation returned with more disturbing news. The agent told them he did not mind complaints from Indians about missionaries. But, he said, Kirkland had told some whites the Indians were so unrepentent that he had written the Governor of New York asking for four thousand men to punish them. Kirkland was shocked when he heard this, and indeed he expressed doubt of the translation's accuracy. Joseph Brant was the translator, and the three headmen insisted that Guy Johnson would verify the accusation if Kirkland wrote him. Conoghquieson told the gathering that Joseph Brant had encouraged him to make the accusations against Kirkland,[18] who sought an explanation from Johnson, but little ever came of it, so the dispute simmered.

All this quarreling made the Iroquois uneasy. The strife between the white brothers was nothing that the Confederacy wanted to get involved in. The Oneidas responded typically to Governor Trumbull on the matter:

> We are unwilling to join on either side of such a contest, for we love you both—old England and new. Should the Great King of England apply to us for our aid—we shall deny him—and should the colonies apply—we will refuse.[19]

Nevertheless, the Oneidas as well as the rest of the Iroquois would soon be embroiled in the war for American independence, on one side or the other.

There were other New Englanders who attempted to sway the Confederacy to the American cause. In March 1775, James Dean, one of Eleazar Wheelock's students, was sent to the Caughnawaga Indians to secure bonds of friendship. Wheelock had educated a number of students from leading families at Caughnawaga, and he felt that religion and education could be put to good use in the field of international diplomacy. Dean was a good choice to send the Mohawks. He spoke their language fluently and without an accent. Before entering Dartmouth under Wheelock's tutelage, Dean had served at Onoquaga as an interpreter for the missionaries at that Mohawk village. Dean felt confident he could influence the Confederacy to support the American side. He declared, ". . . if there should be occasion, and he should be properly authorized for it, he could influence all those Six Nations to join these colonies against any invasion that should be made or attempted against them."[20]

James Dean remained in Montreal (nine miles from Caughnawaga) and continued his mission there until the summer of 1775. He tried to

Illustration from Lafitau, early French chronicler, showing a council meeting as seen by the artist. Note the wampum belts, one on the ground and one held in the hand of the speaker. (From a 1724 edition of Lafitau.)

persuade the Caughnawagas to be neutral in the conflict. Initially, the council of chiefs supported him in this policy. However, Governor Guy Carleton pressured the Caughnawagas into taking a stand on the British side, by threatening to take their land away if they did not comply. Consequently, the Caughnawagas told Carleton they would defend him to the best of their abilities, should he be besieged in Montreal by the American troops.[21] But the Caughnawagas declined any further involvement in British military affairs. Dean's mission was moderately successful. He would later have more success among the Oneidas.

By the spring of 1775, Kirkland was actively engaged in political intrigue on behalf of the patriots. The missionary wrote Andrew Eliot of Boston that it was necessary for the patriots to secure the friendship of the Iroquois. Kirkland suggested that a formal speech be made to the Six Nations, but he asked not to be credited with the idea. Eliot replied he would follow the advice and asked the clergyman to explain to the Iroquois that they would invite ruin upon themselves if they took a stand against the colonists.[22]

Not only were the Oneidas and Tuscaroras being torn by political maneuvering, but also the Mohawks; their dilemma was much more pressing, since they were being overrun by white settlers. Kirkland was advising the Mohawks to hold a neutral course. When the Indian superintendent returned from a visit with the Iroquois nations, he found the Mohawk Valley whites were now suspicious of him. The settlers thought he was inciting the Iroquois against the rebel frontiersmen. Johnson again left for Indian country, holding councils with the Six Nations at Oswego and Montreal. Although rebel rumors reported he was still inciting the Iroquois against white settlers and rebels, he was actually advocating a policy of neutrality to avoid frontier incidents. At Oswego, the eastern tribes of the Confederacy listened to Johnson's logic and decided to continue their classic policy of neutrality. Furthermore, they agreed they would permit neither English nor patriot troops to pass through Iroquois country.[23]

With events becoming more critical after Lexington and Concord, Johnson decided to prevent pro-American propaganda from circulating among the Iroquois. In May 1775, Reverend Kirkland was ordered to remain at the superintendent's house, instead of continuing on his way to the Oneidas. Johnson also sent out word that all other New England missionaries must be relieved of their duties, ". . . Until the difficulties between Great Britain and the Colonies are settled—as it cannot be supposed but the N. England Missionaries, from their Native attachment to their country, may be led some way or other to bias the Indians against government."[24]

On their part, the colonials feared that Johnson would influence the Iroquois to support the British, so the Tryon County Committee of Safety required a loyalty oath of suspected individuals. These men were to give no aid to Johnson in any form. The Tryon County people also suspected that John Stuart, an Anglican missionary to the Mohawks, and Colin McLeland, their schoolmaster, were prodding the Iroquois to ally themselves with the English. Since Stuart and McLeland were at Fort Hunter at the request of the Mohawks and protected by the British authorities, they decided not to remove them forcibly, but to call the two men before the Committee of Safety and warn them not to interfere in the British and American conflict.[25]

During the summer of 1775, both the patriots and the Tories had become wary of one another's actions with regard to the Iroquois. The Americans feared that Johnson and Joseph Brant would muster a large force and attack them along the New York frontier. General Phillip Schuyler appealed to the Continental Congress to alleviate this situation. Meanwhile, Kirkland journeyed to Philadelphia on July 10, 1775, to testify before Congress. He spent several days discussing Indian affairs, and the proper procedures concerning Indian diplomacy. Indian commissioners were appointed following Kirkland's visit.[26]

At this very same time, Johnson was leaving his council at Oswego and proceeding to Montreal with a force of nearly three thousand Indians and whites. This group arrived at Montreal July 17, and he now called another conference to treat with the northern Indians. But Johnson and Governor Carleton disagreed on matters of strategy. Johnson wanted to use Indian troops outside the province of Quebec, while Carleton wanted to depend upon the Canadian militia, which he was beginning to muster. He believed the Indians should be used only in a defensive posture. The conference should not be convened at Lachine, he decided, but at Montreal, so he could keep an eye on events.[27] Johnson and the chiefs had agreed that the conference should be at Lachine, so that consumption of liquor could be curtailed. It was only with difficulty that he was able to persuade the chiefs to meet in the shadow of Montreal.

Despite these differences, the outcome of the meeting pleased Johnson and Carleton. The Caughnawagas and other northern tribes were now persuaded to join the British. The Indians had been disheartened by the lack of support the Crown was receiving from Canadian *habitants,* but they now seemed willing to rally 'round the King. Thus, the earlier work of James Dean seemed undone. Abraham Nimham, a Stockbridge Indian, had also gone to Canada, asking the Caughnawagas to support the patriots, as his tribe had done. Nimham also carried an interesting message to the Caughnawagas from Ethan Allen of Vermont. Allen urged them to join the Americans, because the King was wrong and the Americans were very similar to the Indians in their mode of fighting. He offered evidence of his own military prowess in these words:

> I know how to shute and ambush just like Indian and want your Warriors to come and see me and help me fight Regulars you know they Stand all along close together Rank and file and my men fight so as Indians Do and Abush the Regulars, if you will I will give you Money Blankets Tomahawks Knives and Paint and the Like as much as you say because they first killed our men when it was Peace time.[28]

After the Montreal conference, the Indian superintendent invited the Caughnawagas to a feast. The British provided an ox roast and plenty of wine for the occasion. In the next few days the Indians were placed in various camps around Montreal to defend it and a small force went with a white officer to St. John's to defend that outpost on the American border.[29]

In early August, Johnson's Indian allies discovered a group of Americans above St. John's. Wishing to attack immediately, Johnson told General Prescott, who was then acting in Carleton's place while he was away at Quebec, about the enemy's movements. Prescott told Johnson not to allow the Indians at Montreal out of the province. But the Indians were eager for action, and Johnson insisted that only action would keep their morale up. Prescott would not relent, and so the superintendent had to be content with handing out war belts to each tribe, ". . . to be held ready for service."[30]

Most of Johnson's Indian contingent drifted away in early August due to lack of action. But they promised to return when needed, and they took their war belts with them to Onondaga. Johnson was disheartened with Carleton's tactics, and Prescott's approval of such tactics, regarding the use of Indian support troops.

The Oneida patriot supporters now advised the Americans to be more forceful in their diplomatic and military maneuvers. In June 1775, at German Flats, they had told the Americans, ". . . the gate of Fort Stanwix ought to be shut, that nothing might pass and repass to the hurt of our Country." They urged the patriots to repair and garrison the fortress. They also asked the Committee of Safety at Albany to "relight the council fire" there, and meet with the Six Nations. Phillip Schuyler forwarded this request to the Congress, asking the patriot body to act favorably.[31] The Congress, anxious to establish relations with the Iroquois, seized upon this request and planned a conference at Albany for the end of summer.

When the other five nations in the Confederacy heard of the Oneida appeal, they sent a delegation to remind them of Johnson's request that they stay well away from white settlements. A group of pro-British Mohawks declared that the only motive of the Albany people was to trick them. Moreover, the Mohawks warned, once the Indians were in Albany, the whites would either kill them or enslave them to the New Englanders.

After the assembly had heard the Mohawk orators, Oneida and Cayuga speakers were recognized. They chastized the Mohawks in particular, for insulting the white people and taking up arms at a time when the Confederacy was still at peace. The Mohawks had failed to sway the assembly. They admitted they had taken up arms and would confess their error at the Albany council in August. The assembly then turned to graver matters. Johnson had uttered threats against Kirkland at the Ontario conference. He said he had found evidence of interference by the minister in political affairs. He also warned that any tribe found harboring the missionary would face severe consequences. The Senecas, Cayugas and Onondagas were disturbed at this turn of events. They told the Oneidas they had ". . . all heard Col. Johnson's threats—should he put them in execution and your minister apprehended and taken away by violence, all N. England will blame us—and the whole confederacy bro't into trouble. . ." Therefore it was advised that Kirkland ". . . should retire for the present, or that we all agree to support him, at all hazards."[32] After listening to this advice, the Oneidas decided to keep Kirkland in their midst until Johnson returned from Canada, when they would help him to escape.

With these issues clear in their minds, the Iroquois went to the council at German Flats, called by the American commissioners. Volkert P. Douw and Turbutt Francis represented the Americans, and Kirkland acted as interpreter. Francis addressed the Iroquois, assuring them that the patriots were not hostile to them. On the next day, the Onondaga chief Tianogwando thanked the commissioners. He explained to the Americans that he could not bring representatives to Albany from all the nations of the Confederacy. It would be necessary to send messages to all the nations, then have the messages discussed, the delegates formally assigned; the time consumed in travel would be considerable. Tianogwando also said the Caughnawagas were already allied with the British and probably would not attend a conference with the Americans. He suggested that the Six Nations report the results of the Albany conference to adjacent allied tribes upon its conclusion. Finally, Tianogwando asked that the Indians attending the conference be given safe passage through white settlements on their way to Albany.[33]

The council reconvened at Albany in August. In traditional style, the first meeting was spent in "rekindling the ancient council fire," which was once at Albany. (Sir William Johnson had moved this council fire to Johnson Hall; it was the council fire for talking to the whites. The Confederacy fire remained at Onondaga.) Pledges of friendship were exchanged and a pipe was smoked. These formalities ended, the conference began. The Americans claimed that the King had broken the covenant chain with them. They complained of the British refusal to accord them proper representation in matters concerning taxation. The Continental Congress had no desire, they said, to make demands upon the Iroquois either for support or services. The quarrel was between the Americans and the British. The Americans only wanted Iroquois neutrality.[34]

During the conference, Schuyler left to help conduct the campaign against Canada. The other commissioners continued the meeting. They promised the Iroquois that the roads in their country would be kept open and no one would be hindered in his activities. After some deliberation, the Iroquois reassembled and stated their assessment of what the commissioners had discussed. Little Abraham, chief of the lower Mohawk castle, told the Americans, ". . . we bear as much affection for the King of England's subjects upon the other side of the water as we do you born upon this Island." This statement was not an easy one to make, as the Confederacy was already experiencing internal strife. Many Iroquois present at Albany would not adhere to the decision of the Confederacy, and the Americans would break their word as well. But for the moment, neutrality seemed to be the order of the day. Abraham urged the Americans to take their quarrel outside of Iroquois country. Since some Caughnawagas were friendly to the King, he asked that they not be attacked. This, he insisted, would only complicate matters.

Summarizing the statement of the Confederacy, the Mohawk chief said:

> As for your quarrels to the Eastward, along the Sea Coasts, do as you please but it would hurt us to see those brought up in our Boston ill used. In particular we could mention the Son of Sir William Johnson (Sir John Johnson). He is born among us, and is of Dutch Extraction by his Mother; he minds his own affairs, and does not intermeddle in public disputes. We would likewise mention our Father, the Minister (John Stuart), who resides among the Mohawks, and was sent them by the King. He does not meddle in Civil affairs, but instructs them in the way to Heaven. He absolutely refuses to attend to any political matters, and says they do not belong to

him, they beg he may continue in peace among them. The Mohawks are frequently alarmed with Reports that their Minister is to be torn away from them.[35]

Having concluded political matters, the Confederacy turned to the question of reviving trade at Albany and Schenectady. The quarrel between the colonies and the King had threatened this relationship, and the Iroquois were anxious to exchange furs for white manufactured goods. The American commissioners promised to attend to this request. Abraham also brought up two land grievances against the Albany Corporation, charging it had taken land without paying ". . . so much as a single pipe." Tianogwando also brought up the Wyoming land controversy. While the Iroquois had ceded this land to Pennsylvania, the colony of Connecticut had earlier concluded a fraudulent treaty with some Mohawks and had also laid claim to this parcel of land. Such chicanery in land cession was standing in the way of honest and friendly relations with the Six Nations. The Americans declared they would take the question to Congress for settlement, which would do everything in its power to secure an enduring friendship with the Iroquois.

While matters appeared friendly on the surface, there were long standing doubts about the sincerity of the Albany people. The chiefs realized that the commissioners had avoided directly promising solutions to the land problems and had not given concrete assurances that American troops would not invade their homeland. Abraham replied diplomatically to the vague promises of the commissioners to examine the Wyoming controversy. He said, "In case I was to answer that part of your speech, it might perhaps draw us into an argument."[36] But he expressed pleasure with both the Americans and Johnson in advising the Iroquois to remain neutral.

For the moment, neutrality seemed the natural course for the Indians, and would please both the Americans and the Loyalists. Some leaders, such as Joseph Brant, wanted an alliance with the British, but for the most part the Iroquois were still avoiding the conflict. It was an uneasy neutrality, since it depended upon both the Americans and the British refraining from interfering in the affairs of the Iroquois, particularly in trade and travel. As the Iroquois had done for generations, they were adhering to the diplomacy of playing one white faction against another and demanding the *status quo*.

It would not be easy for those Iroquois near-rebel communities to maintain neutrality, and the Americans were now free to move on to Canada without fear of an Indian attack at their rear. Major General Phillip Schuyler, with Brigadier General Richard Montgomery, commanded the force moving on Canada. About two thousand men moved to positions above Lake Champlain to attack the post at St. John's. Benedict Arnold was proceeding through the hostile terrain of Maine to approach Quebec from the other side. This caused alarm among the British military officers in the province, since they were suspicious of the French *habitants*.[37] Carleton could easily see Quebec falling to the Americans and becoming the fourteenth member of the Continental Congress.

As the Americans approached Montreal, Indian scouts sent word of their movements, and Johnson began to beef up his contingent of Indians. However, Prescott once again directed Johnson to hold his Indian force around Montreal in check, for defensive purposes only. On September 6, 1775, the Americans began landing about a mile away from the unfinished side of the fort at St. John's. Major Charles Preston, British commander of the fort, ordered about ninety Indian scouts to move out for an attack against the enemy as they proceeded to the fort. The Indian force, made up mostly of Caughnawagas, set up an ambush along the route of the Americans. One contingent of American troops was attacked while it was crossing a creek. The fighting was fierce, and the progress of the march was impeded. Both sides claimed victory in this engagement, but one can never completely judge the victor in such wilderness skirmishes. The Indian scouts did stop the Americans however. Casualties were suffered on both sides. In the evening, a man whose name Schuyler would not disclose, came to the American camp and advised him that the fort at St. John's contained most of the British military force in Canada. He reported also that the American force would not be joined by many Canadians since most wished to remain neutral. The man concluded that an attack on St. John's would be imprudent.[38]

The next day, Schuyler held a meeting with his officers and shared this intelligence. Apparently they trusted Schuyler's word and the intelligence of the mysterious man, and the officers decided to withdraw to Isle aux Nois. Schuyler also took into account the resistance he had met and the failure to provide him with adequate artillery. At any rate, he retreated to reconsider the situation. Schuyler did not know that the Caughnawagas were disgusted with their lack of white support. They believed that Major Preston had deliberately tried to sacrifice them, while protecting his own soldiers within the fort. Angered, the Indians left St. John's and went home.[39] Such exploitative behavior towards Indian auxiliary troops would be repeated on both sides throughout the American war for independence.

On September 10, Montgomery and a force of eight hundred Americans attacked St. John's again, but the green recruits were easily defeated. The Americans returned to the Isle aux Nois. Subsequently, fevers set in at the encampment because of its swampy location. Schuyler himself became ill and turned the command over to Montgomery. On September 16, Montgomery mounted another attack on the fort. It was repulsed. The Indian ambush of American troops played a crucial role in retarding, for almost two weeks, the American advance upon the province of Quebec. This gave the British time to repair the fort and bring in more men and supplies. Carleton issued a statement to his Indian allies on September 13 in which he gave thanks ". . . to the Indian Chiefs and Warriors who behaved so gallantly in the action of the 6th Instant near St. Johns and desires that the same may be communicated to them by Col. Johnson their Superintendent."[40]

St. John's stood siege for another two months. But this delay cost the Americans the campaign for the province of Quebec; they were able to take Montreal after the fall of St. John's, but failed to take the city of Quebec. Then the first military campaign bogged down in the winter snows of Canada.[41]

However, things remained relatively calm in Iroquois country. The Americans were upset over the machinations of Colonel Johnson. After a December meeting with some Iroquois at Albany, Schuyler received the war belt that had been given to the Mohawks at Montreal. The indignant Schuyler wrote John Hancock, President of the Continental Congress, "We now have a full proof that the Ministerial Servants have attempted to engage the Savages against Us."[42]

The official policy of the Iroquois was still neutrality. In the fall of 1775, a council was held at Fort Pitt, attended by the Seneca, Shawnee, Delaware, and Wyandot nations and the Americans. The Congressional commissioners wanted a commitment to neutrality from the dependent nations of the Confederacy, similar to the one they had received earlier from the Six Nations at Albany. The Seneca half-king, Guyasuta, promised neutrality among the western nations, even though White Eyes, a Delaware chief, had proclaimed their independence. However, the entire council came to a consensus that neutrality remained the best course. Also, Guyasuta promised to use this influence within the Confederacy to continue the neutrality policy. Cornplanter, the Seneca, and his nephew Blacksnake, were at the meeting. It is believed that Cornplanter's brother, Handsome Lake, was there as well.[43]

When General Thomas Gage was removed and replaced by General William Howe in the fall of 1775, Guy Johnson feared that other appointments in the Indian service might be changed. Very soon, a Major John Campbell appeared from England and presented his papers for his new appointment as superintendent of Indian affairs for Quebec. He replaced Daniel Claus, who had held the post for fifteen years. Also, the new appointment superseded the authority of Guy Johnson. Campbell's appointment appeared to be pure patronage to Johnson and Claus, and they set out for England to argue their case in person against such a political appointment in an area so delicate as Indian affairs. Joseph Brant went with them, as did a Mohawk warrior named John, from the lower Mohawk castle. Captain Gilbert Tice, Joseph Chew, Ensign Peter Johnson, and Ensign Walter Butler joined the party. Brant wanted to learn for himself the true nature of the quarrel between England and America. He was also prepared to present land grievances to the English government.[44]

Early in January 1776, Isaac Paris of the Tryon County Committee of Safety wrote to Schuyler, ". . . inimical preparations are taken against the Friends of the American Cause in Johnstown . . . ." Paris reported that about seven hundred men were already armed and provided with artillery. Congress gave Schuyler the power to investigate these claims.[45]

These accusations proved to be true, and so Schuyler raised a force of seven hundred men by mid-January and went to Johnstown to confront Sir John Johnson. Schuyler sent word ahead to the Mohawks at Fort Hunter that he was on his way to Johnstown. But the Six Nations had concluded an agreement with the Americans at Albany the summer before, and had not expected such troop movements, nor the attacks on John Johnson. The Mohawks at Fort Hunter asked Schuyler not to hurry to Johnstown; perhaps a body of three or four people could persuade Sr. John to ". . . remain silent and be at peace." Furthermore, the Mohawks informed Schuyler that they wished to adhere to the Albany agreement. Schuyler was urged to do likewise, and to refrain from bringing troops into Iroquois territory.[46]

Subsequently, a group of Mohawks set out for Albany to talk with Schuyler, but met him at Schenectady at the head of his army, now numbering nearly three thousand (Schuyler picked up militiamen along his route). Little Abraham expressed his disappointment in Schuyler's breaking the Albany agreement so soon and without provocation. He also told Schuyler the Mohawks only wanted peace and suggested they be mediators in the dispute. Schuyler would not turn his force back, but did permit the Mohawks to send a delegation of chiefs to accompany him to Johnstown.

Schuyler arrived at Johnstown within a few days and began negotiations with Sir John. His terms were severe and inflexible. He demanded that Johnson give him all ". . . cannons, arms, and other military stores" at Johnstown. He requested that Johnson be confined to a restricted area of Tyron County unless the Congress decided he be removed to another colony. He also asked that Johnson's Scottish tenants disarm themselves and present the Americans with six hostages. Other Loyalists in the area were to give up their arms as well, and Johnson was directed to turn over all Indian trade goods in his possession.

Sir John was irate at such treatment and sent a compromise offer to Schuyler, but the Americans would not relent. The American officer then issued an ultimatum: Johnson must either comply by 12:00 A.M., January 18, or the patriot fury would be unleashed upon him and his comrades. Johnson capitulated, keeping a few family firearms and promising not to take up arms against the rebels. But he asked to be free to travel more extensively.

Schuyler agreed. He could travel to the interior of the eastern seaboard, as long as he did not visit any seacoast cities. While Johnson felt he could not provide the six Scottish hostages, the Scots agreed among themselves to send General Schuyler six people in order to comply with the agreement. So on January 20, 1776, Sir John and his tenants met with Schuyler and settled the matter.[47]

The disarming of Sir John increased tensions within the Confederacy. The Mohawks resented the intrusion upon their land, which violated the agreement made earlier at Albany. This intrusion on the part of the Americans would make it difficult for the chiefs to control the warrior contingent within the Six Nations. Although the neutrality was not truly broken, it was now less secure than before, a tenuous thing indeed.

As spring came in 1776, the Mohawks became more anxious, as they were confronted with the continuing abuses of the patriots. In the face of such tensions, they began to leave the Mohawk River Valley. A deputation of Iroquois leaders went to Philadelphia in the spring of 1776 to talk to the Continental Congress and were again exhorted to remain neutral. On May 20, 1776, a group of Mohawks fought against the Americans at the Battle of the Cedars. The Americans were defeated handily as they were retreating from Canada. Atrocity stories about alleged Mohawk excesses were circulated after this engagement, and Congress excoriated the English for using Indian troops. Apparently Congress had a quick change of mind on the issue, because on May 25, 1776 it passed a resolution that, ". . . it was highly expedient to engage the Indians in the service of the United Colonies . . ." The resolution also empowered the commander-in-chief to recruit two thousand paid Indian auxiliaries.[48] The shaky neutrality was now broken on both sides.

During this flurry of activity, the American commissioners were conferring with the Iroquois. Volkert Douw and a secretary, Robert Yates, went to the home of Little Abraham on May 19, 1776. They requested a council to talk about some of the military and trade problems the Americans were encountering in their efforts to live up to their promises at Albany. But before the council could be assembled, a young warrior named Jan burst into the meeting and charged the Americans with treachery in sending yet another army, under Colonel Elias Dayton, into Mohawk country. Jan stated he would defend Sir John in the face of Colonel Dayton's attempt to seize Johnson. After this disruption, the council was put off until the next day.

When the meeting was reconvened, the Americans (including Colonel Dayton's force) were confronted with a fully armed contingent of Mohawk warriors, resolute in their desire to defend Sir John. Dayton warned the Mohawks that though he was a friend, he came as a soldier to arrest Sir John. He asked the Mohawks not to place themselves between ". . . us and our Enemies who are watching an opportunity to destroy us, our Wives, and Children." He told the Mohawks not to try to stop him for, "We love you Brothers. When we shed your Blood, we shall shed tears." The Mohawk warriors discussed Dayton's speech for about two hours and then expressed a concern for the safety of Sir John and other whites among them. The sachem, Little Abraham, told the warriors he was disappointed in them and he insisted the chiefs intended to keep the covenant with the colonies.[49]

Colonel Dayton assured the Mohawks that neither the minister nor the schoolmaster would be harmed. According to Dayton, Sir John was summoned to appear before the Congress as a condition of his parole; he would not be harmed if he would go peaceably, they had promised. By May 21, the Mohawks had calmed down and Dayton went to Johnstown. Sir John had taken advantage of the delay to flee with a large contingent of Tories. His party contained about one hundred and seventy, including scouts and white settlers. Upon arriving in Canada after nine days of hardship, he began to organize the Royal Yorkers, or as the Americans called them, *Johnson's Greens*.[50]

To the west at Niagara, Colonel John Butler, acting in Guy Johnson's absence, was trying to persuade the western tribes of the Confederacy to break the policy of neutrality and declare themselves for the Crown. It was a difficult diplomatic game, since such a decision would involve the repudiation of the covenant of friendship with the Americans.[51] Besides, many of the leading men and women of the Confederacy were strongly inclined towards peace and neutrality, even though many Iroquois warriors had already gone to fight with the English in Canada.

For all the controversy, the Americans had not yet threatened the

Iroquois heartland. Schuyler wanted to press westward to Niagara but was powerless without the consent of the Six Nations. So he suggested that Congress bribe the Iroquois to obtain permission for such an expedition. He promised that he would let the Indians have all the stores within Fort Niagara except the cannon, for the privilege of marching through their land.[52] Nothing ever came of the proposal, but the delay only postponed the coming of the war to the Iroquois until 1777.

In May 1776, a council was held at Niagara to discuss the Iroquois neutrality decision. Leaders from the Six Nations explained to Colonel Butler that the Confederacy during the Grand Council in March had decided they were ". . .all united and resolved to maintain peace, both with the king and the Bostonians . . ." Butler was angered by this reply and tried to persuade the Iroquois to join him against the Americans. He expressed surprise at their intention to remain neutral, saying that Schuyler "has no men, cannon, and ammunition or cloathing, and should he survive the summer he must perish by the cold next winter for want of blankets." But the King, he boasted, lacks neither men nor money. He bluntly told them to "recall" their resolutions, or they must be in a "wretched situation," when the King occupies "all the seaports in America and comes in earnest to sweep off the Americans." This drew a response from the sachems, who said, "We will support the Kings Peace or Government and now we speak from our very inside." Butler then enlisted some fifty Iroquois into the King's service, calling for them to help find Colonel Johnson. (The Niagara commander claimed Johnson was in Quebec; however, he was still in England.)

Butler was also disturbed about the American treaty with the Iroquois and the dependent nations at Fort Pitt, which was concluded in the fall of 1775. Openly criticizing the Iroquois for this decision, he charged that the Americans were deceiving them, and meant to cheat them. The Americans' intent, he said, was to take all the Indian land from them. After these ominous remarks, the leaders discussed, for two days, the commander's proposal to join the British cause. They remained resolute, and chose Guyasuta to reply. The Indian retorted: "It is three nights since you told me the Americans, with whom you are at War, are all mad, foolish, crazy and full of deceit . . . I now tell you that you are mad, foolish, crazy and deceitful person—for you think we are fools and advise us to do what is not in our interest.[53]

Guyasuta said the Americans are "the wise people so far as they have yet spoke to us . . . they tell us your quarrel is between yourselves and desire us to sit still and they tell us right." On the other hand, the Indian declared, ". . .you want us to assist you which we cannot do." What would the Iroquois do, queried the Indian leader, if ". . .the Americans conquer you." Finally, Guyasuta flung these words at Butler, ". . .I tell you Brother you are foolish and we will not allow you to pluck up the Tree of Peace nor raise the Hatchet. We are strong and able to do it ourselves when we are hurt."

Butler, taken aback by this retort, adjourned the council for the day. But on the next day, a Mohawk spokesman addressed the council on behalf of Butler. He spoke of friendship between the tribes and the English. He pointed out the vastness of the King's armies and the superiority of English powder, promising "You therefore need not be afraid, but take up the Hatchet and your old Men and Women your wives and children shall be well taken care of."

These attempts to sway the tribes to the active support of the British came to nothing, however. After some deliberation, the tribes responded, saying they had lived in peace with the Americans, and wished to continue. ". . .when they hurt us it is time enough to strike them." Continuing, the chiefs admitted, "It is true they encroach'd on our Lands, but of this we shall speak to them." They asked a searching question of Butler, "If you are so strong Brother, and they but as a weak Boy, why ask our assistance." Denying the claims of American weakness, the sachems declared, "You say their Powder is rotten. We have found it good. You say they are all mad, foolish, wicked, and deceitful. I say you are so and they are wise for you want us to destroy ourselves in your War and they advise us to live in Peace." Finally, the Indians' response was to follow the Americans' advice. Chagrined and defeated at this time, Butler ended the council and distributed some goods.[54] The council was not a total failure for the Niagara commander, however; about thirty Senecas and a few Chippewas and Ottawas engaged in a brief expedition in Canada on behalf of the English. This was an opening wedge, Butler thought. He would not end his efforts to obtain Iroquois support for the British.

On May 24, 1776, a delegation of Iroquois reached Philadelphia and was presented to Congress after visiting New York and Boston. While they were there, the Congress modified its demands for strict neutrality. The next day, a resolution was passed requesting military assistance from the Iroquois and authorizing Washington to raise a contingent of Indian troops. This resolution was not conveyed to the Iroquois delegation then visiting Philadelphia.[55] The Continental Congress was as yet unaware of the difficulties in store for the patriot cause as a result of this change in policy.

Elements within the Iroquois were now reevaluating their stand on the American War for Independence. A considerable segment of the Oneidas viewed Colonel Dayton's leniency to the Mohawks as damaging, and were convinced that the Mohawks now looked upon the Americans as cowards. At the same time, they were also concerned over Butler's machinations with the western tribes of the Confederacy at Niagara. The pro-American Oneidas asserted that he ". . . has by threats and proffers prevailed upon the greater part of the Senecas, Cayugas, and Onondagas to renounce the cause of the colonies and engage on the King's side."[56] But Butler's small successes in luring away a few warriors of the western tribes shook the resolve of the Confederacy. Slowly, the Iroquois were being caught up in the bitter struggle between the Americans and the English. The tension became so great that many of the Oneidas and Tuscaroras came to believe that neutrality was no longer possible. By the end of May, the Oneida chiefs told Kirkland they had forged an alliance with the Tuscaroras, Ononquagas, and Caughnawagas to protect themselves against pro-English sentiment among the other members of the Confederacy. The Oneidas also confided they would stand by the Americans if the other members of the Confederacy joined the British.

Kirkland left for Fort George on May 29, to tell Schuyler of the Oneida and Tuscarora position. Arriving on June 7, he could report that a split existed within the Confederacy. Schuyler decided to act, and drafted a letter to Congress requesting permission to take the ". . . post at the place where Fort Stanwix formerly stood."[57]

In May 1776, George Morgan had sent Simon Girty to the Six Nations council at Onondaga with a belt of peace and friendship. Girty was a rough hewn frontiersman who had lived for a time with the Indians and knew the language. He was made interpreter for the Six Nations and had served the United States ably, until he defected to the British side. He arrived at Onondaga about the middle of June, just as the council was assembling. All the members of the Confederacy were represented except the Mohawks. Girty delivered the belt to the chiefs and brought a message of friendship from the Americans. Concluding his remarks, he asked for continued Iroquois neutrality.

The ensuing council sessions were filled with anxiety about the English and their ability to win the Iroquois over, thus breaking their neutrality. It was decided that a delegation go to Fort Niagara and demand that Butler bring back the warriors he had sent to Canada. Another messenger went to Oswego to recall the warriors personally, if Butler refused. The council sent reassuring words to the Americans. They hoped for continued friendship and good will between the Iroquois and the colonists. The Indians told Morgan that ". . . among all people there are evil minded persons who try to spoil good arguments and good resolutions but they cannot turn the minds of the Chief Men and Warriors of this Council for we look on Peace and want to enjoy it."

The chiefs then sent the following message to their southern and western allies:

> Brothers and Nephews, We desire you to continue to sit still
> and preserve the Peace and Friendship with all your
> neighbours—remain firm and united with each other so as to be
> like one Man. We desire you to be strong and keep your coun-
> try in peace.[58]

But the Confederacy was unable to recall the warriors who had gone to
Canada. However, the delegation to Fort Niagara did persuade the
men encamped there to leave, thus thwarting Butler's efforts to bring
them over to the British.

Hence, the majority of the Confederacy was still inclined to peace
and neutrality. However, the council was having a difficult time enforcing its will. It had become impossible to control local units within the
Confederacy. Perhaps the influence of Christianity among the Tuscaroras and Oneidas contributed to this drifting away from adherence
to tradition. Certainly the colonial government's degenerating into a
shambles, and the war for independence itself, placed great strain upon
the kinship state of the Iroquois Confederacy.

In July 1776, Joseph Brant and Guy Johnson returned to America,
just as the spirit of independence was beginning to sweep the eastern
seaboard. With the Declaration of Independence, the English felt
compelled to press for Iroquois support. This political environment
paved the way for the rise of Joseph Brant as a key figure among the
Iroquois.[59]

Guy Johnson retained the same commission that his uncle had
received in 1756, and Joseph Brant had talked to prominent leaders in
England about their view of the conflict in the colonies. Englishmen of
various political persuasions had been sought out by Brant. As a result
of his discussions, Brant was convinced that the Americans intended to
become the dominant force on the North American continent. Clearly,
the American cause was not in accord with the interests of the
Iroquois. Brant knew it was the Crown that had consistently inter-
vened on behalf of the Indians, in the face of the colonists' westward
movement.

While in England, Brant and Johnson had presented their land
grievances to officials of the Crown. The faulty boundary written into
the 1768 Treaty of Fort Stanwix was described as an injustice, and
Lord Germain had listened with a sympathetic ear. The claims of the
Corporation at Albany against Mohawk lands were also discussed. In
the final analysis, both Brant and Johnson liked what they had heard in
England, and they in turn made a favorable impression upon the British
government.

Brant also made a favorable impression upon society in London. He fascinated the English, since he spoke good English and had a white man's education. He was also a Mason, a staunch churchman, a translator of the Bible into his native tongue. The government provided him with personal guides to the sights of the city, and a noted English artist, George Romney, did a portrait of him.

But the British were not as faithful in their friendship as Brant had come to believe. The Mohawk chief was unfamiliar with the British view of territorial sovereignty. As early as 1765, the attorney general of the province of New York, John Tabor Kempe, had given his interpretation of the Crown's jurisdiction over those Indian lands that had not been ceded by treaty. Kempe asserted the King was sovereign over Indian lands, despite Indian occupancy, in these words:

> . . . it is the Policy of our Constitution, that wheresover the Kings Dominions extends he is the Fountain of all Property in Lands, and to Deny that Right, in the Crown, in any place, is in Effect denying his Right to Rule there—Hence it follows, that in a legal Consideration the King can grant Lands within his Dominions here, as well without previous Conveyance from the Indians . . . .[60]

Had Brant understood the ramifications of such legal concepts about British sovereignty, he might not have been so anxious to join the cause of the King. He would not discover the legal impact of this statement until after the American Revolution, when the British ceded Iroquois lands to the Americans without their consent. In effect, Kempe believed the treaties to have no legal standing.

As Brant and Johnson returned to America in July 1776, Schuyler was assembling the Iroquois at German Flats to negotiate another treaty. Because of the distance people had to come and the short notice for the meeting, it was not until early August that the council opened at German Flats. Shortly before the meeting, two sachems approached the Americans about holding a public condolence ceremony for a Seneca chief who had been slain while attacking an American relief party on its way to reinforce the post at the Cedars. Failing to understand the nature of the request, Schuyler and the other American delegates were insulted and refused.

The conference began in earnest on August 7. Schuyler thought about offering the Iroquois the hatchet, but decided to wait until he saw their reaction to the American speech. He knew the Iroquois had used the American argument for neutrality in order to defeat efforts by the British to break that neutrality. The Americans were frequently referred to as independent and able to fight their own battles; the British did

82

not appear in that light to the Iroquois. Schuyler felt he had to maintain that image.[61]

During the meeting, Schuyler warned the nations which had taken up arms against the Americans that the Congress would not tolerate such activities. He praised the nations that remained neutral. He asked for a renewal of the promise of friendship and neutrality from the Iroquois instead of offering the hatchet, because he felt Indian neutrality was too important to risk breaking for an uncertain alliance.[62]

Once again, the Six Nations reiterated its pledge of neutrality and requested forgiveness for past transgressions by their warriors. A formal ceremony at the conference showed the Iroquois intentions, since the chiefs symbolically "took the hatchet out of the head of the Americans," burying it so deeply that no one would be able to find it. Apparently the Iroquois were quite satisfied with the results of the meeting as "The Indians returned to their homes well pleased that they could live on neutral ground . . . ."[63]

To the south of German Flats in New York City, both Brant and Johnson were bottled up for the summer, unable to penetrate enemy lines to enter Indian country. During the Battle of Long Island at the end of the summer in 1776, Joseph Brant had distinguished himself. British officers were impressed with his ability as a soldier and strategist. Subsequently, Brant requested that he be allowed to slip through the American lines; because of his valor at the Battle of Long Island the request was granted. Brant wanted to tell the Iroquois leaders what he had heard in England about the consequences of an American victory. He also intended to remind the Confederacy of the old alliance with the King.

In the last part of November, Brant and Captain Gilbert Tice, a Mohawk Valley Tory, set out for Iroquois country in disguise. To further protect the two, Johnson gave his instructions orally to Brant. Johnson told Brant to make a wampum belt upon his arrival that would speak in favor of the King's cause.[64]

Traveling by night and hiding in the day, the two made their way to the Susquehanna River settlement of Ononquaga in a few days. Upon their arrival, the Oneidas, Tuscaroras, Mohawks and Mahicans gathered around the two travelers to hear the news. Brant told them of his trip to England and his consultations with men high in the British government. He talked of his military exploits on Long Island and how the Americans were defeated there. He was given a hero's welcome and his ideas were readily accepted as he explained the danger to Indian country and its liberty if the Iroquois did not resist the Americans.

Thus, Joseph Brant had rallied most of the village to the King's service. From Ononquaga, he traveled along the west branch of the Susquehanna to the Genessee Castle of the Senecas. From there, he went to Fort Niagara, reporting to Colonel Butler. Brant told Butler of Johnson's plans and his own activities in Indian country. Unfortunately for both men, they were unable to establish a relationship of trust. Neither Brant nor Butler could agree on many things and both men remained cool to each other throughout the War of Independence. Butler probably resented Brant's authority and abilities and felt that the Mohawk chief was infringing on his domain.[65]

After talking to Butler, Brant had a wampum belt made and traveled throughout Iroquois country advising alliance with the King. When he had completed this tour, he deposited the belt at Onondaga. His efforts were generally successful among all the tribes except the Oneidas and Tuscaroras. The Oneidas rebuffed the Mohawk war chief for seeking to break the pledge of neutrality. When told that the King's troops were crushing the Americans, the Oneidas replied that the King did not need help if that were true. Brant had to use all his powers of persuasion throughout the winter to get people to start thinking about breaking the covenant of neutrality with the Americans. Circumstances, however, would begin to work more in Brant's favor in the near future.[66]

By early 1777, internal disagreement within the Confederacy, American chicanery and British pressure would finally force the Iroquois to take up the hatchet. In January, the council fire at Onondaga had to be extinguished since three sachems and some eighty seven others died in an epidemic. A condolence ceremony was scheduled. All major political decisions were postponed. Such activities were difficult to conduct at midwinter and the divisive times made it even more difficult for the Confederacy to heal its wounds of grief and act wisely for all the Iroquois. Consequently, power began to flow to the warriors and the various village and national councils.[67]

With such activities in Indian country, the Americans decided to call a conference of the Six Nations in Albany on July 15. But the British had already moved to bring most of the Iroquois to the Tory fold. At Irondequoit, a council was called in the early summer to hear the King's agents request that the Six Nations declare themselves in favor of the British cause. All the tribes were present except the Oneidas and Tuscaroras. The British distributed rum and trinkets, and began to talk of the rebellious Americans. They urged the Iroquois to accompany them in the taking of Fort Stanwix and the Fort at Wyoming.[68]

However, the decision to take up the hatchet had not been formally made, despite Brant's efforts. So after hearing the British, the warriors met in council to discuss the British appeal to arms. The council could not reach a consensus. Brant spoke eloquently about the necessity of taking up the hatchet, stating that neutrality would lead to disaster and that the Americans or the British might turn on the Confederacy with a vengeance. Red Jacket and Cornplanter argued against Brant. They insisted that this quarrel was among the whites; interfering in something they did not fully understand was a mistake. As the meeting broke up in a furor, Brant called Cornplanter a coward. The people gathered at Irondequoit divided into two camps and discussed the issue of going to war. In general, the Senecas were disposed to neutrality. Handsome Lake also advocated neutrality. However, the words of Brant stung the ears of the Senecas. They could not bear to be called cowards. Finally, after lengthy discussion, the Senecas were swayed along with other wavering groups to take up the King's cause. Of great importance was the consent of the clan mothers. The Senecas took this defeat gracefully and exhorted the warriors to unite in the fight against the Americans.[69] With this meeting, the resolution was made unanimous. Thus did the Six Nations break its neutrality and take up the British cause.

With the rupture in the Confederacy complete and the warriors in control, the teachings of Deganawidah were ignored. The Great Council at Onondaga had failed to stem the warriors' impetus to war. Iroquois warriors now freely enlisted in the service of the King. At Oswego alone, several hundred Iroquois joined Colonel Barry St. Leger's small army. St. Leger was to sweep down the Mohawk Valley while General John Burgoyne would march down the Hudson Valley, thus splitting New England from the rest of the colonies. St. Leger was to meet Burgoyne at Albany and they were to march to New York City. However, an Oneida sachem named Thomas had heard of the Burgoyne plan while he was at Caughnawaga, and warned the Americans in the Mohawk Valley. Thomas told the Americans to defend Fort Stanwix. He also informed Schuyler that pro-American Indians had not been permitted to take up the hatchet against the British. This intelligence gave the Americans time to reinforce Fort Stanwix before the coming of the British and their Iroquois allies.[70]

Supply problems plagued Burgoyne's expedition as well as spies. Daniel Claus was having difficulty finding the materials of war for his Iroqouis warriors. Because intelligence about the activities of the Americans seemed inadequate to Claus, he sent John Hare, an officer in the Indian department, and John Deserontyon, to spy on Fort Stanwix. After gathering a party and proceeding to Stanwix, the group had a brush with some Americans, then reported to Claus that the Americans were expecting Burgoyne and St. Leger. They also revealed that Stanwix had six hundred men garrisoned, and plenty of supplies. When

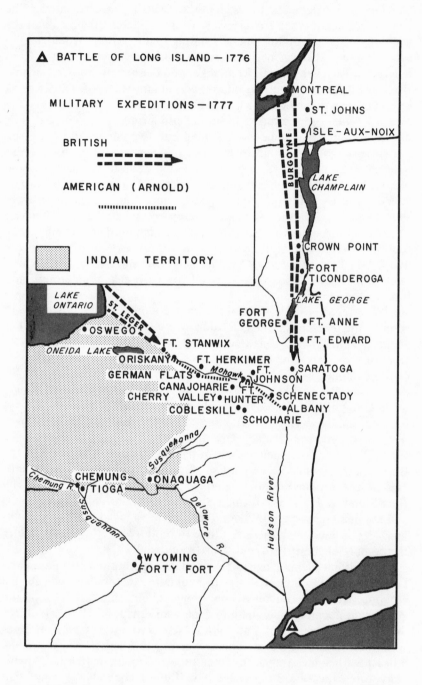

St. Leger received the information, the British Colonel admitted he did not have the firepower to take such a strongly held garrison, but was determined to press on in spite of it.[71]

By the time St. Leger arrived at Fort Stanwix on August 3, he found it heavily fortified. He ordered the rebel commander to surrender; he was refused. St. Leger made preparations to lay siege to the fortress and cut off any reinforcements to the Americans. Three days later, the provincial militia under General Herkimer was attacked by Brant and a group of Johnson's Royal Yorkers at Oriskany. Herkimer had sent word ahead that he was coming, and a force of Americans had sallied forth to meet him at the very time the battle of Oriskany was raging. Brant had cleverly laid a trap for Herkimer at Oriskany Creek. Herkimer had about sixty Oneidas with him as he entered the prepared trap. As they marched into a ravine, John Johnson and his Yorkers were to fire a volley at Herkimer. Butler with his rangers, and Brant, were on Herkimer's flanks to close the trap, as Herkimer's force fully entered the ravine. But before the trap could be completely closed the Indian auxiliaries attacked. It was too soon. Herkimer and his men were able to escape the ravine and maintain a defensive position on a wooded plateau west of it. But the rest of the day saw some of the fiercest hand-to-hand fighting in the War for Independence. Herkimer's strategy showed that he was well acquainted with frontier warfare. He placed two men behind a tree and when one man had shot his musket, the Indians would rush in to attack the man that was loading his gun. However, the second man would step out and shoot the approaching Indian, thus luring him into a trap. By the time the second man had fired, the first man was ready to shoot again. It was a bloody battle. Some Senecas like Red Jacket fled in the face of the fighting and did not stop except for sleep until he had reached the Genessee. The Seneca, Blacksnake, recalled that he had ". . . seen the most Dead Bodies all . . . over that I never Did see, and never will again. I thought at that time the Blood Shed (was) a Stream Running down on the Decending ground during the afternoon, and yet some living crying for help. But have no mercy . . . for them."[72]

The bitter battle ended when the British and the Indians left the field to stop Lieutenant Colonel Marinus Willett and his expedition from looting their camp. Willett led the sortie from Fort Stanwix; he found kettles, blankets, muskets, ammunition and confidential British papers. These captured documents gave the Americans an idea of the strategies of St. Leger and Burgoyne. When the Loyalist forces began to leave the field of battle, the Americans retreated down the valley, carrying with them the mortally wounded Herkimer. The losses were staggering. From two to four hundred of Herkimer's men were estimated killed and several hundred more were wounded, captured, or deserted in the face of battle. One hundred Iroquois died and another hundred Loyalists lost their lives.[73] The British claimed victory at Oriskany because they had stopped the advance of reinforcements and inflicted heavy casualties on the Americans. The rebels claimed victory since they were in possession of the battlefield at the end.

The tragedy of war had fallen hardest on the Indians. Thirty-six Senecas died, including several sachems. Red Jacket's reputation lay in ruins. He had fled in the face of battle. A couple of days after the Battle of Oriskany, the British advised the Iroquois to go home. The Iroquois at Oriskany had faced the heaviest fighting so far in the War for Independence. Mary Jemison, a white woman living among the Seneca, sadly described the return of the warriors. When the full extent of the losses was made known to the Seneca villagers, the entire community was paralyzed with grief. However, Iroquois resolve was not shaken within the Cofederacy, since Brant believed he could raise a force to harass the retreat of the American militia.[74]

The battle of Oriskany was the start of civil war within the Iroquois' League. Pro-British Indians later attacked the Oneida settlement of Oriska, burned the crops, and ran off the cattle. Lines of loyalty were now being drawn within the Confederated tribes according to one's stand on the American war for independence. The Great Peace and the idea of the Extended Lodge were discarded for the ideological conflicts of the white man. Abandoning tradition, the Iroquois would follow the advice of the whites during the American Revolution. Divisions among the Europeans had spilled over to the Confederacy. The old unity was divided. Clan would fight against clan and nation against nation. Oriskany stymied the British attempt to take Fort Stanwix, and the Indian losses made them less willing to fight in future pitched battles.[75]

With Herkimer retreating, St. Leger resumed his efforts to take Fort Stanwix on August 7, 1777. Getting his battery in place, St. Leger saluted the fort at dusk. The next day, Butler went to demand Colonel Peter Gansevoort's surrender. Butler told Gansevoort that the anger of the Iroquois was hard to restrain after Oriskany and if the commander would turn the fort over to the Loyalists, he would spare them being massacred and devastation would not be visited upon the Mohawk Valley. According to Butler, Burgoyne was already in Albany; the fort was cut off. Gansevoort replied to this bluff in straightforward language: ". . . it is my Determined resolution with the forces under my Command to defend this Fort to the last Extremity in behalf of the United American States who have placed me here to Defend it against all their Enemies."[76]

After Gansevoort's refusal to surrender, St. Leger continued the siege of Fort Stanwix for more than two weeks. He also tried to gain the support of the Mohawk Valley settlers, but to little avail. The siege lasted until August 22, when General Benedict Arnold's trickery forced St. Leger to withdraw. A mentally retarded Tory by the name of Han Jost Schuyler was arrested and sentenced to death by the Americans. But his mother begged for mercy and Arnold agreed not to execute the man if he would go ahead of his army to St. Leger's camp and give the Loyalists an exaggerated account of the size of Arnold's relief force and his closeness to Fort Stanwix. To add authenticity to the story, Arnold had Schuyler's coat riddled with bullet holes to make it appear that Arnold was in hot pursuit. Han Jost Schuyler agreed to the ruse and went to St. Leger's camp, telling them that the approaching American army was as numerous as the leaves on the trees. This news alarmed the Iroquois because they felt that St. Leger's artillery and the little Loyalist army was not capable of meeting a sizeable American force.[77]

In the face of such intelligence, St. Leger attempted to boost the morale of his Indian contingent, saying he would lead three hundred men against Arnold's advance. The chiefs agreed to this proposal and chose a spot where they planned to ambush the Americans. But Arnold's ruse was most effective. An Oneida appeared in St. Leger's encampment the day after Han Jost's visit. The Indian reinforced the story of Schuyler; and other messengers began to drift in, telling of Arnold's force and Burgoyne's surrender. To quiet the growing anxiety, St. Leger called a council, urging his Indian allies to remain with him, but during the council, he learned that two hundred of his Indian allies had already left. The Iroquois who remained urged him to leave Stanwix and retreat to Oswego to obtain heavier artillery and more men. As his Indian force ebbed away, St. Leger realized he was helpless. He decided to retreat.[78]

The British officer began his retreat at night, sending the wounded and sick ahead. But more false intelligence came into the camp, claiming that Arnold was only two miles away. Panic reigned, and the orderly retreat became a frenzied flight. Much of the war material that St. Leger had brought with him was left behind. He was quick to blame the Mississaugas for plundering the boats during the retreat. Uneasy elements among the tribes attacked some of the white stragglers, thus turning on their own allies.

In his report to Carleton, St. Leger placed the blame for his failure upon the Indians. However, his superiors tell the story more accurately:

St. Leger's retreat, as it is called, turns out to be a downright flight, if leaving his tents, baggage, ammunition, and hiding his artillery can be called so. Nor do I find that it was owing to the cowardice or bad disposition of the Indians that they came away. Nor did they plunder until the camp was abandoned. Then indeed they got drunk with liquors they found there and afterwards as you may imagine did a great deal of mischief. In short it is a most unaccountable and strange affair . . . Luckily, indeed, for them and everybody else, not a man stirred from the fort, and it is now said that the rebels in the fort excepted, not another was within forty miles of it.[79]

The white soldiers took flight more readily than the Indians, it would appear, since the military stores left behind at the site of the siege were extensive. The Americans found such items as these in the abandoned camp: eighty felling axes, one hundred spades, one hundred picks, fifty-four tents, nineteen wagons, fifteen batteaux, forty canteens, ten knapsacks, forty coats, six mattresses and an extensive amount of artillery and ammunition.

Arnold arrived at Fort Stanwix on August 24, with about a thousand men. Another force of militiamen followed in Arnold's rear. The besieged Americans at Fort Stanwix cheered the arrival. Gansevoort stated that the reason for the failure of St. Leger's expedition to take Fort Stanwix was ". . . the want of heavy Cannon." The commander also commented that, ". . . had the Enemy come . . . with a few Eighteen and twelve pounders the Fort must inevitably have fallen."[80] Claus had warned St. Leger about his lack of firepower in Canada at the start of the campaign, but St. Leger had been unwilling to heed his advice.

By August 26, St. Leger had reached Oswego and distributed supplies to his beleaguered Indian and white troops. Most of the Senecas had left him during the retreat. Blacksnake recalled the reasons for the Seneca withdrawal after the retreat:

We then Retreated for the winter . . . we Replace ourselves, at Near home for our hunting till Spring, Some of those which were family went on home But when we got Ready and hunt Deers & Bears and Elks and other game—for Provisions for the Next for to play upon, and for our childrens and for the old folks, which we have to provide for, all their wants, which we always amken preparation for them before we leave them.[81]

St. Leger now retraced his steps to join Burgoyne. Brant told Claus that he and a party of warriors were going to Mohawk country to bring back the women and children and get more warriors to join Burgoyne's force. Brant and his warriors skirted Fort Stanwix on their journey and some scouts attacked them, seriously wounding the

Mohawk, Captain John Deserontyon. Brant joined Burgoyne, but did not stay long. He was becoming disgusted with the British mismanagement of the campaign, so he decided to return to Iroquois territory.[82]

The bitterness aroused within the Confederacy at Oriskany and Fort Stanwix caused havoc among the Indian people in the Mohawk Valley. The Oneidas and Americans raided Mary Brant's home in Canajoharie. Although she managed to escape, the dwelling was pillaged because she was responsible for sending word to the Loyalists that Herkimer was moving toward Fort Stanwix. In the face of American and Oneida wrath, Mary Brant hurried to Onondaga with her children. But the looters did not stop with plundering the Brant home. The Americans and Oneidas devastated the whole Mohawk settlement, appropriating food and livestock.

The chairman of the Tryon County Committee of Safety enriched himself during the plundering by carrying off wagonloads of goods. The American also urged the Oneidas of Oriska to make up their losses at the hands of the raiding Mohawks. Peter Deygart of the Committee of Safety urged the Oriskas to take two cows, horses, sheep, and hogs for every one that the Mohawks had taken from them. The Oneida, Honyery Doxtater, and Deygart divided the booty obtained from Mary Brant's home. Among the things they took were "Sixty half Johannesses, two quarts full of silver several Gold Rings, Eight pair silver Buckels; a large quantity of Silver Broaches, Together with several silk Gowns." Doxtater moved into the Brant house finally. The Fort Hunter Mohawks were later looted also. Many of the Mohawks had lived in greater comfort than the struggling white settlers. Thus, the settlers were only too pleased to loot Indian homes. A cursory glance at some of the articles taken in these raids reflects the wealth of these Indian communities. Agricultural products like Indian corn, turnips and potatoes were among the things taken as well as livestock, wagons, farm implements, and sleighs. Many Mohawk houses were sturdily built and had window glass, a rare item on the frontier. The result of this devastation was to persuade the Mohawk Nation that their only ally would be the British government. August was a month of victories for the Americans in upstate New York. As Fort Stanwix was being besieged, Colonel John Harper was moving toward Albany to stop the raiding of a force of Tories in the Schoharie area. Harper rallied twenty-eight Continental troops while the militia routed the Tories in the area.[83]

With most of the Iroquois now allied either with the Americans or the British, the American commissioners called another council at Albany in September, 1777. They realized that the Iroquois now respected their abilities in war. On September 14, 1777, about three hundred Iroquois gathered at Albany. Most were Oneidas and Tuscaroras, with a few Onondagas and Mohawks. According to tradition, a fire was kindled on September 15 and the American commissioners asked the assembly if they were disposed to active participation in the war on their side. The warriors were receptive, so the next day a speech was made and a war belt presented to the Iroquois. Each representative from the various nations took hold of the belt, thus accepting the hatchet from the Americans. On September 17, the Iroquois prepared a war feast and the affirmation of the whole assembly was obtained. The ancient unity of the Iroquois Confederacy was now completely broken.

For the next few days, General Schuyler issued supplies and equipment to his new Indian allies. On September 19, he received word of a skirmish between Burgoyne's army and the American force at Freeman's Farm. The news came while he was dining with some of his leading warriors, so Schuyler asked the Indians to help the American army, and to leave at once. The warriors agreed, and hastened, in the middle of the night, to aid the patriots.[84]

Burgoyne's expedition had left Canada in June 1777, to capture the Hudson Valley and split New England from the rest of the colonies. He had a force of seven thousand English regulars and German mercenaries and some two hundred and fifty Tories and Canadians. His Indian contingent numbered about five hundred men, mostly from Caughnawaga, St. Regis, St. Francis, and some Huron settlements.[85]

By July 6, Burgoyne had taken Fort Ticonderoga, and Americans were fleeing in the face of superior manpower at Hubbardton. For awhile it seemed as though nothing could stop the advance of the British. But Burgoyne was not familiar with American modes of warfare, and he was unable to understand his Indian auxiliaries. Indeed the British cause was of only secondary consequence to many of Burgoyne's warriors. They had joined forces with the lesser of two evils. But the situation was aggravated by the weakness of the Indian Department in Canada. Since the removal of Claus and the appointment of Major John Campbell, the Indian administration had been hampered by men such as Campbell, who could not speak an Indian language and had no understanding of Indian customs.[86]

As Burgoyne was hacking his way through upstate New York in July, an incident involving his Indian troops caused an uproar among the Americans. A young woman, one Jane McCrea, had gone to Fort Edward to be reunited with her fiance, David Jones, an officer in Burgoyne's army. Miss McCrea and her friend, Mrs. McNeil, were captured by two of Burgoyne's Indians. The unfortunate Miss McCrea was killed. When Burgoyne heard of this, he demanded that the guilty person be executed. However, his Indian advisors told him this would cause his Indian force to desert, possibly to pillage Canada in retaliation. Burgoyne relented, and let the incident pass without punishment. But the news of this incident helped rally Americans to fight Burgoyne.[87]

Since Schuyler had hastily retreated in the face of Burgoyne's forces, he was removed in August and replaced by General Horatio Gates. Gates used the McCrea incident to recruit troops throughout New England and the Mid-Atlantic colonies. The Americans turned out in droves, fearing that such an event could occur in their own villages.

As Burgoyne plodded through the wilderness and met increasing resistance from American forces all around him, his Indian contingent began to dwindle. Many Mohawks went home to help gather crops. The war had caused a severe scarcity of food. The western Indians also departed, and many others went home disillusioned, as Burgoyne bogged down in the woods of upstate New York.

The source of all this resentment was the mismanagement of Indian affairs by Burgoyne, but then the whole expedition had been mismanaged on all fronts. The value of the Indian contingent during the campaign was summed up in the memoirs of Thomas Ansbury, a soldier with Burgoyne:

They were of vast service in foraging and scouting parties, it being suited to their manner; they will not stand a regular engagement, either through the motives I formerly assigned, or from fear, but I am led to imagine the latter is the case, from the observation I have made of them in our late encounter with the enemy. The Indians were running from wood to wood, and just as our regiment had formed in the skirts of one, several of them came up, and by their signs were conversing about the severe fire on their right.[88]

While the British under Burgoyne were having trouble with their Indian allies, the American Gates was pleased with the Oneidas and Tuscaroras who had joined him on September 20. They were described as steady, dependable and loyal. Their bravery in the campaign against Burgoyne was unquestioned and they ". . . fought like Bull dogs." Gates openly declared that the Iroquois were of great service to him at Saratoga.[89]

With the surrender of Burgoyne's ragged army on October 17, 1777, the nature of warfare in New York would be different in the future. Peace would probably have reigned in the Mohawk Valley had the British been successful. However, the Tories and Brant's warriors would require a change in their strategy. They would now pursue a scorched earth policy in the Mohawk Valley. If the British could not hold this grain producing area, they could at least render it useless to the enemy.

The war of attrition was beginning. The League was split. The Great Tree of Peace stood tall no more. The people of the Extended Lodge were no longer as one. The White Roots of Peace were ripped up and the weapons underneath were exposed, so that Iroquois would fight Iroquois once again as they had done in the days before Hiawatha and Deganawidah. A sadness settled upon the Iroquois as they were drawn into the white man's quarrels. White and Indian states were crumbling in the face of revolution.

Most important, the old kinship state, which had remained strong, wavered, and finally toppled, as the intensity of the War for Independence heightened. The Iroquois were surrounded by warring whites and could no longer detach themselves from the struggle. In any case, it was too late. The Confederacy failed to unite the Iroquois, because both the Americans and British were unable to comprehend the complex relationship within the Confederacy, and the whites were unable to unite themselves during the revolution. A string of unfortunate events also weakened the position of the peace chiefs at a crucial moment, thus allowing the warriors to assert their power without the counterbalancing force of the older men within the Confederacy. And so the Confederacy that had endured for hundreds of years was put aside for a struggle among the whites. Changes in religion, lifestyle, and technology altered the lives of the Iroquois, causing the Laws of the Great Tree of Peace to fail at a time of stress. The people who had helped to nurture the colonists and teach them the way of democracy succumbed to the enticements of both sides in the war. But the heart and spirit of the Confederacy was not wholly extinguished, certainly not in the minds and hearts of the people. It would live on even within the new governments that the white colonists would create and would eventually be rekindled by the Iroquois themselves.

REFERENCES CHAPTER THREE

1. Gipson, *Revolution,* pp. 215-234.

2. Quoted from Cohen, ed., *Felix Cohen Papers,* pp. 321-323.

3. Quoted from Felix Cohen, "Americanizing the White Man," in Roger L. Nichols and George R. Adams, ed., *The American Indian: Past and Present* (Waltham, Massachusetts, 1971).

4. John Adams to Abigail Adams, July 24, 1775, in Margaret W. Willard, ed., *Letters of the American Revolution* (Boston, 1925), p. 188.

5. Wallace, *Seneca,* p. 126.

6. G. Elmore Reaman, *The Trail of the Iroquois Indians* (New York, 1967), p. 50.

7. General Gage to Lord Dartmouth, July 18, 1774, No. 5, *Gage Papers,* English Series, Vol. XXV, Clements Library, University of Michigan; and John Tebbell and Keith Jennison, *The American Indian Wars* (New York, 1965), pp. 109-110.

8. *Ibid.*

9. Wallace, *Seneca,* p. 126.

10. *Ibid.,* p. 127.

11. See Journal of Samuel Kirkland, June 10, 1774-January 1775, p. 19, *Kirkland Papers.*

12. John Deserontyon to Daniel Claus, December 3, 1778, *Claus Papers,* VI, Public Archives of Canada; and Tebbel and Jennison, *Indian Wars,* Chapters 5 and 6.

13. See Harvey Chalmers, *Joseph Brant: Mohawk* (East Lansing, 1955) for a more detailed treatment of Joseph Brant.

14. Journal of Samuel Kirkland, June 10, 1774—January 1775, pp. 19-20, 26-27, *Kirkland Papers.* See also William T. Hagan, *Longhouse Diplomacy and Frontier Warfare* (Albany, New York, 1975), p. 1.

15. *New York Colonial Documents,* VIII, p. 517.

16. Journal of Samuel Kirkland, January 1775-March 20, 1775, p. 20, *Kirkland Papers.*

17. *Ibid.,* p. 17; and Hagan, *Longhouse Diplomacy,* p. 10.

18. *New York Colonial Documents,* VIII, pp. 538-539.

19. Journal of Samuel Kirkland, January 1775-March 20, 1775, pp. 29-33, *Kirkland Papers.*

20. Speech of Oneidas to Governor Trumbull, March, 1775, *Kirkland Papers.*

21. Graymont, Iroquois, p. 59, and Hagan, *Longhouse Diplomacy,* p. 12.

22. "A Short Account of a Tour Undertaken 9th March 1775 from Dartmouth College to Canada," *Schuyler Papers,* Box 13, New York Public Library; Beauchamp, *New York Iroquois,* pp. 225-226.

23. Samuel Kirkland to Andrew Eliot, March 28, 1775 and Andrew Eliot to Samuel Kirkland, April 7, 1775, *Kirkland Papers.*

24. William L. Stone, *Life of Joseph Brant–Thayendanegea* (New York, 1838), pp. 65-70.

25. Graymont, *Iroquois,* p. 63; and Hagan, *Longhouse Diplomacy,* p. 10.

26. Beauchamp, *New York Iroquois,* pp. 223-224.

27. W. C. Ford, *et al.,* eds., *Journals of the Continental Congress 1774-1789* (Washington, 1904-37), II, pp. 93, 174-183.

28. Beauchamp, *New York Iroquois*, p. 226; and Stone, *Joseph Brant*, pp. 86-90.

29. Ethan Allen to Indians of Canada, May 24, 1775, Q11 Public Archives of Canada, pp. 193-194; and Hagan, *Longhouse Diplomacy*, pp. 11-12.

30. Stone, *Joseph Brant*, I, pp. 89-90.

31. *New York Colonial Documents*, VIII, pp. 342-343, 596.

32. Graymont, *Iroquois*, p. 69; and Hagan, *Longhouse Diplomacy*, pp. 11.

33. Comments by Samuel Kirkland on Guy Johnson letter, February 14, 1775, *Kirkland Papers*.

34. Stone, *Joseph Brant*, I, pp. 94-96.

35. Wallace, *Seneca*, pp. 127-128; and Hagan, *Longhouse Diplomacy*, p. 11.

36. *New York Colonial Documents*, VIII, 621-624. See also Hagan, *Longhouse Diplomacy*, pp. 11-12.

37. Wallace, *Seneca*, p. 128.

38. Gustave Lanctot, *Canada and the American Revolution* (Cambridge, Massachusetts, 1967), pp. 43-91.

39. Graymont, *Iroquois*, pp. 75-76; and Hagan, *Longhouse Diplomacy*, pp. 12-13.

40. General Detail of Colonel Claus's Services, *Claus Papers*, XIV, Part I, pp. 24-25, Public Archives of Canada.

41. *New York Colonial Documents*, VIII, p. 661.

42. Stone, *Joseph Brant*, I, p. 116.

43. *Ibid.*, I, pp. 112-113.

44. Wallace, *Seneca*, p. 129.

45. John R. Alden, *General Gage in America* (Baton Rouge, La., 1948), see Chapters 14 and 17.

46. Stone, *Joseph Brant*, I, Chapter 6.

47. *New York Colonial Documents*, VIII, p. 651.

48. Stone, *Joseph Brant*, I, Chapter 6.

49. Wallace, *Seneca*, p. 131.

50. "Minutes of the Proceedings of the Commissioners for the Northern Department Commencing 29 April, 1776," *Schuyler Papers*, Box 13, New York Public Library.

51. John Johnson to Daniel Claus, January 20, 1777, *Claus Papers*, I, pp. 232-233, Public Archives of Canada.

52. Washburn, *Indian in America*, p. 148.

53. Phillip Schuyler to John Hancock, February 15, 1776, *Papers of the Continental Congress*, R. G. 360, I, 541, in National Archives.

54. *New York Colonial Documents*, VIII, pp. 688-690.

55. See George Morgan Letterbook, 1776, pp. 43-49, Pennsylvania Historical and Museum Commission.

56. *Journals of the Continental Congress*, IV, pp. 394-396.

57. Graymont, *Iroquois*, p. 100.

58. Phillip Schuyler to Congress, June 8, 1776, *Papers of the Continental Congress*, R. G. 390, II, pp. 192-196.

59. See George Morgan Letterbook, 1776, passim, Pennsylvania Historical Museum Commission.

60. Beauchamp, *New York Iroquois*, p. 227.

61. *Sir William Johnson Papers*, XI, pp. 817-819.

62. See Indian Records, R.G. 10, ser. 2, XII, 130, Public Archives of Canada.

63. Graymont, *Iroquois*, p. 107.

64. Seaver, *Mary Jemison*, p. 73.

65. *New York Colonial Documents*, VIII, pp. 687-688.

66. Graymont, *Iroquois*, p. 109; Hagan, *Longhouse Diplomacy*, pp. 15-17.

67. "Anecdotes of Brant," *Claus Papers* reprinted in Frank Severance, ed., *Publications of the Buffalo Historical Society* (Buffalo, 1896), IV, pp. 24-31.

68. Washburn, *Indian in America*, p. 148.

69. Graymont, *Iroquois*, p. 100, 122-124.

70. Wallace, *Seneca*, p. 132.

71. *Ibid.*, p. 134.

72. Stone, *Joseph Brant*, I, p. 209.

73. John R. Alden, *The American Revolution* (New York, 1954), pp. 138-139.

74. *Ibid.*, p. 140.

75. See Seaver, *Mary Jemison*, pp. 76-77; and Stone, *Joseph Brant*, I, pp. 209-264.

76. Washburn, *Indian in America*, p. 149.

77. Gansevoort's answer to St. Leger, August 9, 1777, *Gansevoort Military Papers*, III, New York Public Library; and Alden, *American Revolution*, pp. 138-139.

78. Alden, *American Revolution*, p. 140.

79. *Ibid.*, pp. 140-141.

80. Montreal, September 4, 1777, *Germain Papers*, VI, Clements Library, University of Michigan. See also Hagan, *Longhouse Diplomacy*, p. 23.

81. Graymont, *Iroquois*, p. 146.

82. Blacksnake's Memoirs, *Draper Papers*, State Historical Society of Wisconsin.

83. "Anecdotes of Brant," *Claus Papers*, *Buffalo Publications*, IV, pp. 24-31.

84. Graymont, *Iroquois*, pp. 146-147; and Hagan, *Longhouse Diplomacy*, pp. 23-24.

85. Phillip Schuyler to John Hancock, September 27, 1777, *Papers of the Continental Congress*, R. G., p. 360.

86. Alden, *American Revolution*, p. 141.

87. John Burgoyne, *A State of the Expedition from Canada* (London, 1780), pp. 99-101, Appendix xx-xxi.

88. F. J. Huddleston, *Gentleman Johnny Burgoyne* (Indianapolis, 1927), pp. 164-165.

89. Thomas Anbury, *With Burgoyne from Quebec* (Toronto, 1963), p. 178, and Alden, *American Revolution*, p. 136.

90. General Gates to John Hancock, October 12, 1777, *Emmet Papers*, New York Public Library; and Hagan, *Longhouse Diplomacy*, pp. 23-24.

GUS-TO-WEH WITH BROKEN ANTLER. The broken antler represents the loss of certain Iroquois chiefs because they chose the path of war for personal gain.

Chapter Four
THE WAR OF ATTRITION

W ITH THE GREAT TREE OF PEACE UPROOTED, the fury of war was
unleashed among the Iroquois. In many cases, kinsman would
fight kinsman. The old Iroquois policy of balancing one white power
against another failed them now, and the divisive factors within the
white community had spread to the Iroquois. The effect was civil war
among the Indians, and disunity among the Six Nations worked to
destroy, at least for the time, the teachings of Deganawidah. The campaign of 1777 had split the Confederacy and forced each tribe to take
sides in the American War for Independence.

While the winter of 1777-1778 was uneventful, the seeds of a border war between Indians and white frontiersmen were being sown.
Congress tried to gain the favor of the four hostile tribes of the Confederacy (Mohawk, Onondaga, Cayuga, Seneca), claiming that the Shawnee and Delaware were friends of the Americans; therefore the
Iroquois could benefit by such a strong alliance. Ostensibly, the frontier remained quiet, but Joseph and Mary Brant were laying the basis
for Confederacy support of the British cause throughout the long
winter. Mary Brant received invitations to settle in several Iroquois
villages after her home was plundered. She eventually decided to remain at Cayuga. She was a woman of influence among the Iroquois, a
clan mother, the granddaughter of Hendrick, and the widow of Sir
William Johnson. Joseph Brant also made Cayuga his home base.
Daniel Claus encouraged the Brants' pro-British sentiments further, by
sending two officers from the Indian department. Lieutenant John
Dockstader was sent among the Cayugas, and Captain John Johnson
lived among the Senecas for the winter. The Widow McGinnis, a white

Loyalist, also stayed the winter at Cayuga.[1] All three of these emissaries knew the language and customs of their hosts. However, both the agents of the Indian department and the Brants found it difficult to persuade the Iroquois to stand firm in the British cause.

After the Battle of Saratoga, General Schuyler had sent a wampum belt to the Six Nations, telling them of the great victory over Burgoyne and asking them to make peace with Congress. As the wampum belt made its way westward, pro-American Iroquois rejoiced and pro-English factions began to waver. At Cayuga, the Widow McGinnis seized the belt[2] and had another one made that read more favorably for the British cause.

British losses at Fort Stanwix, Oriskany, and Saratoga had damaged the fighting image of the British among the Iroquois. Many pro-British Iroquois seemed to be leaning toward neutrality again. Mary Brant sought to stem this feeling of futility toward the British. Due to her position, she was actually more influential within the Confederacy than her younger brother, Joseph. As a clan mother and consort of Sir William Johnson, she was a powerful figure within the traditional framework and also knew the ways of the white man. Claus understood the enormous power Mary Brant wielded. He observed that, "one word from her goes farther with them than a thousand from any white Man. . . ."[3]

As winter set in, the Iroquois began to assess the benefits of their recent alliance with the English Crown. The four hostile tribes had lost many lives in the campaign of 1777, but they had inflicted even greater casualties upon the enemy. The British had conducted an exhausting campaign, with embarrassingly poor results. St. Leger and Burgoyne had both failed, but signs pointed to tactics that were even less encouraging. The Iroquois saw that the English had evacuated Fort Ontario on the Oswego River; this left the tribes exposed to the wrath of the Americans.[4] Their traditional friendship to the Crown was now on shaky ground.

Influential chiefs such as Sayenqueraghta again began to talk of peace and neutrality. During the Revolution, Sayenqueraghta was the most respected of all the chiefs in the Confederacy. While Joseph Brant was well known among the Iroquois, his youth and his acculturated manner often worked against him. In council, Sayenqueraghta had voiced his doubts. Mary Brant was quick to defend the British cause. She reminded the chief that his family had been loyal to the Crown since the time of Queen Anne. Mary also talked, with tears in her eyes, of the friendship between Sayenqueraghta and Sir William Johnson. The council was deeply touched by her eloquent plea, and Sayenqueraghta decided to continue supporting the Crown.[5]

Joseph Brant and Sayenqueraghta spent the winter mapping

strategy for the coming spring campaign. Sayenqueraghta decided to move against the Pennsylvanians, and cut off the Wyoming Valley. Brant centered his activities in the Mohawk Valley region. Before the winter had set in, the Senecas had sent war parties to the Virginia and Pennsylvania frontiers to harass settlers.[6] The Senecas were becoming more keenly aware of the fact that the Americans could be expected to cheat Indian people out of their land.

By the fall of 1777, Major John Butler had returned to Fort Niagara, and he invited Mary Brant to come to the frontier to live. The Iroquois clan mother hesitated, not wanting to alienate her friends and relatives at Cayuga. Later, however, she did move to Niagara. While there, she maintained an open house for all the leading men and women of the Confederacy. Niagara was a busy place, as the Iroquois were constantly visiting the post to trade. She freely gave her advice on affairs of state and encouraged people to remain loyal to the English cause, listening sympathetically to the grievances of the influential chiefs and providing counsel to those in doubt.[7]

In December, 1777, Butler held another council with the Iroquois. He found them ready to fight, in spite of their losses in the disastrous summer campaigns, and he plied the Iroquois with gifts to compensate for the losses. Several Onondaga and Tuscarora chiefs who had been friendly to the Americans attended the meeting and gave Butler the war belt they had received from the United States at an earlier conference. However, they were not speaking for their entire consitutency, since the Onondagas were uncertain of joining the British until 1779, and many Tuscaroras continued to fight on the American side throughout the Revolution.[8]

The Oneidas remained steadfast in their support of the American cause. As Washington's army shivered in the snow at Valley Forge, Skenandoa and the Oneidas carried baskets of corn to the starving Continental Army. Clearly, the members of the Confederacy were continuing to act at cross purposes to each other.

General Schuyler was aware of British activity among the Iroquois. During the winter, he sent a wampum belt to the Six Nations, calling for a council at Johnstown in February, 1778. The Senecas refused the invitation outright, as did the Cayugas. These refusals caused delays, and the council was not held until March, 1778.[9]

Early in 1778, Joseph Brant left Niagara to spend the winter among the Iroquois and stood prepared to defend the heartland of the Six Nations if the Americans provoked him. Although Butler was jealous of Brant, he realized that his cooperation was crucial in keeping Iroquois as allies. Butler recommended to General Carleton that Brant be supported for his services to the Crown.[10] Both men were uneasy about each other, but such differences were glossed over for the sake of the British cause.

On March 7, several hundred Iroquois assembled at Johnstown for talks with Schuyler. No Senecas were present and only a few Cayugas and Mohawks bothered to attend. The Onondagas, Oneidas and Tuscaroras were most broadly represented at the council. The Marquis de LaFayette, commander of the northern department, was present. The Americans spoke harshly to the Iroquois, threatening the Six Nations with force if they did not remain strictly neutral. The Americans also wanted the four hostile nations (Seneca, Mohawk, Onondaga, and Cayuga) to meet at the council fire at Onondaga to discuss their proposals. This request was denied, since only Tenhoghshweaghta of the Onondagas agreed to the idea. The failure of the League to settle their differences at this point was aptly explained by Tenhoghshweaghta:

> Times are altered with us Indians. Formerly the warriors were governed by the wisdom of their uncles the Sachem but now they take their own way and dispose of themselves without consulting the Sachems. While we wish for peace and they are for War, Brothers they must take the Consequences. As for the Senecas, they have long since forsaken our Council Fire.[11]

But the Onondaga spokesman promised to try to rekindle the council fire and bring the dissident groups back under the Tree of Peace. Plainly, the old ways of the Iroquois were giving way to newer, more individualistic patterns. The warriors were following their own course without the consent or advice of the older sachems. The educated and urbane Joseph Brant played a key role in this process. Not only were individuals within the Confederacy following their own convictions, but also a whole nation, the Senecas, refused to take part in the activities at Onondaga.[12]

While the Tuscaroras and Oneidas continued to ally themselves with the Americans, they also warned the commissioners at Johnstown that the Onondagas could not be trusted. Since the Oneidas were becoming staunch allies of the Americans, they feared attack from the other tribes as well as from the British. Consequently, the Oneidas asked that a fort be established at Kanowalohale, the main village. The Oneidas also requested that American troops be sent among them. LaFayette heeded their requests and built a small picket fort immediately after the close of the council. In concluding this council, the Tuscaroras and Oneidas reminded the Americans that establishing a trading post at Fort Stanwix was crucial to maintain friendly relations with the tribes. They wanted clothing, explaining that British influence increased in proportion to the amount of goods they were able to provide the Iroquois.[13]

In Schuyler's report to Henry Laurens, President of the Congress, the general stressed that the wisest strategy would be to carry the war to Indian country in the spring. Schuyler knew that border warfare would start as soon as winter ended. He reasoned that putting Americans in Iroquois country would serve as protection for frontier inhabitants and, if necessary, would enable the Americans to destroy hostile Indian settlements. He feared the English would fully garrison the post at Oswego and thus move closer to the American frontier. Indeed, strengthening Oswego would make it impossible for many Iroquois to side with the American cause, because the British would then dominate the area. Schuyler advised Laurens that prompt measures were needed to thwart the English. There were other problems. Schuyler wanted the Tryon County Committee of Safety to find the guilty parties in the sacking of Canajoharie, a Mohawk settlement, so that restoration could be made. He also discouraged the patriots' tendency to incite Indians in pillaging Tory homes.[14]

The British failure to garrison Fort Ontario early in the war was caused by their refusal to follow the advice of their Indian allies. As a supply base, it was crucial. It was capable of providing shelter and protection for the Indian people in the event of an invasion. The British had tarried too long in their decision to garrison Fort Ontario, and the consequences of this decision would be disastrous.[15]

With the spring thaw, war began in earnest. Springfield, a town at the head of Otsego Lake, was attacked by pro-British Iroquois. The fort was burned, and some American men were slain. Others were captured. Despite American accounts of atrocities, the style of warfare pursued by the Iroquois was humane. The primary concern of all their raiding parties was the destruction or seizure of property. Expulsion of the rebels was a factor also. If the men resisted, they were killed or captured. Women and children were usually left alone or taken prisoner. There were no instances of torture in Iroquois raids except for some soldiers captured during Sullivan's campaign. Indeed, there were no wholesale massacres by the Iroquois at all.[16]

During the spring of 1778, Schuyler and LaFayette recruited about fifty Oneidas and Tuscaroras to serve in the Continental Army. Congress had sought to get four hundred volunteers, but this proved to be unrealistic. In May, 1778, the Oneida and Tuscarora force of fifty men fought with LaFayette at the Battle of Barren Hill in Pennsylvania. But no other Iroquois people were willing to commit themselves to the American cause.[17] In fact, Joseph Brant was busily consolidating the efforts of the four other tribes in order to raid the American frontier more effectively.

After gathering warriors at Ononquaga in the spring, Brant advanced to Cobleskill with over three hundred Tories and Indians. On May 30, 1778, Captain Samuel Patrick, with a force of about fifty American regulars and militiamen, ran into a party of Brant's scouts. The scouts ran, in a maneuver intended to draw Patrick and his men to the main body of Brant's men. The Americans pursued them for about a mile and then realized they were being led into a trap. When the full size of Brant's force was discovered, a retreat was ordered by Captain Christian Brown, who had assumed command when Patrick fell in battle. The total American loss is said to have been about half the force, dead and wounded. The same number of casualties, about twenty-five, was suffered by Brant. As a result of his victory over the Americans, Brant laid waste to Cobleskill. He burned about ten houses with their barns and drove off most of the cattle. He took five prisoners and sent them to Niagara to await an exchange. A neighboring settlement, Durlach, was also taken.[18]

With the frenzy of border warfare unleashed, Brant headquartered himself at Onoquaga, increasing the size of his army, as well as his supplies. He roamed about Tryon and Ulster Counties gathering supporters and protecting Loyalists. After a few more minor raids in June, the entire Mohawk Valley seemed powerless to stop the onslaught. People flocked to the larger settlements of Cherry Valley and Schenectady seeking safety. Schenectady sent an urgent appeal to Governor George Clinton for military protection. The whites of the Mohawk Valley felt they were exposed both to British and Indian attacks without any protection. Fort Stanwix would not be helpful to the settlers of the Mohawk Valley if it were cut off from supplies and endangered through Brant's forays.[19] The situation looked bleak for the Americans.

The response of Congress to these raids was swift and deliberate, but ineffectual. An expedition against Detroit, Niagara, and Oswego was suggested. Congress reasoned that by mounting an offensive they would gain more security for the American frontier. Major General Horatio Gates was named to organize the campaign, and $932,743 was set aside for an Indian campaign.[20] However, the plan was not implemented in 1778.

The first major battle of the 1778 campaign was the famous battle at Wyoming. A force of several hundred Tories under Butler and Johnson was outfitted at Niagara. Most of the Seneca warriors joined them as they moved into Pennsylvania. Early in July, this force appeared at Forty Fort, the rebel stronghold in the Wyoming Valley. On July 3, 1778, about four hundred Americans left the fort to confront the

Tories and Indians. Both sides arranged themselves in a skirmish line, but the Senecas and other Iroquois warriors managed to outflank the American troops; the rebels were forced back, and began to retreat. Very soon, the retreat turned into a rout. About three hundred and forty of the four hundred rebel men were killed outside of Forty Fort that day. Tory and Indian losses were much lighter. The Senecas claimed they had lost only five men. On July 4, 1778, the fort surrendered to the superior force of Tories and Indians. As a result of this victory, the entire Wyoming Valley was laid waste by Loyalist forces. Settlements were burned and pillaged and most of the inhabitants fled to the nearby mountains. The survivors invented outlandish tales about atrocities and Wyoming became an American symbol for Indian savagery in war. The "monster Brant" was accused of murder even though he was elsewhere, in the Mohawk Valley. While the news of the Wyoming Valley campaign was being distorted all out of proportion along the American frontier, the Indians and Tories returned to Fort Niagara with fifteen prisoners whom they turned over to the British. The Senecas received some money for their efforts, as well as some clothes, and were told to go home.[21]

Fearing a concerted effort along the frontier, Peter Gansevoort, the American commander at Fort Stanwix, sent a detachment of men under Lieutenant McClellan to destroy the buildings at Oswego, early in July, 1778. The troops burned the buildings so that the British would have to completely rebuild the installation to take post there. On July 10, McClellan returned and reported that Oswego was destroyed.[22] Thus, a strategic point was devastated; it would prove to be a stumbling block for the British.

Brant was increasing his activities in the Mohawk Valley. At Oriska, the Oneidas were attacked. They sent word to Schuyler that German Flats would be the next place attacked. Schuyler continued complaining to Governor Clinton that the finest wheat country in the state was being ". . . ruined for want of a body of Continental Troops." He was also busy trying to organize Oneida and Tuscarora resistance against Brant. Four Oneida and Tuscarora chiefs told Schuyler they could not persuade the Cayugas and Senecas to remain neutral, so they wanted American help to fight the western members of the Confederacy. The American commander ordered some Oneida scouts to German Flats and the Schoharie area. The chiefs wanted commissions in the Continental Army for some of their head warriors, and Schuyler relayed the request to Congress, reporting they did not want any pay and ". . . I should be happy to comply with their request."[23]

With the defeat of the rebels at Wyoming, the Continental Congress decided to speed up its plans to attack the Iroquois. Brant's summer camps at Unadilla and Onoquaga for refugee Tories and Mohawks seemed to be the Mohawk leader's headquarters. American intelligence reported that Brant was fortifying his post at Unadilla, and the rebels in the neighboring Cherry Valley were sending out parties to thwart Brant's efforts. Congress reduced its grandiose project of attacking Detroit and the Ohio Valley, to one of merely trying to protect the Susquehanna River Valley.[24]

In September, 1778, a force of Americans swept into the upper Susquehanna Valley region and destroyed Unadilla and Onoquaga. By then the towns were abandoned, but the Americans burned the houses to the ground, including the sawmill and gristmill. At the same time, about two hundred American militiamen, commanded by Colonels Denniston and Hartley, marched up the Susquehanna River from the Wyoming Valley, destroying deserted Indian towns at Tioga, Queen Esther's Town, and Sheshequin. When rumors reached the Americans that Butler was near Tioga, the militiamen retreated to Wyoming. During the retreat, Butler's Indians attacked them, and the force suffered minor casualties.[25]

These feeble threats only hardened Brant's determination to protect the Iroquois heartland. He saw now that the home of the Six Nations was threatened by land-hungry frontiersmen who wanted to sweep aside all Indians. The result of these American retaliations swayed the Seneca sachem, Big Tree, to support the warriors. Until the destruction of Indian towns in the upper Susquehanna Valley, Big Tree had continued to negotiate with the Americans through the Oneidas, but as a result of the destruction he grew to believe that the British were the only true allies of the Iroquois.[26]

To retaliate for the attacks on Unadilla and Onoquaga, Butler's rangers and Brant's men attacked Cherry Valley with about three hundred men. Red Jacket was expected to accompany Brant, but he turned back with three other men, complaining that winter was upon them, and it was too late for a campaign. This was the second time the Seneca warrior had decided to avoid fighting. The strategy planned by Brant and Butler was to paralyze the militia in the fort by snipers from Butler's ranks. While the militia was being diverted, Brant and his men captured some men, women and children, drove off the livestock and took some supplies. The houses, barns and haystacks were burned. A number of Americans were killed, and about forty women and children were captured. Most of the captives were released a few miles outside of the settlement. A few were kept, to be held as hostages for the release of Walter Butler's wife and family. The Americans were holding the Butler family for the return of Walter Butler himself, although they had sentenced him to death.[27] An exchange was eventually worked out.

The Cherry Valley attack generated many atrocity stories among the Americans, just as the Wyoming Valley attack had done. However, this time the stories had an element of truth. Brant and Butler were unable to restrain their men as they had at Wyoming. About thirty civilians were killed at Cherry Valley. Through his correspondence with both General Schuyler and General Clinton, Butler denied the widespread killing of women and children. He asserted that the killing of civilians was in revenge for the atrocities committed by Americans. But stories about the excesses at Cherry Valley continued to spread. Rumors about atrocities sent the frontier into a panic, causing hatred for the Iroquois and the Tories.[28]

With the spring of 1779, the raids along the frontier began again. For almost two years, the Americans were at the mercy of the Iroquois and the Tories along the northern frontier. They were anxious to retaliate. The state of New York was being devastated by these attacks, and the Continental Army was deprived of valuable foodstuffs through the destruction of these frontier areas. The frontier was also being pushed farther eastward as a result of the attacks, and Washington feared the Iroquois might eventually join the major forces of the British. Consequently, Washington and Congress deemed it necessary to secure the hinterland of New York from Indian raids.

The Iroquois had no idea that such a campaign was being mounted against them. The Confederacy was still divided. The Oneidas and Tuscaroras were pressured by the Cayugas to abandon the American cause, but the two tribes remained steadfast in their friendship with the rebels. The Onondagas were divided as a nation into three parties: pro-American, pro-British, and neutral. As early as January, 1779, a delegation of eight Onondaga chiefs went to the Oneidas and pledged their support to the American cause. General Schuyler received a report on the Onondagas, saying ". . . they now let go their Hold of peace; extinguished the Council Fire; sunk the Tree of Peace into the Earth and caused total darkness to overspread the Confederacy. . . ." The decision of the Onondagas was ". . . to join their Children the Oneidas and Tuscaroras to oppose any invaders."[29]

The Onondaga chiefs insisted that everyone within the nation declare himself for one side or the other. This statement caused considerable dismay. Several Onondagas told the delegation they had done what others could not do. Furthermore, the villagers said, ". . . that they looked upon that land as given to them by the Great Spirit." The chiefs were reminded that they ". . . had nothing to do with the Fire; nor would they who were the Guardians of it consent that it should be put out. . . ." Despite these protests, about forty Onondagas left in

February to live with the Oneidas. They gave the Americans a medal they had received from the British. In moving to Oneida country, these Onondagas escaped the impending destruction of their town.[30]

Meanwhile, Brant was attacking settlements from the Mohawk River to the Minisinks on the Delaware River. The Senecas and Cayugas captured Fort Freeland (near Sunbury, Pennsylvania). About thirty soldiers were taken prisoner. Western Pennsylvania was raided by smaller bands, as far west as Pittsburgh. While the loss of life in the raids was small for the Americans, they were effective in destroying the military and economic resources of the American frontiersmen. These blows battered the American mobilization effort and struck at the morale of the Pennsylvania frontiersmen. In New York, Brant was following a similar course. At German Flats, a rich and productive agricultural area in the Mohawk Valley, Brant successfully attacked the entire area. One hundred square miles of farmland was destroyed, while the Americans defended their small forts (which were not fired upon).[31]

From the Mohawk Valley to the Susquehanna Valley, the frontier was in panic. Hysteria reigned. Appeals for help were desperate. One such appeal pleaded:

> . . . I need not ask what is to be done, Help, Help; our whole frontier laid open, and the Communication with Gen. Sullivan's army is cut off.[32]

Petitions were circulated to bring Sullivan's army to the rescue, since he had been sent to lay waste to Iroquois towns. Many people demanded court proceedings against Sullivan. Forts were left unmanned, and the local milita would not muster to defend the countryside.

A colonel in the militia wrote to the president of Pennsylvania's revolutionary council: ". . . there is nothing to be seen but Disolation, fire & smoak. . . ."[33] Many older inhabitants compared the destruction to the losses during the French and Indian War two decades earlier.

These raids confirmed Washington's worst fears. From the Monongahela River to the Mohawk Valley, a fifty to one hundred mile swath of devastation was cut by Brant and other pro-British Iroquois. All through the winter of 1778, Washington laid plans to strike at the Iroquois. It was to be the major campaign of 1779. Washington first offered the command of the proposed Indian expedition to Major General Horatio Gates and then to Major General John Sullivan, who accepted reluctantly and assumed command of his force in early spring of 1779. Sullivan's campaign was to be one of the most carefully organized raids of the whole war. Washington realized the Iroquois were doing enormous damage to the American cause. The Americans were facing defeat; the economy was disrupted. When militiamen were called from their fields during planting and harvesting, this meant that agriculture would deteriorate.[34] The burning of these crops meant less food for the American people as well as for Washington's army.

During the spring and summer of 1779, there were several invasions into the heartland of the Iroquois by American forces. In April, 1779, Colonel Goose Von Schaick was ordered by General James Clinton to strike the Onondagas. Even at this late date, the Onondagas were still trying to remain neutral. While it was true that many of the men had participated in attacks on the Americans, the Onondaga chiefs frequently proclaimed their neutrality at Albany. Moving from the Mohawk Valley, General Clinton in August, 1779, proceeded towards Sullivan at Tioga.[35]

The attack on the Onondaga villages convinced those who were still talking of neutrality to align themselves with the British. The Onondagas retaliated against Clinton's raids by attacking Cobleskill, New York, just east of Schoharie. About three hundred Onondaga warriors (nearly every able bodied man in the tribe) burned the village and fort at Cobleskill. Twenty-two soldiers were killed; and two prisoners were taken. The Senecas also were incensed at the treacherous attack upon the neutral Onondagas.[36]

During his invasion of the Onondagas, Clinton issued orders containing statements that reflected the Iroquois' humane treatment of prisoners of war:

> Bad as the savages are, they never violate the chastity of any women, their prisoners. Although I have very little apprehension that any of the soldiers will so far forget their character as to attempt such a crime on the Indian women who may fall into their hands, yet it will be well to take measures to prevent such a stain upon our army.[37]

Actually, this was a startling realization for many American officers, that Indian people would often treat prisoners more humanely than the rough hewn militiamen and regulars in the Continental Army.

After plundering the land of the Onondagas, General Clinton, with 1,500 men on 220 flatboats, floated down the Unadilla River from Otsego Lake to join General Sullivan and his troops at Tioga. Clinton was able to make the trip quite easily; he broke a dam at the mouth of Otsego Lake and rode the crest of a flood down the Unadilla. The flood served another purpose: it destroyed Indian cornfields all along the way. Clinton burned three Tuscarora villages on his way down the Susquehanna (it appeared that the pro-American stand of most of the Tuscarora did not make them immune to the ravages of the American

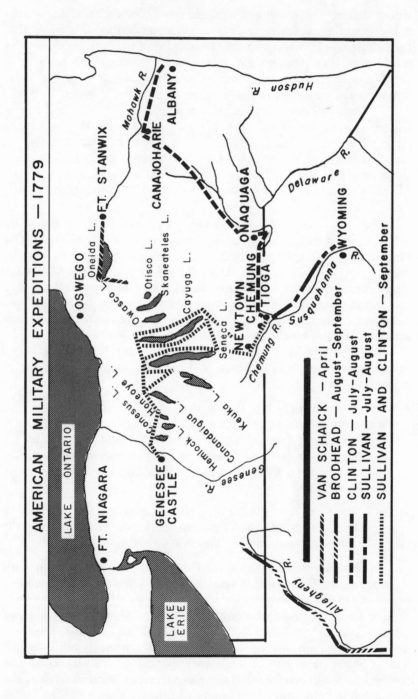

AMERICAN MILITARY EXPEDITIONS — 1779

VAN SCHAICK — April
BRODHEAD — August-September
CLINTON — July-August
SULLIVAN — July-August
SULLIVAN AND CLINTON — September

army). The whole trip from Otsego Lake to Tioga took a little less than two weeks (August 9-22). When Clinton arrived at Tioga on August 22, General Sullivan took command of the combined forces, amounting to a little over 4,000 men.[38]

Sullivan's campaign was planned for late summer so that there could be no replanting of crops after they had been burned. Unlike Clinton's first attack on the Onondagas, the second, third and fourth attacks would be done simultaneously by Generals Clinton and Sullivan, and Colonel Brodhead. Washington's orders to Sullivan were explicit; he was to totally destroy the Iroquois villages and take as many prisoners as possible. He was to devastate the Iroquois from the Mohawk Valley to Niagara. While Sullivan and Clinton marched through the Finger Lake Region, a smaller force under Colonel Daniel Brodhead proceeded up the Allegheny River from Fort Pitt. Now the dogs of war were unleashed in the heart of Iroquois country. Many military historians view Sullivan's campaign as one of the first examples of modern strategies of total war. The methodical Sullivan moved up the Chemung River and then into the Finger Lakes region with a vengeance. He maintained strict discipline and kept his supply lines open during this campaign. He also sent out Oneida spies to prevent his lines from being ambushed. Sullivan knew he had the element of surprise with him when he moved into Iroquois country, since the British and Iroquois were not expecting so extensive an expedition. Neither Brant nor Butler had the forces to stop the American advance.[39]

At Newtown on the Chemung River, Brant and Butler assembled about seven hundred and fifty men, without artillery, in an effort to stop Sullivan's advance. On August 29, 1779, Brant, Butler and the Johnsons fought the Americans from foxholes and hastily constructed breastworks. Sullivan's artillery gave him a definite advantage as he sprayed the enemy with shrapnel. The British and Iroquois were outnumbered three to one, so Sullivan was able to turn their flank and route them. But the fighting was hand-to-hand and spirited, until superior numbers won the day. Brant and the British fell back and regrouped beyond the Genesee. Here they prepared to meet Sullivan again. The battle at Newtown was the only major military engagement of the campaign. But Sullivan's purpose was to lay waste to the productive resources of the Iroquois. He destroyed all the surviving towns on the Susquehanna River and its branches. He plundered all the important Cayuga villages and most of the Seneca strongholds. He systematically destroyed the Iroquois villages, much the same as Brant and the Senecas had done to American lands in New York and Pennsylvania. The Americans burned all the houses and outlying buildings, cut down fruit orchards, and put acres of corn and other vegetables to the torch. Most of the Iroquois abandoned an area when Sullivan moved in, so he could take only a few prisoners. The extent of his destruction was staggering. He destroyed three towns on the Chemung River, three more on the Tioga, about a dozen Cayuga and Seneca towns on Seneca and Cayuga Lakes, about six Seneca towns on his path westward to the Genesee, and the cluster of settlements around Genesee. Sullivan never encountered the regrouped Tory and Indian force he met at Newtown since he had turned back at the Genesee River. By the time he reached the river, his men were on half rations and he had only a couple of cannons, so he decided to return to Tioga.[40]

Sullivan had missed a few settlements on the upper and lower Genesee River and several small settlements west of the Genesee Valley. But Colonel Daniel Brodhead, with about four hundred men, was also proceeding up the Allegheny River from Pittsburgh. Brodhead planned to pillage the Seneca villages on the upper Allegheny. He burned the town at Jenuchshadago and several small settlements, but he failed to reach the large settlements along the oxbow of the upper Allegheny. Most of the villages he burned were deserted. Brodhead met very little resistance (one or two small skirmishes with small parties of Seneca warriors), but he burned huge expanses of cornfields and took no prisoners.[41]

While winding up the expedition, Sullivan sent a small contingent of troops to the Lower Mohawk Castle, where a few people had remained behind, living in peace with their white neighbors. These Mohawks were taken prisoner. Their houses and farms were confiscated and given to the surrounding white population. Eventually released with apologies, it is safe to assume that the Lower Castle Mohawks did not get their land back, but the record in this regard is unclear.[42]

While the immediate effect of Sullivan's raid was to strengthen the determination of the Iroquois, the Continental Congress and George Washington gained a dubious reputation among the Indians. Washington won the name of "Town Destroyer" among the Iroquois for his role in planning Sullivan's camapign. To this day, the Iroquois name for the President of the United States remains "Town Destroyer," and with good reason. In 1790, Cornplanter summed up the Iroquois view of the 1779 campaign:

> When your army entered the country of the Six Nations, we called you Town Destroyer; and to this day when that name is heard our women look behind them and turn pale, and our children cling close to the necks of their mothers.[43]

The devastation caused by the Continental Army could not be easily forgotten.

As the summer of 1779 came to a close, the Onondagas, Mohawks, Cayugas, and Senecas found themselves in a perilous situation. All their towns had been destroyed or were abandoned in the heat of the American attack. The devastation was as complete as the Iroquois expeditions into the Mohawk Valley and Pennsylvania had been earlier. Towns on the Upper Susquehanna that were dependent on the Iroquois were burned and all but two of the larger Seneca towns were ravaged. The Oneida towns were left untouched because of their friendliness to the Americans. However, Brant's forces and a group of Tories swept down on the Oneida settlement in the winter and burned it. The fort, houses, and Kirkland's mission were razed, and the Oneidas took refuge among the whites at Schenectady until the end of the Revolutionary War.[44]

Prior to the Revolution, the Iroquois and other dependents had lived in about thirty villages, from the Mohawk River to Lake Erie. These were thriving villages until the ravages of war hit them. In the spring of 1780, only two Seneca towns remained unscathed. The others were deserted, burned, or severely damaged. Some people tried to return and begin anew in their old villages, but most were dispersed, or crowded into other settlements. Many went to camp in flimsy cabins on the banks of the Niagara River with their British allies. The winter of 1779-1780 was a time of hunger, cold, and disease. As the surviving Iroquois huddled together that winter, they talked of replanting and rebuilding, and revenge.[45]

However, despite the deep winter snows and the enormous job of taking care of the displaced, the Iroquois warriors were ready to raid again in the spring. In July of 1780, Guy Johnson reported that:

> The Number of Men of the Six Nations Confederacy is about sixteen hundred, about twelve hundred of whom are Warriors, and of the latter, eight hundred and thirty are now on service agst the frontiers. . . .[46]

The war parties from Fort Niagara, Lake Champlain and Crown Point were on the move in March, 1780. A few of the Iroquois' western allies came from as far away as Sandusky and Detroit.

The Iroquois raids along the American frontier devastated the land from the Mohawk Valley, the Catskills, the central and western part of Pennsylvania, to the Ohio Valley. By August, 1780, Brant and his forces seemed to be gaining. Early in August, the Canojoharie District was burned by about four hundred Tories and Indians. Cornplanter, Sayenqueraghta, and Brant led the forces. The Senecas were the largest group at this raid. A few women had come along; their main purpose was revenge. When the attack had ended, fifty-three houses and barns were burned, as were a church, gristmill, and two small forts.

Ironically, one of the houses destroyed was owned by the old Indian trader, John O'Bail. After the aged O'Bail was taken captive, he was recognized by the Senecas. He was Cornplanter's father. Cornplanter was informed immediately that his father was among the prisoners. He apologized to the old man for the ravaging of his farm, offering to take care of him for the rest of his life. But the aging O'Bail wanted to return home, so Cornplanter dispatched several men to bring him safely home. Many other whites were released as a tribute to Cornplanter. After they had concluded their business at Canojoharie, a party of about thirty Senecas drifted southward to the Susquehanna, attacking the countryside.[47]

The most important campaign of 1780 was the Schoharie Valley expedition. This was led by Sir John Johnson, accompanied by Brant and a large contingent of Senecas. The results of the expedition were disastrous for the Americans. The destruction was on a large scale, such as Sullivan's earlier raid on the Iroquois had been. Tories and Indians converged on the Schoharie Valley in the fall of 1780. They were unopposed; then, meeting the Mohawk River, they marched up that river, raiding. This wiped out all white settlements west of Schenectady. The total amount of damage Americans suffered at the hands of the Iroquois during 1780 was staggering. About three hundred and thirty Americans were killed (fourteen were officers), and over seven hundred houses burned, six forts and several mills. Almost a thousand head of cattle were confiscated by the Iroquois. A huge amount of grain was burned. It was a grave time for the whites of New York.[48]

Governor Clinton of New York appealed to the Congress for help:

We are now arrived at the year 1781, deprived of a great Portion of our most valuable and well inhabited Territory . . . We are not in a Condition to raise Troops for the Defense of our Frontier, and if we were, our Exertions for the common cause have so effectively drained and exhausted us, that we should not have it in our power to pay and subsist them. In short, Sir, without correspondent Exertions in other States and without Aid from those for whom we have not hesitated to sacrifice all, we shall soon approach to the Verge of Ruin.[49]

The Loyalist Iroquois campaign of 1780 demonstrated the inability of Sullivan's strategy in preventing raids along the frontier. Both Loyalists and Americans were agreed on this point. James Madison stated in June, 1780, that Sullivan's expedition made the Iroquois more resolute than terrified.[50] The pro-British Richard Cartwright wrote in his memoirs that:

the rebels must have found that their grand Western Expedition, attended with such vast labour and enormous expense, instead of conquering, had only served to exasperate the Indians.[51]

But the Iroquois as a body were pushed back beyond the Genesee River, even though they fought at will to the east. They were also made more dependent now on the British for supplies in order to continue their efforts.

Those Iroquois who were supporting the Americans suffered a harsh fate in the winter of 1780-1781. After Brant's raids on their villages, the remains of the Tuscarora and Oneida nations took up residence around Schenectady. Their condition was deplorable. General Schuyler evicted some French people to give these friends of America better living conditions. However, many Oneidas and Tuscaroras survived the winter in small huts that were described in the bleakest terms:

These huts are like our barracks in time of war, or like those built in vineyards or orchards, when the fruit is ripe and has to be watched at night. The framework consists only of two uprights and one crosspole; this is covered with a matted roof, but is well lined within by a quantity of bark. The inner space is rather below the level of the ground, and the entrance by a little side door; in the middle of the hut is the fireplace, from which the smoke ascends by an opening in the roof. On each side of the fire are raised two platforms, which run the length of the hut and serve as beds; these are covered with skins and bark.[52]

Huddled in these dwellings and in some army barracks, were about four hundred men, women and children. The Oneidas and Tuscaroras were often reduced to seeking charity, since they had no land and no crops. Many died during that winter. Smallpox broke out in the camp and took its tragic toll. These tribes, that had fought so hard for the American cause, were now virtually forgotten. Although they were dispossessed by the pro-British Iroquois for their support of the Americans, they still refused to desert the Americans and go to Niagara. There are those who believe they would have been treated better by the British.

War was taking its toll on all sides, and the bitterness intensified. During the campaign of 1781, sixty-four war parties raided along the

New York, Pennsylvania and Ohio frontier. About three thousand Indians participated in these raids against the Americans. They were mainly Iroquois, with a few of the traditional allies of the Six Nations. Many war parties revisited settlements previously destroyed, to raze what had been rebuilt. A party of fourteen Delawares ranged as far as the Hudson River in early January. A Mohawk party under David Karaghqunty followed the path of the Delawares a few weeks later. Captain Shinop and nine Nanticokes raided the Susquehanna region in January.[53] The spring and summer of 1781 was one of constant raids along the American frontier. Although the groups were small, they moved swiftly and did considerable damage to the American crops.

By October 1781, Cornwallis had surrendered at Yorktown. Traditionally, this has been treated as the last battle of the American Revolution. However, raids along the frontier were continuing.[54] On November 18, Lieutenant Adam Crysler attacked Schoharie with twenty-eight Indians. They killed one man, drove off fifty head of cattle, burned a few houses, and drove off several horses. The Caughnawagas were anxious to go raiding. Just before winter at a council near Niagara, two Onondagas and a Huron asked Colonel Johnson for British troops to help the Hurons and Shawnees destroy Fort Pitt.[55] After Yorktown, peace between England and America seemed closer, but the Iroquois had no such desire.

The news of peace negotiations was slow to reach the frontier. The Virginia militia attacked some Shawnee towns in 1781 and 1782. Perhaps the most brutal act of the whole Revolutionary War came during March, 1782. A colony of Delawares who were converts to the Moravian Church had settled along the Muskingum River in Ohio. However, their peaceful policy made them suspect to other warring tribes, so they moved to Sandusky in the fall of 1781. In the spring of 1782, a delegation of these Delawares returned to their towns along the Muskingum to bring back their corn and other supplies. At the same time, an Irishman, William Wallace, and his entire family was killed on Raccoon Creek nearby. Some militiamen under Colonel David Williamson set out to find the raiders who had committed the murders. When the militia came upon Gnadenhutten, the Delawares were just preparing to leave. They greeted the Americans with friendly gestures, suspecting no violence. But a detachment of militia had found the hat and coat of Hugh Cameron in one of the villages, which seemed to prove that these pacifist Delawares could not be trusted. They took them prisoner. Proceeding on the assumption that the only good Indian is a dead Indian, the militiamen decided on reprisals. A few men would not participate in what was to follow, but they were a decided minority. Colonel Williamson was unwilling to interfere with the majority, so he took his gun and walked out of sight, saying to the men, "Do as you please with the prisoners."

The Delawares pleaded for their lives, professing their innocence, explaining they were pacifists. Finally, as their situation became clearly hopeless, they huddled together, singing and praying. They were then gathered together and shot, tied to stakes or tomahawked by the militiamen. The village was burned. The carnage was horrible and has been regarded as the most brutal act of the American Revolution, performed not by Indians but by whites. When it was over, ninety-six Delawares lay dead. The old and the young were not spared. Women and children were slaughtered indiscriminately. Returning home with the loot from the Delaware villages, the militia received high praise for their efforts from the white settlers.[56]

Two months later, an expedition under the command of Colonel William Crawford, with Williamson second in command, suffered a defeat at the hands of the Delawares. The outrage for what had befallen their Moravian brothers could not be contained. Crawford and two other prisoners were tortured, and Crawford was killed. The inhumanities of war had now reached its highest level on all sides.[57]

In the spring of 1782, the Iroquois were still sending out war parties. Both Isaac Hill and John Deserontyon helped to destroy a mill at Little Falls on the Mohawk River. Sayenqueraghta moved toward Wheeling with three hundred Senecas. Other parties set out for the Pennsylvania frontier. However, the raids were intermittent and peace seemed on the horizon. In that same year, Lord North's ministry fell in Parliament. Rockingham succeeded North, and then Shelburne became Prime Minister. The British sent delegates to Paris to negotiate with the Americans and French. An order to stop all hostilities was issued. Shelburne's cabinet opposed North's armed intervention in the colonies. However, they now had no interest in Britain's Indian allies. These allies, in the view of the Shelburne ministry, should be discarded; the government had no more need of them.[58]

Before word of the British treachery could reach North America, Brant and a group of warriors left in June, 1782, to take post at Oswego. On June 18, he arrived at Oswego with about three hundred warriors. He was dismayed to find that no war supplies were there as planned. He needed moccasins and ammunition. Failing to have supplies, Brant and his force contented themselves with repairing the fort. Major John Ross, who was slated to become the commander, commented on the Iroquois' and Brant's enthusiasm in rebuilding the facility at Oswego: "I never saw men work so hard, and it greatly encouraged the troops."[59]

Early in July, Brant and about four hundred men left Oswego for the surrounding frontiers. Some of Ross' men went out also. Scarcely had they departed when word arrived of peace negotiations, and a message was sent to bring Brant and his men back to Oswego. He returned with his men, but they were disappointed in not being allowed to attack. Ross praised Brant for his restraint.[60]

Nevertheless, many Iroquois were displeased about being denied the right to continue the war. Indeed they had not been consulted during the peace negotiations and were dismayed at being treated so cavalierly. They considered themselves to have been allies, nations that had allied themselves with another nation. Many chiefs felt that peace between England and America would ignore the Indian, and they were right. By the fall of 1782, all the Indian warriors who had gathered at Oswego were back in their villages. Sir John Johnson and Brant toured the upper posts in New York and told the Iroquois that conditions would turn out for the best under the new system being developed. They would never be forgotten,[61] was the promise.

As the American War for Independence was coming to a close, the pressure for westward expansion grew. The frontiersmen knew that the British were restraining their Indian allies, so they flocked into the Ohio region, staking out claims, clearing land, and building cabins. At this time also, a force of Americans attacked a lower Shawnee village at Standing Stone. While the men were away hunting, they killed the women and children. The Iroquois were furious about this attack on their younger brothers in the Confederacy, so they called a council at Niagara to ask for British aid in retaliating against the frontiersmen. Sayenqueraghta, the Seneca chief, reported that the Americans

> gave us great Reason to be revenged on them for their cruelties
> to us and to our Friends, and if we had the means of publishing
> to the World the many Acts of Treachery and Cruelty commit-
> ted by them on our Women and Children, it would appear that
> the title of Savages wou'd with much greater justice be applied
> to them than to us.[62]

Despite these pleas for help, the British did nothing to end the cruelties inflicted upon Indian people along the American frontier.

Britain's inability to protect her Indian allies along the frontier quickly caused resentment among the Six Nations. Brant complained to Sir John Johnson that the Iroquois were in a vice; the Americans were attacking them on one side and the British were grumbling about the cost of supplying their allies on the other. This situation would continue for many years. The British had abandoned their allies.

The fort at Oswego played an important role in the final campaign, in the winter of 1782-1783. Oswego was strategic for both sides, because it gave the British closer access to the American frontier, and it would be a good supply point for both Loyalists and Indians. Consequently, Colonel Marinus Willett received orders from General Washington to take the post at Oswego. Willett planned a surprise night attack, using scaling ladders and bayonets. On February 9, 1783, Willett and his men left Fort Herkimer with an Oneida scout, Captain John Otaawighton. The men marched to Oneida Lake, crossed it, and proceeded up the Oswego River. As they traveled along the river, they stopped for awhile to build their ladders. On the evening of February 13, they were only a few miles from the fort. They walked for several miles along the ice of the river until it became too hazardous. Captain John assured the expedition they would soon find the path to the fort. But the Americans became lost in the woods and wandered around aimlessly all night, thus losing the element of surprise. Finally, the colonel realized that Captain John and his men were lost. Disgruntled, he placed the Captain under guard and ordered his men to turn back. At dawn, the party was discovered by some English scouts. Three Senecas came upon the gloomy party and professed friendship as they hurried away. The Americans ignored them. Their goal had been the fort, and they had failed.

Willett was suspicious of Captain John's intentions, but his suspicions were groundless; the Oneida chieftain was noted for his integrity. The American force and Captain John had really lost their way in the deep winter snows and the dark. Later, Washington wrote to Willett seeking to salve his feelings.

The loss of Oswego mattered little, however, in the final course of events. The war was at an end. On November 30, 1782, the British and Americans had agreed upon the Preliminary Articles of Peace. Word of this agreement would finally reach the frontier in the spring of 1783. However, the Iroquois were to face still another desperate struggle, the effort to hold their land.[63]

In spite of the British defeat, the war seemed to be going well for the Six Nations. At the end of the 1783 summer campaign Blacksnake and other Senecas at Fort George were told by treacherous British officials that Washington had surrendered. The real truth, that it was the British who had surrendered, began to dawn upon the warriors at Fort George and Fort Niagara despite the false report.[64] Only slowly, however, did the Iroquois come to believe that the British had actually been defeated by the rebels, and a peace had been concluded between the two warring nations. Of far more importance was the realization that the peace had been negotiated and signed without Iroquois participation. The interests of those Indians supporting the Americans as well as those supporting the British had been equally ignored at the Peace of Paris.

The war had ended along the American frontier, but the efforts of the Iroquois went unrewarded by both sides. The British discarded their Mohawk, Onondaga, Cayuga, and Seneca allies at the earliest convenience. The Americans would do the same to their loyal allies, the Tuscaroras and Oneidas. All past declarations of friendship were forgotten. In fact, the American frontiersmen were now poised on the edge of Indian land, waiting to make up for lost time during the War for Independence. The Iroquois began to rebuild the Confederacy, but this would be no easy task.

REFERENCES CHAPTER FOUR

1. Wallace, *Seneca,* p. 136; and Daniel Claus to Guy Johnson, November 12, 1777, *Clinton Papers,* Clements Library, University of Michigan.

2. "Claim of Sarah McGinn," *American Loyalists,* XXI, pp. 400-406, New York Public Library; and Hagan, *Longhouse Diplomacy,* p. 23.

3. See "Molly Brant—Loyalist," *Ontario History,* XLV, 3 (Summer 1953), pp. 97-108; and Daniel Claus to General Frederick Haldimand, *Claus Papers,* XXV, p. 119, Public Archives of Canada.

4. Graymont, *Iroquois,* p. 159.

5. "Anecdotes of Brant," *Claus Papers, Buffalo Publications,* IV, pp. 24-31.

6. Wallace, *Seneca,* pp. 136-137.

7. Daniel Claus to General Frederick Haldimand, August 30, 1779, *Claus Papers,* II, pp. 132-133, Public Archives of Canada.

8. Major John Butler to Sir Guy Carleton, February 2, 1778, Q15, pp. 123-145, Public Archives of Canada.

9. Beauchamp, *New York Iroquois,* p. 234.

10. Major John Butler to Sir Guy Carleton, February 2, 1778, Q15, pp. 123-145.

11. See Indian Council, March 1778, *Schuyler Papers,* Box 14, New York Public Library; and Hagan, *Longhouse Diplomacy,* pp. 28-29.

12. *Ibid.*

13. Stone, *Brant,* I, pp. 306-307.

14. General Phillip Schuyler to Chairman of General Committee of Tryon County, March 11, 1778, Schuyler Mansion Document 12, New York State Library; and Tebbel and Jennison, *Indian Wars,* p. 120.

15. Graymont, *Iroquois,* p. 164.

16. Wallace, *Seneca,* pp. 136-137.

17. "Minutes of the Indian Commissioners, April 15, 1778," *Papers of the Continental Congress,* III, pp. 298-300.

18. Beauchamp, *History of the Iroquois,* p. 235; and "Anecdotes of Brant," *Claus Papers, Buffalo Publications,* IV, pp. 24-31.

19. Hugh Hastings, ed., *Public Papers of George Clinton* (Albany 1900-1914), III, pp. 409, 418, 476, 542-543.

20. "Report of the Board of War, June 10, 1778," *Papers of the Continental Congress,* II, 81-85; and Henry Laurens to General Horatio Gates, June 13, 1778, *Papers of the Continental Congress,* I, p. 366.

21. Beauchamp, *New York Iroquois,* pp. 235-236.

22. Colonel Peter Gansevoort to General Phillip Schuyler, July 10, 1778, *Gansevoort Military Papers,* IV, New York Public Library; and Hagan, *Longhouse Diplomacy,* p. 33.

23. *Clinton Papers,* III, 565; and General Phillip Schuyler to Henry Laurens, July 19, 1778, *Papers of the Continental Congress,* III, p. 350.

24. Wallace, *Seneca,* p. 138.

25. Beauchamp, *New York Iroquois,* p. 236.

26. Wallace, *Seneca,* p. 139.

27. Graymont, *Iroquois,* pp. 186-189.

28. Stone, *Brant*, I, passim; and Blacksnake's Memoirs, *Draper Papers*, State Historical Society of Wisconsin.

29. James Dean to General Phillip Schuyler, January 18, 1779, *Papers of the Continental Congress*, II, pp. 420-423; and Wallace, *Seneca*, p. 140.

30. Beauchamp, *New York Iroquois*, p. 238; and Graymont, *Iroquois*, p. 193.

31. Wallace, *Seneca*, p. 140.

32. *Pennsylvania Archives*, First Series, VII, p. 593.

33. Wallace, *Seneca*, p. 141.

34. Charles P. Whittemore, *A General of the Revolution: John Sullivan of New Hampshire* (New York, 1961), pp. 115-116; and "The Committee appointed by the Assembly of the State of Pennsylvania to confer with a Committee of Congress," *Papers of the Continental Congress*, II, p. 55.

35. Beauchamp, *New York Iroquois*, pp. 238-239.

36. Wallace, *Seneca*, p. 142.

37. Stone, *Brant*, I, p. 404.

38. Beauchamp, *New York Iroquois*, p. 240.

39. Wallace, *Seneca*, pp. 142-143.

40. Beauchamp, *New York Iroquois*, pp. 240-241.

41. Wallace, *Seneca*, p. 143.

42. *Ibid.*, pp. 143-144.

43. Beauchamp, *New York Iroquois*, p. 243.

44. Wallace, *Seneca*, p. 144.

45. For a detailed description of Sullivan's raid see Stone, *Brant*, II.

46. *New York Colonial Documents*, VIII, p. 797.

47. Wallace, *Seneca*, p. 145.

48. Beauchamp, *New York Iroquois*, p. 244.

49. Governor George Clinton to President of Congress, February 5, 1781, *Papers of the Continental Congress*, II, pp. 351-352.

50. James Madison to Thomas Jefferson, June 2, 1780 in Edmund C. Burnett, ed., *Letters of Members of the Continental Congress* (Washington, 1923-1933), V, p. 181.

51. Graymont, *Iroquois*, pp. 240-241.

52. Francois Jean de Chastellux, Howard C. Rice, Jr., eds., *Travels in North America in the Years, 1780, 1781, and 1782* (Chapel Hill, 1963), II, p. 208.

53. Graymont, *Iroquois*, p. 245.

54. Alden, *American Revolution*, p. 247; and Marjory Barnum Hinman, *Onaquaga: Hub of the Border Wars* (Windsor, N.Y., 1975), pp. 90-91.

55. Graymont, *Iroquois*, p. 251.

56. Stone, *Brant*, II, pp. 215-225.

57. *Ibid.*, II, pp. 225-226.

58. Alden, *American Revolution*, pp. 250-251.

59. Joseph Brant to Major John Ross, June 18, 1782, B124, pp. 10-11, Public Archives of Canada; and Major John Ross to General Frederick Haldimand, June 27, 1782, B124, pp. 6-7, Public Archives of Canada; and Charles M. Johnston, ed., *The Valley of the Six Nations* (Toronto, 1964), pp. xxxiv-xxxv.

60. Graymont, *Iroquois*, p. 255.

61. Captain Matthews to Captain Ross, September 9, 1782, B124, pp. 178-180, Public Archives of Canada, Hagan, *Longhouse Diplomacy*, p. 52.

62. Council at Niagara, December 11, 1782, B115, pp. 170-179, Public Archives of Canada; Hagan, *Longhouse Diplomacy*, pp. 52-53.

63. See Stone, *Brant*, II, 233-236 for a detailed account of Willet's expedition; and Beauchamp, *New York Iroquois*, pp. 246-247.

64. Wallace, *Seneca*, p. 148.

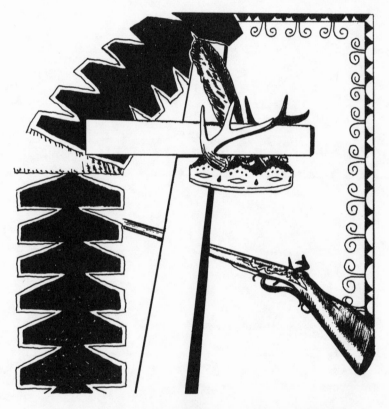

WAMPUM, CROSS, GUS-TO-WEH
WITH ANTLER AND MUSKET. This array of objects symbolizes the tension and conflict that came with the arrival of Christianity and European technology. Ultimately, these factors would
weaken the effectiveness of Iroquois unity during the American
Revolution.

Chapter Five

THE LEGACY
OF THE REVOLUTION

W ITH THE REVOLUTION ENDED, THE CONTRIBUTIONS OF the Iroquois in political and military affairs were ignored by the infant Republic as well as by the British Crown. The Iroquois did-not consider themselves a vanquished people in 1784. They were capable of continued resistance, but since the Americans and British had settled their differences, the Indians decided to negotiate a treaty at Fort Stanwix. This new treaty seemed necessary since Great Britain had made no terms for her Indian allies in the Peace of Paris. They had promised the Mohawks much for their aid in the war; it seemed clear that Iroquois interests had been abandoned.

In deciding the fate of the Mohawks and other pro-British Iroquois, the British had played a key role. For a time, the Mohawks remained on the American side of the Niagara River, and the Senecas offered them land in the Genesee Valley. However, Brant and his followers had no desire to remain in New York. Subsequently, Governor Haldimand consented to purchase a tract of land at the Bay of Quinte for Brant and his people. But the Senecas wanted Brant's people closer, so Haldimand secured a 1200-square mile tract on the Grand River in 1784. While most of the Iroquois moved to the Grand River Reserve, some refused to move after they had settled at the Bay of Quinte. The Quinte location was farther from the Americans. Also, some friction had developed between John Deserontyon and Joseph Brant. Deserontyon, speaking for the Fort Hunter Mohawks at

125

Quinte, wrote to John Johnson stating their dismay about Brant's leadership:

> I indeed foretold you that we could not depend on our Friends (I meant Capt Brants party) and you see how they have acted so shameful a part in giving up or sacrificing their country.[1]

But there were representatives from other nations in the League who came to the Grand River Reserve. Some Delawares, Nanticokes, Tuteloes, Creeks and Cherokees also moved to these new lands. In 1785, some one thousand eight hundred and forty-three Indians had resettled along the Grand River. With all the Six Nations represented, the League of the Iroquois was brought to life again. Somehow, the Old Law was to survive.[2]

Negotiations on the American side would be different. The Iroquois who assembled at Fort Stanwix in 1784 felt that most of western and central New York was still theirs, but the American commissioners showed them the peace conditions signed between the English and Americans, which ignored the Iroquois claims. Factionalism was also manifested among the Iroquois along pro-British and pro-American lines. Sickness also haunted the Iroquois, and weakened their position at Fort Stanwix, since many people could not attend the meeting due to illness in their family. These unfortunate events converged to damage the abilities of the Iroquois to negotiate from a strong position.

On October 11, 1784, the American commissioners at Fort Stanwix ordered all liquor confiscated. Agents of New York, Peter Schuyler and Peter Ryckman, were trying to usurp the power of the commissioners, so they were ordered to stay away from the council house. October 12, guards were placed outside the council house to keep the New York agents away, but the Pennsylvania commissioners who cooperated with the American commissioners were permitted to attend the council. Captain Aaron Hill, a Mohawk, opened the council on October 12 on a friendly note. Arthur Lee then spoke, on behalf of the American government. Lee claimed sovereignty over all Indian lands and asked that the prisoners still held by the Iroquois be delivered to the Americans. They were most anxious to obtain Skenandoa, Good Peter, and Johannes Schrine. All three of these men were made prisoners when they went to Niagara in 1780 for peace talks. Finally, the commissioners announced that they wanted an adjustment of present boundaries, to end the friction between whites and Indians along the frontier. Lee spoke bluntly with a sharp edge to his words, and this set the mood for the remaining treaty negotiations.[3]

After a few days' deliberations, Captain Hill asserted it was not the right of the Six Nations to make peace with the Americans unilaterally. He said the Iroquois were ". . . free and independent, and at present under no influence." Therefore, he claimed to speak not only for the Iroquois but for the tribes to the west and to the south. He rejected the American claim of sovereignty, declaring that the United States must send a delegation among the Iroquois to gather up the prisoners they wanted.

The Americans replied in harsh and uncompromising terms. Lee rejected the position that the Iroquois spoke for any tribes other than themselves. He pointed out that they showed no wampum to verify their claim. He chastized them for supporting the King, while also pledging neutrality to the Americans. The commissioner denied Hill's contention that the Iroquois were independent. Arrogantly, he pronounced, "you are subdued people; you have been overcome in a war which you entered into with us, not only without provocation, but in violation of most sacred obligations." He concluded that the Iroquois stood alone against the might of America, and the acceptance of the treaty was their best choice. He then read the provisions of the treaty, the only terms the Americans would agree to for cessation of hostilities.[4]

Hostages were to be returned, and the Americans demanded a cession of land including parcels along the Niagara frontier. They also demanded that the Iroquois abandon all claims to lands in the Ohio region. Tuscarora and Oneida territorial integrity was not to be endangered. Finally, gifts would be presented to the Six Nations for their "use and comfort" in exchange for agreement to these provisions. Lee warned that if there were any further objections to the land cession demand, the government might claim the whole of New York by right of conquest, since the King had ceded the area to the Americans in the peace agreement. But, Lee pointed out, the Americans were willing to take only a part, to make amends for the ". . . blood and treasures which they have expended in the war."[5]

The second Fort Stanwix treaty was signed October 22, 1784. When the Americans had completed their negotiations, the Pennsylvania agents, Francis Johnson, William McClay and Samuel Atlee, moved in for their turn with the Iroquois. Through negotiations, they pressured the Six Nations to grant a tract of land that encompassed most of the northwestern part of Pennsylvania. Only the Cornplanter Reserve remained as Indian land (this would be just south of the present Allegheny Reserve) in Pennsylvania. The Pennsylvania commissioners argued, as the American envoys had done, that the King had ceded all Indian land to Pennsylvania, but they wished to provide some form of compensation, so that they would not be accused of taking advantage of Indian people. Cornplanter and others had at first refused. However, the Pennsylvania delegation offered an array of goods amounting to about $4,000, for the whole area. The Iroquois were advised they had no choice but to accept quickly, since the next day was Sunday and they would do no business on the Sabbath. They were also most anxious to return home. The Iroquois accepted the offer, with the provision that another $1,000 worth of goods be given them the following year. It was agreed to, and a deed was prepared for the Six Nations to sign, October 23, 1784. Consequently, the Iroquois had ceded still another large tract of land for $5,000 Continental dollars. It was quite a bargain.[6]

When the Iroquois delegates at Fort Stanwix returned to their people, they were received with disdain. Because much of the negotiations were done at gunpoint, most of the tribes felt they had been betrayed by their leaders. The chiefs involved with the Treaty of Fort Stanwix were berated by their own tribes for years to come. Holding council at Buffalo Creek, the Six Nations asserted that the delegates were not authorized to cede the land. The council asked the Americans to return the deeds, and the Confederacy would grant a few parcels of land to repay them for the gifts that had been received at Fort Stanwix. This request was ignored, or treated scornfully by the Americans.[7]

But the Iroquois were still a strong and independent people at the end of the American Revolution. However, the consequent peace was to create even more devastation than the war had done. Land was taken indiscriminately from former allies such as the Oneidas and Tuscaroras, as well as from the tribes that had supported the British. In the early Nineteenth Century, the Seneca prophet Handsome Lake would preach a message of spiritual rebirth through the old ways that would give strength not only to the Senecas but to the rest of the Six Nations tribes. Handsome Lake condemned the use of alcohol, witchcraft and magic. The result of his message was to give the Iroquois renewed strength to resist the cultural domination of the white man. To this day, the Code of Handsome Lake and the way of the Longhouse provide strength and unity to the Iroquois people.[8]

In a very real sense, the legacy of the Revolution was (and is) a negative one for the Iroquois. Deprived of their land, divided on distant reservations in Canada and the United States, the Iroquois had little to rejoice about in the founding of the United States. Tribal autonomy and the following of the old ways were to be frowned upon by the new government. If there was a promise of freedom or autonomy for the Indians during the American Revolution, it was quickly discarded for quick land acquisitions in order to serve the interests of the restless white frontiersman.

When one understands the legacy of unity and democracy that the

Iroquois provided to the emerging American colonies, it appears clear that these contributions have generally been suppressed. A casual glance at the scholarly literature on the Revolution reinforces this conclusion. Immediately after the Revolution, David Ramsey's *History of the American Revolution* pointed out that geographical distance, ". . . generated ideas in the minds of Colonists favorable to liberty." Ramsey also referred to the absence of a strong sense of social inequality in America, but did not address himself to the origins of such beliefs. It was assumed, then, that these ideas had sprouted spontaneously on American soil. George Bancroft, in his *History of the United States,* written in the antebellum period, considered the Revolution as the final event in the American march towards liberty, stressing the fact that this progression to liberty was self-determined. Historians in the Imperial school, such as Herbert L. Osgood, George L. Beer, and Laurence H. Gipson, saw the Revolution in a different light. They were preoccupied with the transformation of British institutions in the American setting, and in placing the American Revolution in the contemporary realities of the Eighteenth Century, thus giving the interpretation a British background. In a very real sense, the Imperial historians chronicle the gradual disintegration of British feudal and proprietary elements in American society, because they were foreign to frontier life in America.

The Progressive interpretation of the American Revolution emphasizes the conflict of interests and how this conflict was manifested in economic, social and cultural issues in the struggle for independence. Men like Charles Beard, Carl Becker, and Vernon L. Parrington stressed conflict as the catalyst for the Revolution, attempting to pinpoint friction in the mercantile system, taxation, and class struggle. A few Progressive historians also state that the conservatives entered the Revolution to curb the ardor of the dissatisfied masses.

In today's academic world, the Neo-Whig school (Jack Green, Daniel Boorstin, and Edmund Morgan) as well as others, have given the interpretation of social conflict less emphasis. This interpretation stresses the building of a new and distinct society as the major feature of the American Revolution. There are many in this school of thought who talk of a "unique" American environment which produced this new society. A corollary view has also emerged through the work of Sir Lewis Namier, a position which reinforces the American conservative school. Namier contends that the proper view of the Revolution is not through the study of Whig and Tory parties, but through an analysis of "connections," "interests," and patronage. He seeks to modify George IIIs image as a tyrant, thus removing one of the strongest Whig arguments concerning the cause of the American Revolution.

As one can see from this cursory discussion of the causes of the American Revolution as interpreted by historians, the role of the Native American is absent. However, these writers do agree that between 1759 and 1776 America had developed into a separate and distinct society. This fact emerges clearly. What then can we say about the roots of the new society? Where did the Americans gain these new, unique, distinct ideas that made and make them today so different? The answers to such questions are complex, certainly. But the Americans were, on the whole, sensitive to capricious authority and attempts to usurp colonial self-determination. This free and non-feudal American society faced a series of bureaucratic irritations before the Revolution, causing increasing criticism and a heightened sense of unity among the colonies. The Revolution was originally a movement to restore the rights they believed they had, to be enjoyed as free-born Englishmen. In the end, separation seemed to be the only alternative.

At the Albany Conference of 1754, Old Hendrick of the Mohawks spoke to the colonial delegates about their disunity, holding up the Iroquois League as an example for the "thirteen fires" to emulate, as previously here discussed.[9] The French were profoundly influenced by the unique aspects of Indian society, and this was expressed by many prominent philosophers of the Enlightenment. In turn, these thinkers were read by literate American revolutionaries like Franklin and Jefferson.[10]

Indeed, Thomas Jefferson believed Indian society ought to be emulated. He noted that Native Americans had:

> never submitted themselves to any laws, any coercive power, any shadow of government. The only controls are their manners, and that moral sense of right and wrong . . . an offense against these is punished by contempt, by exclusion from society, or, where the case is serious, as that of murder, by the individuals whom it concerns.[11]

Jefferson also developed ideas that came close to a rejection of European values. In one of his more critical statements, he says:

> As for France and England, with all their pre-eminence in science, the one is a den of robbers, and the other of pirates, as if science produces no better fruits than tyranny, murder, rapine and destitution of national morality, I would rather wish our country to be ignorant, honest and estimable as our neighboring savages are.[12]

Early in the history of the American Republic, we find Iroquois democratic traditions being compared to the classical Greek model. In 1814, DeWitt Clinton asserted that all of the proceedings of the

130

Iroquois ". . . were conducted with great deliberation and were distinguished for order, decorum, and solemnity." The New Yorker also pointed out that in ". . . eloquence, in dignity, and in all characteristics of profound policy, they surpassed an assembly of feudal barons, and were perhaps not far inferior to the great . . . Council of Greece."[13] According to Jefferson, "Every man with them, is perfectly free to follow his own inclinations."[14]

Paradoxically, the League of the Iroquois was used as an integral part of Marxist theory in the late Nineteenth Century. Friedrick Engels, in his *Origin of the Family, Private Property, and the State* describes Iroquois society in glowing terms:

> And this gentile construction is wonderful . . . Everything runs smoothly without soldiers, gendarmes or police; without nobles, kings, governors, prefects or judges; without prisons; without trials . . . Blood revenge threatens only as an extreme or rarely applied measure . . . . The household is run in common and communistically by a number of families, the land is tribal property . . . . All are free and equal, including the women. And the kind of men and women that are produced by such a society is indicated by the admiration felt by all white men who came into contact with uncorrupted Indians, admiration of personal dignity, straightforwardness, strength of character and bravery of these barbarians.[15]

Engels had been inspired by the reading of Lewis Henry Morgan's work on the Iroquois, and had come in contact with Morgan's "Ancient Society." He was enthralled, thinking that here is the final counterpart of a classless, democratic society free from restraints of government and operating on the basis that land and goods belong to all, so that "To each according to his needs, from each according to his abilities" could be a viable and practical solution to the ills of society.

Engels sought to prove that social institutions are subject to change under socio-economic conditions. In studying the Iroquois, using Morgan's work as well as various reports, he hoped that a new society would emerge as ". . . a revival in a higher form, of the liberty, equality and fraternity of the ancient gentes." In other words, the ultimate goal of Marxian socialism is to return to a state on a higher and more complex level, analogous to that of the ancient Iroquois.[16] Engels had not been in contact with the Iroquois themselves, nor had he ever visited their country.

It is interesting that the ideals of the Iroquois Confederacy serve as examples both for the democratic societies as well as for the communist. Both of the world's major ideologies seem to be attempting to recapture, through programs, theories, and various institutions, the spirit of the Iroquois Confederacy. America tries to gain liberty through political institutions, while the Communist countries are trying to accomplish their goal through state planning and national control of the forces of production as well as the land and resources. However, the Marx-Engels ideal of the withering away of the state as a political institution, appears to be just as far from realization in the prototypes of Communist society that we see today, as it was when their governments were first formed as "dictatorships of the proletariat." There can be no doubt, however, that Iroquois society holds a great fascination for the democratic and communist ideologies of our contemporary world.

The Albany Plan of Union and the Laws of the Iroquois Confederacy are strikingly similar in their structure and philosophy. The principal component in the Iroquois Confederacy, unity, is a concept foreign to European democratic thinkers. Yet, Franklin and others seized upon this idea and utilized it effectively through the "Join, or Die" slogan publicized in the *Pennsylvania Gazette.*

It is indeed strange that the discussion continues after these many years, as to whether or not the Iroquois Confederacy *really* had an effect on the founding of the American Nation. It would appear that little short of a signed affidavit bearing the stamp of any year from 1600 to 1780 is acceptable to the scholars and politicians who deny the role of the American Indian as a force for progress, as a force for good. There are, however, some scholars who have emphasized the role of the Iroquois in the formation of the United States. Morgan, mentioned above, was the first serious student of the Iroquois. He asserted that the "People of the Longhouse ". . . commended to our forefathers a union of colonies similar to their own as early as 1755. They saw the common interests and common speech of the several colonies the elements for a confederation."[17] Morgan also states that the League was the ". . . germ of modern parliament, congress and legislature."[18] In the 1930s, Matthew W. Stirling suggested that the Albany Plan of Union was greatly influenced by the League of the Iroquois. He writes that the Iroquois had a profound impact upon the formation of the American state.[19] The distinguished American legal scholar, Felix Cohen, has also argued that the Iroquois and other Indian peoples exerted a sustained and marked influence upon the political development of the United States.[20]

But the political acumen, the democratic philosophy, and the concepts of private property and natural resources (which belong to all mankind and cannot be used for profit or personal gain), which are the heart of the Iroquois Great Law, have not entered into the American consciousness. The predominant public image of the Iroquois in textbooks and other media is one that fails to acknowledge their significant contributions. The American Nation has deep ties with its aboriginal peoples, but these common traits usually go unrecognized and unsung. One of the most eloquent pleas to further understanding of Indian contributions comes from the late President John F. Kennedy:

> Before we can set out on the road to success, we have to know where we are going, and before we can know that, we must determine where we have been in the past. It seems a basic requirement to study the history of our Indian people. America has much to learn about the heritage of our American Indians.[21]

Unfortunately, President Kennedy's fine words did not prevent him from signing the law passed by the United States Congress, which led to the building of the Kinzua Dam, inundating Seneca land and homes, nearly wrecking the Seneca Nation, and violating its own treaty with these Indians.

The Native people are an enduring, a forgiving, and a strong people. The Senecas endured and are improving their lot. The Iroquois Confederacy, in a different world, with different technology and within a different political structure, will be completely revived. The Iroquois believe it, and it will be done. The heart and spirit of the Confederacy has never been completely destroyed, at any rate. Always there has been a small seed with which it could be rebuilt.

Basically, the formation of the United States was influenced by Iroquois political and philosophical traditions. The ideas of freedom and equality stimulated and then transformed the transplanted Europeans who came to American soil. These immigrants were receptive to such concepts because they had in one way or another repudiated, to a degree, the values of the mother country. Militarily, the Iroquois made a contribution to the formation of the United States. Although divided on the issue of American independence, their strategies about frontier fighting shaped the mind of the youthful, as well as the mature George Washington. These are but a few examples of Indian and white interaction in the colonial period. More needs to be done. Especially if America continues to view itself as a distinct entity set apart from many of the values of Western Civilization. Thus, the values of the Iroquois Confederacy live on in the Longhouse today, and these same concepts have a pale reflection in American institutions also. The United States Constitution would subvert the Articles of Confederation in order to give the state more power, but the Bill of Rights that

Jefferson and others insisted upon represent the survival of political freedom and unity through discussion and consensus. Thus, the legacy of Hiawatha and Deganawidah survives among the Iroquois and in the heritage of the American people. If the political and philosophical gifts of the Iroquois could be brought to a full level of awareness in the American mind perhaps the bitterness, insensitivity and paternalism towards Indians in the government as well as in the popular press would subside. Once this happens, contributions of Indian people can be fully appreciated without the shadow of racial arrogance and conceit. Knowledge and awareness is always a humbling experience if it is truthful, but unity and a renewed sense of strength and freedom can also emerge through a new consciousness of the roots of American democratic thought.

For the Iroquois, the legacy of the American Revolution was much different. They became disunited during the American Revolution when many chiefs became opportunistic. Although most of the Iroquois resisted the American Revolution, this was not because they could not see what the Americans were fighting to obtain. On the contrary, the Iroquois sided predominantly with the British as a result of the course of the Revolutionary War and the consequent conflict between America and England. In a sense, the Iroquois nurtured freedom and talked about it to their white neighbors, and then they became the victims of that revolution for a newly conceived democratic society. The Americans understood the confusion of the Iroquois. As early as 1777, the Continental Congress published a book entitled *Apocalypse de Chiokoyhekoy, Chief des Iroquois,* which allegedly claimed that an Iroquois prophecy of the apocalypse was coming to pass. Basically, the book argued that several beasts were fighting for control of Iroquois territory. Eventually, the better beast (U.S.) won out over the worst beast (England). This triumph of the Americans was supposed to allow the Iroquois to return ultimately to their traditional way of life.[22] This piece of propaganda is significant because it demonstrates the understanding that the colonists had for the Iroquois ways, and it also forecasts the decline and subsequent rejuvenation of the Iroquois traditions. In the vision, the U.S. emerges as the lesser of two evils, since it is somewhat similar to the Iroquois ways of governing society.

Even after the Revolution the Iroquois continued to play a key role in the forming of the political institutions of America as well as the world. The ideals of the Iroquois Confederacy serve as cornerstones for democratic societies, and as an inspiration to the peoples of the world. Furthermore, the very concept of a United Nations is similar to the broad principles of the Great Tree of Peace of the Iroquois. It may be symbolic that this world institution, dedicated to peace among all peoples, is located in New York City near the eastern edge of the Iroquois Confederacy.[23]

Literary fascination for the Iroquois' way of life continued into the Nineteenth Century through Henry Wadsworth Longfellow's *Hiawatha*. Also, the "Leatherstocking Tales" of James Fenimore Cooper expressed a naive, vulgarized, but respectful attitude toward the Indians of America. Although neither Longfellow nor Cooper gave the American people an accurate reflection of Indian ways, they fashioned a literary tradition about the Indian guide, the frontiersman, and ultimately the cowboy. This tradition of courageous, reverent and just men (both Indian and white) persists today in American as well as "spaghetti" westerns. This tradition of freedom and justice has a tremendous attraction to the European and American mind, just as it did for the French *philosophes* more than two centuries ago.

Europeans often speak of a distinct American character that is different from the European mentality. No less a psychologist than Carl G. Jung thought he perceived an Indian segment in the character of many of his American patients. Jung observed that his American patients were significantly different from Europeans and thought that frontier contact with Indians might be the answer to the differing characters.[24]

Another foreign observer, Mrs. Francis Trollope, would pass through Iroquois country in the 1820s and comment on the dignity of the Iroquois. In conversing with some Iroquois, Mrs. Trollope learned that the Six Nations had a "senate and . . . at several of their meetings . . . the power of their eloquence was evident from the great effect it produced among themselves." She also hinted, after this experience, that the civilizing white man should continue to take some lessons from the "indigenous manners" of Indians.[25]

The fascination for Indian confederacies and their liberties continued into the Nineteenth Century through the institution of Tammany Hall. Taking its name from the Delaware leader, Tamenend, the New Yorkers founded the Tammany society with different lodges called "tribes" and its leaders "sachems." The meeting place was a "wigwam." Tammany's original purpose was admirable. After the Revolution, the society dedicated itself to liberty, independence and federal union. It worked against powerful forces that wanted to institute an oligarchy or monarchy in the new nation. Subsequently, the Tammany society advocated other libertarian ideals in the United States. In 1826, Tammany was instrumental in developing a law to abolish imprisonment for debt in New York City. Later, Tammany became a corrupt political machine, but its early record is notable in its dedication to freedom and justice, as well as in its desire to cloak its ideology within the Indian tradition.[26] Perhaps the most contradictory experiment in confederation was the constitution of the Confederate States of America. With its emphasis on state's rights, a weak executive, and slavery, the document must stand as a gross perversion of Indian democratic ideals.

Certainly the vision of freedom, justice, liberty and peace in the Iroquois Confederacy has persisted in many ways until today. A clearer understanding of this heritage may make those ideals more possible of attainment. The greatest lesson to be learned from the Iroquois is one of balance and unity. Unlike democratic and communist ideologies, the Iroquois fostered economic and political democracy through spiritual and kinship harmony. The Iroquois experience is not theoretical and unattainable; it is practical.

The governments of ancient and medieval societies are studied assiduously by scholars. Mankind turns its creative powers to the question of devising new, humane laws and governments. Yet here, in the ancient constitution of the Iroquois Confederacy are the precepts of democratic unity, based on a philosophy of fairness and strength.

It would seem that this constitution deserves the serious attention of scholars, and at least an examination of its principles, for a study of comparative government.

The *Constitution of the Five Nations* (see Appendix A), provides enormous ideas for study of a unique ancient society, whose precepts are still alive and indeed are being revived today.

Probably the first reference in North American history to a "United Nations" is that found in the Iroquois Constitution. The formulation is found in Paragraph 61, as "the Five United Nations." The precise policies, structure, conditions and ritual binding the Indian nations into a confederacy is found in this remarkable document of human endeavor and creativity.

In Paragraph 84, the right of self-determination is found as a firm philosophy of government.

Paragraph 95 deals with the role of women, who stood in a relationship level with their men in the functions of government.

Government by the people, "by consent of the governed," as so often is found in referring to the type of democracy in the United States, is guaranteed in Paragraph 96. Also, in Paragraph 98, there is definite provision for such consent of the governed and controls by those governed. Freedom of religion is provided for in Paragraph 99.

Of particular interest to those searching for a governing structure that would insure oversight and provide searching examination of the way a government is performing, is the provision that the Iroquois Council must meet once every five years for the purpose of reaffirming its goals, and have an opportunity to dissolve, and in this way submit to a searching analysis of its functions and performance. Thus, the freedom to continue in the confederate structure is guaranteed, and the people know they have the right to decide, indeed the *right to self-determination*.

The unique and rich observances and rituals of the Confederacy are interlaced with provisions of government, throughout the constitution. Its purpose is clear: to endow with observance and ceremony the sacred principles of the United Nations.

Here is a wealth of information and ideas to be examined. There is no suggestion that the Iroquois ritualistic observances should be observed by all. Each people has its own rich ceremonial, and in native North American society there was great variety. A study of the Pueblo government and observances will provide a fascinating view of comparative native societies, as only one example. But the philosophy and even the structure of the confederacy can and should be studied for adoption of certain features by peoples of the world who long for a better life, a peaceful existence, and the self respect of a responsible and responsive government existing by consent of the governed.

To what extent do the principles and observances of the ancient constitution exist today? That is a matter for further study. However, it may come as a surprise to some people, that the Iroquois nations are still functioning, and many of their observances are still alive.

The Iroquois hold land in New York State and Southern Ontario. The Caughnawagas are just outside of Montreal in Quebec. Many Oneidas were relocated on a reservation near Green Bay, Wisconsin. Some Cayuga-Senecas were removed to Southeastern Kansas and Northeastern Oklahoma. Until a few years ago, a few of the Cornplanter Senecas had a reserve near Warren, Pennsylvania. The construction of the Kinzua Dam caused their relocation to the Allegany Reservation in New York State.

The Mohawks have a reservation (Akwesasne) in the North country of New York. The Onondagas have a reservation outside New York. The Tuscarora reservation is located near Niagara Falls, New York. There are four Seneca reservations in Western New York: Tonawanda, Cattaraugus, Allegany, and Oil Springs.

The Iroquois have survived, and have maintained their culture in various ways. The Mohawk language is still spoken, and indeed is being taught both to Indian and nonIndian students. Steps are being taken to revive and preserve the other Iroquois languages. But all cultures change if they are dynamic. The culture of the Iroquois has also changed, as it must if the people are to endure. The Iroquois work in many of the same professions as the dominant society. They are iron workers, steel workers, teachers, businessmen, artists. But many maintain the traditional culture in the modern setting. The chiefs of the confederacy still gather at Onondaga to carry on the business of the League. The Great Law is recited today as in ancient times, and such meetings are well attended by both city-based and reservation Iroquois.

The Longhouse persists as a focus of religious and ceremonial life, although the traditional way has been somewhat modified by the Code of Handsome Lake. The great festivals and thanksgiving observances continue as part of the life of the people. They are forging a lifestyle for themselves that includes the wisdom of their ancestors and the benefits of modern technology, to create a culture in which they can live comfortably and at peace.

The Iroquois are stirring in other ways as well. They are insisting on their treaty rights. Continuing over many years, are the annual "border crossings" into Canada in the summer, to assert their right through the Jay Treaty to have uninhibited passage across the American and Canadian border.

Working through the legal structure of the United States, as well as through demonstrative activities, the Iroquois nations are trying to regain some of their land and protect their rights. They are a people with a tremendous sense of endurance and inner strength. Their persistence as a viable and cohesive culture is a monument to human values that have meaning in spite of persecution and defeat by a militarily stronger culture. The League of the Iroquois lives on as a testimony to freedom,for all who care to examine it. Its spirit endures as a vision and a goal for the betterment of all mankind.

REFERENCES CHAPTER FIVE

1. John Deserontyon to John Johnson, February 15, 1785, *Claus Papers,* IV, p. 69, Public Archives of Canada.

2. Census of the Six Nations, B103, p. 457, Public Archives of Canada in Johnston, *Valley of Six Nations,* p. 52.

3. Neville B. Craig, ed., *The Olden Time* (Pittsburgh 1848), II, pp. 413-415.

4. *Ibid.,* pp. 418-420.

5. *Ibid.,* pp. 423-427; and David Hill to a friend, November 2, 1784, *Claus Papers,* IV, pp. 45-48, Public Archives of Canada; and Johnston, *Valley of Six Nations,* pp. 50-55.

6. Graymont, *Iroquois,* pp. 282-283.

7. Wallace, *Seneca,* p. 152.

8. See Arthur C. Parker, *The Code of Handsome Lake* (Albany, New York, 1912).

9. *New York Colonial Documents,* VI, pp. 853-891.

10. Peter Farb, *Man's Rise to Civilization* . . . (New York, 1968) pp. 95-111.

11. William Peden, ed., *Notes on the State of Virgina* (Chapel Hill, 1955) p. 93.

12. Lester J. Cappon, ed., *The Adams-Jefferson Letters* (Chapel Hill, 1959), II, p. 291.

13. Quoted from DeWitt Clinton, "A Discourse Delivered Before the New York Historical Society . . ." New York Historical Society, *Collections* II (1814), p. 50; and Peter Farb, *Man's Rise,* pp. 95-96.

14. Andrew A. Lipscomb and Albert E. Beagh, eds., *The Writings of Thomas Jefferson* (Washington, 1903-1904), XV, p. 25.

15. Frederick Engels, *The Origin of the Family, Private Property and the State* (New York, 1972), p. 100.

16. *Ibid.,* p. 22.

17. Lewis H. Morgan, *Houses and House-Life of the American Aborigines* (Chicago, 1965), p. 32.

18. See William N. Fenton, "The Iroquois Confederacy in the Twentieth Century: A Case Study of the Theory of Lewis Henry Morgan in 'Ancient Society,' " *Ethnology,* IV (July 1965).

19. Matthew W. Stirling, "America's First Settlers, the Indians," *National Geographic Magazine,* LXXII, 5 (November 1937).

20. Felix Cohen, "Americanizing the White Man," *The American Scholar,* XXI, 2 (Spring 1952).

21. President John F. Kennedy, introduction to William Brandon, *The American Heritage Book of Indians* (New York, 1961), p. 12.

22. Dwight W. Hoover, *The Red and Black* (Chicago, 1976), pp. 56-57.

23. Wallace, *White Roots,* passim.

24. See Carl Gustav Jung, *Contributions to Analytical Psychology,* translated by H. G. and Cary F. Baynes (New York, 1928) for a discussion of this concept.

25. Donald Smalley, ed., *Domestic Manners of the Americans By Mrs. Francis Trollope* (New York, 1949), p. 392.

26. Brandon, *Book of Indians,* p. 241.

SOURCES

I. PRIMARY MATERIAL

A. Manuscript sources
  Clements, William L., Library (Ann Arbor, Michigan).
    Clinton Papers
    Gage Papers
    Lord Germain Papers
  Hamilton College Library (Clinton, New York).
    Samuel Kirkland Papers
  National Archives (Washington, D.C.).
    The Papers of the Continental Congress, 1774-1789, Record Group 360.
  New York Public Library (New York, N.Y.).
    American Loyalists
    Emmet Papers
    Gansevoort Military Papers
    Schuyler Papers
  New York State Library (Albany, New York).
    Schuyler Mansion Documents
    Schuyler Papers
  Pennsylvania Historical and Museum Commission (Harrisburg, Pennsylvania).
    George Morgan Letterbooks
  Public Archives of Canada (Ottawa, Canada).
    Claus Papers
  State Historical Society of Wisconsin (Madison, Wisconsin).
    Draper Papers

B. Printed sources and collections

Benson, Adolph (ed.). *Peter Kalms Travels in North America.* New York, 1937, 2 vols.

Brock, Robert E. (ed.). *The Official Records of Robert Din-widdie, Lieutenant Governor of Virginia, 1751-1758*, in Virginia Historical Society *Collections.* Richmond, Virginia, 1883-1884.

Burgoyne, John. *A State of the Expedition from Canada.* London, 1780.

Burnett, Edmund C. (ed.). *Letters of the Members of the Continental Congress.* Washington, 1923-1936. 8 vols.

Cappon, Lester J. (ed.). *The Adams-Jefferson Letters.* Chapel Hill, 1959.

Cohen, Lucy K. (ed.). *The Legal Conscience: Selected* Papers of Felix S. Cohen. New Haven, 1960.

Colden, Cadwallader. *The History of the Five Indian Nations.* New York, 1922. 2 vols.

Fitzpatrick, John C. (ed.). *The Diaries of George Washington, 1748-1799.* New York, 1925. 4 vols.

Ford, W. C. *Journals of the Continental Congress, 1774-1789.* Washington, 1904-1907. 34 vols.

Hastings, Hugh (ed.) *Public Papers of George Clinton.* Albany, New York, 1900-1914. 10 vols.

Hooker, Richard J. (ed.) Charles Woodmason, *The Carolina Backcountry on the Eve of the Revolution.* Chapel Hill, 1953.

Johnston, Charles M. (ed.). *The Valley of the Six Nations.* Toronto, 1964.

Labaree, Leonard W. and Bell, Whitfield J. (eds.). *The Papers of Benjamin Franklin.* New Haven, 1962. 18 vols.

Lederer, Lawrence R. (ed.). *The Livingston Indian Records*, 1666-1723. Gettysburg, Pennsylvania, 1956.

Lipscomb, Andrew A. and Beagh (eds.). *The Writings of Thomas Jefferson.* Washington, 1903-1904. 30 vols.

McIlwain, Charles Howard (ed.). *An Abridgement of the Indian Affairs Contained in Four Folio Volumes, Transacted in the Colony of New York, from the Year 1678 to the Year 1751 by Peter Wraxall.* Cambridge, 1915.

O'Callaghan, E. B. (ed.). *Documents Relative to the Colonial History of the State of New York*, Albany, New York, 1853-1887. 15 vols.

Peden, William (ed.). *Notes on the State of Virginia*. Chapel Hill, 1955.

Pennsylvania. *Minutes of the Provincial Council of Pennsylvania from the Organization to the Termination Proprietary Government*. Philadelphia, 1851-1853. 10 vols.

Poore, Benjamin P. (comp.). *The Federal and State Constitutions, Colonial Charters, and Other Organic Laws of the United States*. Washington, 1878.

Rice, Howard C., Jr. (ed.). *Francois Jean de Chastellux Travels in North America in the Years, 1780, 1781, and 1782*. Chapel Hill, x963.

Severance, Frank H. (ed.). *Publications of the Buffalo Historical Society*. Buffalo, 1896-1903. 6 vols.

Sherover, Charles (ed.). *Annotated Edition of the Social Contract*. New York, 1974.

Sherover, Charles (ed.). *The Development of the Democratic Idea*. New York, 1974.

Smalley, Donald (ed.). *Domestic Manners of the Americans* by *Mrs. Francis Trollope*. New York, 1949.

Smythe, Albert Henry (ed.). *The Writings of Benjamin Franklin*. New York, 1905-1907. 10 vols.

Sullivan, James, et al. (eds.). *The Papers of Sir William Johnson*. Albany, New York, 1921-1965. 13 vols.

The Great Law of Peace of the Longhouse People. Akwesasne, 1971.

Thwaites, Reuben Gold (ed.). *The Jesuit Relations and Allied Documents*. Cleveland, 1869-1901. 73 vols.

Willard, Margaret W. (ed.). *Letters on the American Revolution*. Boston, 1925.

II. SECONDARY MATERIAL

A. Articles

Clinton, Dewitt, "A Discourse Delivered Before the New York Historical Society," in New York State Historical Society *Collections*. New York, 1811-1859.

Fenton, William N. "The Iroquois Confederacy in the Twentieth Century: A Case Study of the Theory of Lewis Henry Morgan in 'Ancient Society,' " *Ethnology*, IV (July 1965).

Fenton, William N. "This Island, the World of the Turtle's Back," *Journal of American Folklore*, LXXV, (October-December 1962), 283-300.

Grinde, Donald A., Jr. "A Historical Sketch of the Ereiz Indians," *Journal of Erie Studies*, II, 2 (Fall 1973), 25-27.

Gundy, H. Pearson. "Molly Brant—Loyalist," *Ontario History*, XLV, 3 (Summer 1953), 97-108.

Hewitt, J.N.B. "Review of Parker's Constitution of the Five Nations," *American Anthropologist*, XIX, 3 (July-September 1917), 432-433.

Jacobs, Wilbur R. "Wampum, the Protocol of Indian Diplomacy," *William and Mary Quarterly*. Third Series, IV (October 1949), 596-604.

Sosin, Jack. "The Use of Indians in the War of the American Revolution: A Re-Assessment of Responsibility," Canadian Historical Review, XLVI, 2 (June 1965).

Stirling, Matthew W. "America's First Settlers, the Indians," *National Geographic Magazine*, LXXII, 5 (November 1937).

"The Founding of the League of the Iroquois," *The Conservationist*, XXX 4 (January-February 1976), 4-5/

Wallace, Anthony F.C. "The Origins of Iroquois Neutrality; The Grand Settlement of 1701," *Pennsylvania History*, XXIV (July 1957), 223-235.

B. Books

Alden, John R. *The American Revolution*. New York, 1954.

Alden, John R. *General Gage in America*. Baton Rouge Louisiana, 1948.

Ansbury, Thomas. *With Burgoyne from Quebec*. Toronto, 1963.

Beauchamp, William M. *A History of the New York Iroquois*. Port Washington, New York, 1961.

Bond, Richmond P. *Queen Anne's American Kings*. Oxford England, 1952.

Brandon, William. *The American Heritage Book of Indians*. New York, 1961.

Canfield, William W. *The Legends of the Iroquois: Told by "The Cornplanter."* Port Washington, New York, 1902.

Chalmers, Harvey. *Joseph Brant: Mohawk*. East Lansing, 1955.

Craig, Neville B. (ed.). *The Olden Time*. Pittsburgh, 1848.

Eccles, William J. *The Canadian Frontier, 1534-1760*. New York, 1969.

Engels, Frederick. *The Origin of the Family, Private Property and the State*. New York, 1972.

Farb, Peter. *Man's Rise to Civilization* . . . New York, 1968.

Gipson, Lawrence Henry. *The Coming of the Revolution*. New York, 1954.

Gipson, Lawrence Henry. *The Great War for the Empire*. New York, 1954-1967. 11 vols.

Graymont, Barbara. *The Iroquois in the American Revolution*. Syracuse, 1972.

Hagan, William T. *Longhouse Diplomacy and Frontier Warfare*. Albany, 1975.

Hertzberg, Hazel W. *The Great Tree and the Longhouse: The Culture of the Iroquois*. New York, 1966.

Hinman, Marjory Barnum. *Onaquaga: Hub of the Border Wars*. Windsor, New York, 1975.

Hodge, F.W. (ed.). *Handbook of American Indians North of Mexico*. Washington, 1907. 2 vols.

Hoover, Dwight W. *The Red and Black*. Chicago, 1976.

Huddleston, F. J. *Gentleman Johnny Burgoyne*. Indianapolis, 1972.

Jacobs, Wilbur R. *Wilderness Politics and Indian Gifts*. Lincoln, Nebraska, 1966.

Josephy, Alvin. *The Patriot Chiefs*. New York, 1972.

Jung, Carl Gustav. *Contributions to Analytical Psychology*. New York, 1928.

Lanctot, Gustave. *Canada and the American Revolution*. Cambridge, Massachusetts, 1967.

Lothrop, Samuel Kirkland. *Life of Samuel Kirkland*. Boston, 1847.

Lydekker, John W. *The Faithful Mohawks*. Cambridge, England, 1938.

Morgan, Lewis Henry. *Houses and House Life of the American Aborigines*. Chicago, 1965.

Morgan, Lewis Henry. *League of the Ho-De-No-Sau-Nee or Iroquois*. New York, 1901. 2 vols.

Nash, Gary B. *Red, White, and Black*. Englewood Cliffs, New Jersey, 1974.

Navarre, Robert. *Journal of the Conspiracy of Pontiac, 1763*. Detroit, 1910.

Nichols, Roger L. and Adams, George R. (eds.). *The American Indian: Past and Present*. Waltham, Massachusetts, 1971.

Parker, Arthur C. *The Code of Handsome Lake*. Albany, New York, 1912.

Parker, Arthur C. *The Constitution of the Five Nations*. Albany, 1916; (and herewith in appendix).

Peckham, Howard H. *Pontiac and the Indian Uprising*. Chicago, 1961.

Reaman, G. Elmore. *The Trail of the Iroquois Indians*. New York, 1967.

Schoolcraft, Henry R. *Notes on the Iroquois*. Millwood, New York, 1975.

Seaver, James E. *A Narrative of the Life of Mrs. Mary Jemison*. Batavia, New York, 1842.

Stites, Sara H. *Economics of the Iroquois*. Lancaster, Pennsylvania, 1904.

Stone, William L. *Life of Joseph Brant - Thayendanegea*. New York, 1838.

Sweet, William W. *Religion in Colonial America*. New York, 1947.

Tebbel, John and Jennison, Keith. *The American Indian Wars*. New York, 1965.

Tehanetorens. *Wampum Belts*. Onchiota, New York, n.d.

Tooker, Elisabeth (ed.). *Iroquois Culture, History and Prehistory*. Albany, New York, 1967.

Tooker, Elisabeth. *An Ethnography of the Huron Indians*. Washington, 1964.

Trelease, Allen W. *Indian Affairs in Colonial New York*. Ithaca, New York, 1960.

Turner, Frederick Jackson. *The Frontier in American History*. New York, 1958.

Wallace, Anthony F. C. *The Death and Rebirth of the Seneca*. New York, 1972.

Wallace, Paul A. W. *The White Roots of Peace*. Port Washington, New York, 1946.

Washburn, Wilcomb E. *The Indian in America*. New York, 1975.

Whittemore, Charles P. *A General of the Revolution: John Sullivan of New Hampshire*. New York, 1961.

Wilson, Edmund. *Apologies to the Iroquois*. New York, 1961.

Wissler, Clark. *Indians of the United States*. Garden City, New York, 1967.

Wright, Benjamin F. *American Interpretation of Natural Law*. Cambridge. 1931.

Note: The latest edition date is given for those books that are available in reprint. (See Johnson Reprint and AMS Reprint Co.)

Belt of the Covenant, displayed by the speaker of the Confederate Council.

Appendix A

THE CONSTITUTION
OF THE FIVE NATIONS

(Reprinted from the New York State Museum Bulletin,
Albany, New York, April 1, 1916.)

by Arthur C. Parker

The Council of the Great Peace

The Great Binding Law
Gayanashagowa

1. I am Dekanawidah and with the Five Nations' Confederate Lords[1] I plant the Tree of the Great Peace. I plant it in your territory, Adodarhoh, and the Onondaga Nation, in the territory of you who are Firekeepers.

I name the tree the Tree of the Great Long Leaves. Under the shade of this Tree of the Great Peace we spread the soft white feathery down of the globe thistle as seats for you, Adodarhoh, and your cousin Lords.

We place you upon those seats, spread soft with the feathery down of the globe thistle, there beneath the shade of the spreading branches of the Tree of Peace. There shall you sit and watch the Council Fire of the Confederacy of the Five Nations, and all the affairs of the Five Nations shall be transacted at this place before you, Adodarhoh, and your cousin Lords, by the Confederate Lords of the Five Nations. (I-I-TLL)[2]

2. Roots have spread out from the Tree of the Great Peace, one to the north, one to the east, one to the south and one to the west. The name of these roots is the Great White Roots and their nature is Peace and Strength.

If any man or any nation outside the Five Nations shall obey the laws of the Great Peace and make known their disposition to the Lords of the Confederacy, they may trace the Roots to the Tree and if their minds are clean and they are obedient and promise to obey the wishes of the Confederate Council, they shall be welcomed to take shelter beneath the Tree of the Long Leaves.

We place at the top of the Tree of the Long Leaves an Eagle who is able to see afar. If he sees in the distance any evil approaching or any danger threatening he will at once warn the people of the Confederacy. (2-11, TLL)

3. To you Adodarhoh, the Onondaga cousin Lords, I and the other Confederate Lords have entrusted the caretaking and the watching of the Five Nations Council Fire.

When there is any business to be transacted and the Confederate Council is not in session, a messenger shall be dispatched either to Adodarhoh, Hononwirehtonh or Skanawatih, Fire Keepers, or to their War Chiefs with a full statement of the case desired to be considered. Then shall Adodarho call his cousin (associate) Lords together and consider whether or not the case is of sufficient importance to demand the attention of the Confederate Council. If so, Adodarhoh shall dispatch messengers to summon all the Confederate Lords to assemble beneath the Tree of the Long Leaves.

---

1. Royaneh is always translated "Lord."

2. The abbreviations after each law refer to the sections in the original code and their numbers. TLL, means Tree of the Long Leaves; EUC, Emblematical Union Compact; and LPW, Skanawita's Laws of Peace and War. The first number in Roman numerals refers to the original number of the law, the second number in Arabic numerals, to the section number in the division of the law named by the abbreviation following.

When the Lords are assembled the Council Fire shall be kindled, but not with chestnut wood,[1] and Adodarhoh shall formally open the Council.

Then shall Adodarhoh and his cousin Lords, the Fire Keepers, announce the subject for discussion.

The Smoke of the Confederate Council Fire shall ever ascend and pierce the sky so that other nations who may be allies may see the Council Fire of the Great Peace.

Adodarho and his cousin Lords are entrusted with the Keeping of the Council Fire (4-IV,TLL)

4. You, Adodarho, and your thirteen cousin Lords, shall faithfully keep the space about the Council Fire clean and you shall allow neither dust nor dirt to accumulate. I lay a Long Wing before you as a broom. As a weapon against a crawling creature I lay a staff with you so that you may thrust it away from the Council Fire. If you fail to cast it out then call the rest of the United Lords to your aid. (3-III,TLL)

5. The Council of the Mohawk shall be divided into three parties as follows: Tekarihoken, Ayonhwhathah, and Skadekariwade are the first party; Sharenhowaneh, Deyoenhegwehn and Oghrenghrehgowah the second party, and Kehennakrineh, Aghstawenserrenthah and Shoskoharowaneh are the third party. The third party is to listen only to the discussion of the first and second parties and if an error is made or the proceeding is irregular they are to call attention to it, and when the case is right and properly decided by the two parties they shall confirm the decision of the two parties and refer the case to the Seneca Lords for their decision. When the Seneca Lords have decided in accord with the Mohawk Lords, the case or question shall be referred to the Cayuga and Oneida Lords on the opposite side of the house. (5-V,TLL)

6. I, Dekanawidah, appoint the Mohawk Lords the heads and the leaders of the Five Nations Confederacy. The Mohawk Lords are the foundation of the Great Peace and it shall, therefore, be against the Great Binding Law to pass measures in the Confederate Council after the Mohawk Lords have protested against them. (6-VI,TLL)

No Council of the Confederate Lords shall be legal unless all the Mohawk Lords are present. (13,XIII,TLL).

7. Whenever the Confederate Lords shall assemble for the purpose of holding a council, the Onondaga Lords shall open it by expressing their gratitude to their cousin Lords and greeting them, and they shall make an address and offer thanks to the earth where men dwell, to the streams of water, the pools, the springs and the lakes, to the maize and the fruits, to the medicinal herbs and trees, to the forest trees for their usefulness, to the animals that serve as food and give their pelts for clothing, the great winds and the lesser winds, to the Thunderers, to the Sun, the mighty warrior, to the moon, to the messengers of the Creator who reveal his wishes and to the Great Creator[2] who dwells in the heavens above, who gives all the things useful to men, and who is the source and the ruler of health and life.

Then shall the Onondaga Lords declare the council open.

The council shall not sit after darkness has set in. (7-VII,TLL)

8. The Firekeepers shall formally open and close all councils of the Confederate Lords, they shall pass upon all matters deliberated upon by the two sides and render their decision.

Every Onondaga Lord (or his deputy) must be present at every Confederate Council and must agree with the majority without unwarrantable dissent, so that a unanimous decision may be rendered. (8-VIII,TLL)

If Adodarho or any of his cousin Lords are absent from a Confederate Council any other Firekeeper may open and close the Council, but the Firekeepers present may not give any decisions, unless the matter is of small importance. (9-IX,TLL).

---

1. Because chestnut wood in burning throws out sparks, thereby creating a disturbance in the council.
2. Hodianok'doon Hĕdiohe' (Seneca)

9. All the business of the Five Nations Confederate Council shall be conducted by the two combined bodies of Confederate Lords. First the question shall be discussed and passed by the Oneida and Cayuga Lords. Their decisions shall then be referred to the Onondaga Lords, (Fire Keepers) for final judgment. (10-X,TLL)

The same process shall obtain when a question is brought before the council by an individual or War Chief. (11-X,TLL)

10. In all cases the procedure must be as follows: when the Mohawk and Seneca Lords have unanimously agreed upon a question, they shall report their decision to the Cayuga and Oneida Lords who shall deliberate upon the question and report a unanimous decision to the Mohawk Lords. The Mohawk Lords will then report the standing of the case to the Fire Keepers, who shall render a decision (17-XVIII,TLL) as they see fit in case of a disagreement by the two bodies, or confirm the decisions of the two bodies if they are identical. The Fire Keepers shall then report their decision to the Mohawk Lords who shall announce it to the open council. (12-XII,TLL)

11. If through any misunderstanding or obstinacy on the part of the Fire Keepers, they render a decision at variance with that of the Two Sides; the Two Sides shall reconsider the matter and if their decisions are jointly the same as before they shall report to the Fire Keepers who are then compelled to confirm their joint decision. (19-XVIII,TLL)

12. When a case comes before the Onondaga Lords (Fire Keepers) for discussion and decision, Adodarho shall introduce the matter to his comrade Lords who shall then discuss it in their two bodies. Every Onondaga Lord except Hononwiretonh shall deliberate and he shall listen only. When a unanimous decision shall have been reached by the two bodies of Fire Keepers, Adodarho shall notify Nononwiretonh of the fact when he shall confirm it. He shall refuse to confirm a decision if it is not unanimously agreed upon by both sides of the Fire Keepers. (19-XIX,TLL)

13. No Lord shall ask a question of the body of Confederate Lords when they are discussing a case, question or proposition. He may only deliberate in a low tone with the separate body of which he is a member. (21-XXI,TLL)

14. When the Council of the Five Nations Lords shall convene they shall appoint a speaker for the day. He shall be a Lord of either the Mohawk, Onondaga or Seneca Nation.

The next day the Council shall appoint another speaker, but the first speaker may be reappointed if there is no objection, but a speaker's term shall not be regarded more than for the day. (35-XXXV,TLL)

15. No individual or foreign nation interested in a case, question or proposition shall have any voice in the Confederate Council except to answer a question put to him or them by the speaker for the Lords. (41-XLI,TLL)

16. If the conditions which shall arise at any future time call for an addition to or change of this law, the case shall be carefully considered and if a new beam seems necessary or beneficial, the proposed change shall be voted upon and if adopted it shall be called, "Added to the Rafter." (48-XLVII,TLL)

RIGHTS DUTIES QUALIFICATIONS OF LORDS

17. A bunch of a certain number of shell (wampum) strings each two spans in length shall be given to each of the female families in which the Lordship titles are vested. The right of bestowing the title shall be hereditary in the family of females legally possessing the bunch of shell strings and the strings shall be the token that the females of the family have the proprietary right to the Lordship title for all time to come, subject to certain restrictions hereinafter mentioned. (59-LIX,TLL)

18. If any Confederate Lord neglects or refuses to attend the Confederate Council the other Lords of the nation of which he is a member shall require their War Chief to request the female sponsors of the Lord so guilty of defections to demand his attendance of the Council. If he refuses, the women holding the title shall immediately select another candidate for the title.

No Lord shall be asked more than once to attend the Confederate Council. (30-XXX,TLL)

19. If at any time it shall be manifest that a Confederate Lord has not in mind the welfare of the people or disobeys the rules of this Great Law, the men or the women of the Confederacy, or both jointly,[1] shall come to the Council and upbraid the erring Lord through his War Chief. If the complaint of the people through the War Chief is not heeded the first time it shall be uttered again and then if no attention is given a third complaint and warning shall be given. If the Lord is still contumacious the matter shall go to the council of War Chiefs. (66-LXVI,TLL). The War Chiefs shall then divest the erring Lord of his title by order of the women in whom the titleship is vested. When the Lord is deposed the women shall notify the Confederate Lords through their War Chief, and the Confederate Lords shall sanction the act. The women will then select another of their sons as a candidate and the Lords shall elect him. Then shall the chosen one be installed by the Installation Ceremony. (123,XLI,EUC), (Cf. 42-XLII)

When a Lord is to be deposed, his War Chief shall address him as follows:
"So you, _ , disregard and set at naught the warnings of your women relatives. So you fling the warnings over your shoulder to cast them behind you.

"Behold the brightness of the Sun and in the brightness of the Sun's light I depose you of your title and remove the sacred emblem of your Lordship title. I remove from your brow the deer's antlers, which was the emblem of your position and token of your nobility. I now depose you and return the antlers to the women whose heritage they are."

The War Chief shall now address the women of the deposed Lord and say:
"Mothers, as I have now deposed your Lord, I now return to you the emblem and the title of Lordship, therefore repossess them."

Again addressing himself to the deposed Lord he shall say:
"As I have now deposed and discharged you so you are now no longer Lord. You shall now go your way alone, the rest of the people of the Confederacy will not go with you, for we know not the kind of mind that possesses you. As the Creator has nothing to do with wrong so he will not come to rescue you from the precipice of destruction in which you have cast yourself. You shall never be restored to the position which you once occupied."

Then shall the War Chief address himself to the Lords of the Nation to which the deposed Lord belongs and say:
"Know you, my Lords, that I have taken the deer's antlers from the brow of _ , the emblem of his position and token of his greatness."

The Lords of the Confederacy shall then have no other alternative than to sanction the discharge of the offending Lord. (42-XLII,TLL)

20. If a Lord of the Confederacy of the Five Nations should commit murder the other Lords of the Nation shall assemble at the place where the corpse lies and prepare to depose the criminal Lord. If it is impossible to meet at the scene of the crime the Lords shall discuss the matter at the next Council of their nation and request their War Chief to depose the Lord guilty of crime, to "bury" his women relatives and to transfer the Lordship title to a sister family.

---

1. See sections 94 and 95 for right of popular councils.

The War Chief shall address the Lord guilty of murder and say:
"So you, _____ (giving his name) did kill _____ (naming the slain man), with your own hands! You have committed a grave sin in the eyes of the Creator. Behold the bright light of the Sun, and in the brightness of the Sun's light I depose you of your title and remove the horns, the sacred emblems of your Lordship title. I remove from your brow the deer's antler, which was the emblem of your position and token of your nobility. I now depose you and expel you and you shall depart at once from the territory of the Five Nations Confederacy and nevermore return again. We, the Five Nations Confederacy, moreover, bury your women relatives because the ancient Lordship title was never intended to have any union with bloodshed. Henceforth it shall not be their heritage. By the evil deed that you have done they have forfeited it forever."

The War Chief shall then hand the title to a sister family and he shall address it and say:
"Our mothers, _____ , listen attentively while I address you on a solemn and important subject. I hereby transfer to you an ancient Lordship title for a great calamity has befallen it in the hands of the family of a former Lord. We trust that you, our mothers, will always guard it, and that you will warn your Lord always to be dutiful and to advise his people to ever live in love, peace and harmony that a great calamity may never happen again." (47-XLVII,TLL)

21. Certain physical defects in a Confederate Lord make him ineligible to sit in the Confederate Council. Such defects are infancy, idiocy, blindness, deafness, dumbness and impotency. When a Confederate Lord is restricted by any of these conditions, a deputy shall be appointed by his sponsors to act for him, but in case of extreme necessity the restricted Lord may exercise his rights. (29-XXIX,TLL)

22. If a Confederate Lord desires to resign his title he shall notify the Lords of the Nation of which he is a member of his intention. If his coactive Lords refuse to accept his resignation he may not resign his title.

A Lord in proposing to resign may recommend any proper candidate which recommendation shall be received by the Lords, but unless confirmed and nominated by the women who hold the title the candidate so named shall not be considered. (31-XXXI,TLL)

23. Any Lord of the Five Nation Confederacy may construct shell strings (or wampum belts) of any size or length as pledges or records of matters of national or international importance.

When it is necessary to dispatch a shell string by a War Chief or other messenger as the token of a summons, the messenger shall recite the contents of the string to the party to whom it is sent. That party shall repeat the message and return the shell string and if there has been a summons he shall make ready for the journey.

Any of the people of the Five Nations may use shells (wampum) as the record of a pledge, contract or an agreement entered into and the same shall be binding as soon as shell strings shall have been exchanged by both parties. (32-XXXII,TLL)

24. The Lords of the Confederacy of the Five Nations shall be mentors of the people for all time. The thickness of their skin shall be seven spans—which is to say that they shall be proof against anger, offensive actions and criticism. Their hearts shall be full of peace and good will and their minds filled with a yearning for the welfare of the people of the Confederacy. With endless patience they shall carry out their duty and their firmness shall be tempered with a tenderness for their people. Neither anger nor fury shall find lodgement in their minds and all their words and actions shall be marked by calm deliberation. (33-XXXIII,TLL)

25. If a Lord of the Confederacy should seek to establish any authority independent of the jurisdiction of the Confederacy of the Great Peace, which is the Five Nations, he shall be warned three times in open council, first by the women relatives,

second by the men relatives and finally by the Lords of the Confederacy of the Nation to which he belongs. If the offending Lord if still obdurate he shall be dismissed by the War Chief of his nation for refusing to conform to the laws of the Great Peace. His nation shall then install the candidate nominated by the female name holder of his family. (34-XXXIV,TLL)

26. It shall be the duty of all of the Five Nations Confederate Lords, from time to time as occasion demands, to act as mentors and spiritual guides of their people and remind them of their Creator's will and words. They shall say:
"Hearken, that peace may continue unto future days!
"Always listen to the words of the Great Creator, for he has spoken.
"United People, let not evil find lodging in your minds.
"For the Great Creator has spoken and the cause of Peace shall not become old.
"The cause of peace shall not die if you remember the Great Creator."
Every Confederate Lord shall speak words such as these to promote peace. (37-XXXVII,TLL)

27. All Lords of the Five Nation Confederacy must be honest in all things. They must not idle or gossip, but be men possessing those honorable qualities that make true royaneh. It shall be a serious wrong for anyone to lead a Lord into trivial affairs, for the people must ever hold their Lords high in estimation out of respect to their honorable positions. (45-XLV,TLL)

28. When a candidate Lord is to be installed he shall furnish four strings of shells (or wampum) one span in length bound together at one end. Such will constitute the evidence of his pledge to the Confederate Lords that he will live according to the constitution of the Great Peace and exercise justice in all affairs.
When the pledge is furnished the Speaker of the Council must hold the shell strings in his hand and address the opposite side of the Council Fire and he shall commence his address saying: "Now behold him. He has now become a Confederate Lord. See how splendid he looks." An address may then follow. At the end of it he shall send the bunch of shell strings to the opposite side and they shall be received as evidence of the pledge. Then shall the opposite side say:
"We now do crown you with the sacred emblem of the deer's antlers, the emblem of your Lordship. You shall now become a mentor of the people of the Five Nations. The thickness of your skin shall be seven spans—which is to say that you shall be proof against anger, offensive actions and criticism. Your heart shall be filled with peace and good will and your mind filled with a yearning for the welfare of the people of the Confederacy. With endless patience you shall carry out your duty and your firmness shall be tempered with tenderness for your people. Neither anger nor fury shall find lodgment in your mind and all your words and actions shall be marked with calm deliberation. In all of your deliberations in the Confederate Council, in your efforts at law making, in all your official acts, self interest shall be cast into oblivion. Cast not over your shoulder behind you the warnings of the nephews and nieces should they chide you for any error or wrong you may do, but return to the way of the Great Law which is just and right. Look and listen for the welfare of the whole people and have always in view not only the present but also the coming generations, even those whose faces are yet beneath the surface of the ground—the unborn of the future Nation." (51-LI,TLL).

29. When a Lordship title is to be conferred, the candidate Lord shall furnish the cooked venison, the corn bread and the corn soup, together with other necessary things and the labor for the Conferring of Titles Festival. (50-L,TLL)

30. The Lords of the Confederacy may confer the Lordship title upon a candidate whenever the Great Law is recited, if there be a candidate, for the Great Law speaks all the rules. (XLIV-44,TLL).

31. If a lord of the Confederacy should become seriously ill and be thought near death, the women who are heirs of his title shall go to his house and lift his crown of deer

antlers, the emblem of his Lordship, and place them at one side. If the Creator spares him and he rises from his bed of sickness he may rise with the antlers on his brow.

The following words shall be used to temporarily remove the antlers:
"Now our comrade Lord (or our relative Lord) the time has come when we must approach you in your illness. We remove for a time the deer's antlers from your brow, we remove the emblem of your Lordship title. The Great Law has decreed that no Lord should end his life with the antlers on his brow. We therefore lay them aside in the room. If the Creator spares you and you recover from your illness you shall rise from your bed with the antlers on your brow as before and you shall resume your duties as Lord of the Confederacy and you may labor again for the Confederate people." (XXVII-27,TLL).

32. If a Lord of the Confederacy should die while the Council of the Five Nations is in session the Council shall adjourn for ten days. No Confederate Council shall sit within ten days of the death of a Lord of the Confederacy.

If the Three Brothers (The Mohawk, the Onondaga and the Seneca) should lose one of their Lords by death, the Younger Brothers (the Oneida and the Cayuga) shall come to the surviving Lords of the Three Brothers on the tenth day and console them. If the Younger Brothers lose one of their Lords then the Three Brothers shall come to them and console them. And the consolation shall be the reading of the contents of the thirteen shell (wampum) strings of Ayonhwhathah. At the termination of this rite a successor shall be appointed, to be appointed by the women heirs of the Lordship title. If the women are not yet ready to place their nominee before the Lords the Speaker shall say, "come let us go out." All shall then leave the Council or the place of gathering. The installation shall then wait until such a time as the women are ready. The Speaker shall lead the way from the house by saying, "Let us depart to the edge of the woods and lie in waiting on our bellies."

When the women title holders shall have chosen one of their sons the Confederate Lords will assemble in two places, the Younger Brothers in one place and the Three Older Brothers in another. The Lords who are to console the mourning Lords shall choose one of their number to sing the Pacification Hymn as they journey to the sorrowing Lords. The singer shall lead the way and the Lords and the people shall follow. When they reach the sorrowing Lords they shall hail the candidate Lord and perform the rite on Conferring the Lordship Title. (22-XXII,TLL)

33. When a confederate Lord dies, the surviving relatives shall immediately dispatch a messenger, a member of another clan, to the Lords in another locality. When the runner comes within hailing distance of the locality he shall utter a sad wail, thus: "Kwa-ah, Kwa-ah, Kwa-ah!" The sound shall be repeated three times and then again and again at intervals as many times as the distance may require. When the runner arrives at the settlement the people shall assemble and one must ask him the nature of his sad message. He shall then say, "Let us consider." Then he shall tell them of the death of the Lord. He shall deliver to them a string of shells (wampum) and say "Here is the testimony, you have heard the message." He may then return home.

It now becomes the duty of the Lords of the locality to send runners to other localities and each locality shall send other messengers until all Lords are notified. Runners shall travel day and night. (23-XXIII,TLL)

34. If a Lord dies and there is no candidate qualified for the office in the family of the women title holders, the Lords of the Nation shall give the title into the hands of a sister family in the clan until such a time as the original family produces a candidate, when the title shall be restored to the rightful owners.

No Lordship title may be carried into the grave. The Lords of the Confederacy may dispossess a dead Lord of his title even at the grave. (24-XXIV,TLL)

ELECTION OF PINE TREE CHIEFS

35. Should any man of the Nation assist with special ability or show great interest in the affairs of the Nation, if he proves himself wise, honest and worthy of confidence, the Confederate Lords may elect him to a seat with them and he may sit in the Confederate Council. He shall be proclaimed a *Pine Tree sprung up for the Nation* and be installed as such at the next assembly for the installation of Lords. Should he ever do anything contrary to the rules of the Great Peace, he may not be deposed from office—no one shall cut him down[1]—but thereafter everyone shall be deaf to his voice and his advice. Should he resign his seat and title no one shall prevent him. A Pine Tree Chief has no authority to name a successor nor is his title hereditary. (LXVIII-68,TLL)

NAMES, DUTIES AND RIGHTS OF WAR CHIEFS

36. The title names of the Chief Confederate Lords' War Chiefs shall be:

Ayonwaehs, War Chief under Lord Takarihoken (Mohawk)
Kahonwhadironh, War Chief under Lord Odatshedeh (Oneida)
Ayendes, War Chief under Lord Adodarhoh (Onondaga)
Wenehes, War Chief under Lord Dekaenyonh (Cayuga)
Shoneradowaneh, War Chief under Lord Skanyadriyo (Seneca)

The women heirs of each head Lord's title shall be the heirs of the War Chief's title of their respective Lord. (52-LII,TLL)
The War Chiefs shall be selected from the eligible sons of the female families holding the head Lordship titles. (53-LIII-TLL)

37. There shall be one War Chief for each Nation and their duties shall be to carry messages for their Lords and to take up the arms of war in case of emergency. They shall not participate in the proceeding of the Confederate Council but shall watch its progress and in case of an erroneous action by a Lord they shall receive the complaints of the people and convey the warnings of the women to him. The people who wish to convey messages to the Lords in the Confederate Council shall do so through the War Chief of their Nation. It shall ever be his duty to lay the cases, questions and propositions of the people before the Confederate Council. (54-LIV,TLL)

38. When a War Chief dies another shall be installed by the same rite as that by which a Lord is installed. (56-LVI,TLL)

39. If a War Chief acts contrary to instructions or against the provisions of the Laws of the Great Peace, doing so in the capacity of his office, he shall be deposed by his women relatives and by his men relatives. Either the women or the men alone or jointly may act in such case. The women title holders shall then choose another candidate. (55-LV,TLL)

40. When the Lords of the Confederacy take occasion to dispatch a messenger in behalf of the Confederate Council, they shall wrap up any matter they may send and instruct the messenger to remember his errand, to turn not aside but to proceed faithfully to his destination and deliver his message according to every instruction. (57-XLVII,TLL)

41. If a message borne by a runner is the warning of an invasion he shall whoop, "Kwa-ha, Kwa-ah," twice and repeat at short intervals; then again at a longer interval.
If a human being is found dead, the finder shall not touch the body but return home immediately shouting at short intervals, "Koo-weh!". (23,XXIII, TLL)

---

1. Because, "his top branches pierce the sky and if his roots are cut he will not fall but hang upright before the people."

CLANS AND CONSANGUINITY

42. Among the Five Nations and their posterity there shall be the following original clans: Great Name Bearer, Ancient Name Bearer, Great Bear, Ancient Bear, Turtle, Painted Turtle, Standing Rock, Large Plover, Little Plover, Deer, Pigeon Hawk, Eel, Ball, Opposite-Side-of-the-Hand, and Wild Potatoes. These clans distributed through their respective Nations, shall be the sole owners and holders of the soil of the country and in them is it vested as a birthright. (94-XI, EUC)

43. People of the Five Nations members of a certain clan shall recognize every other member of that clan, irrespective of the nation, as relatives. Men and women, therefore, members of the same clan are forbidden to marry. (98-XV, EUC)

44. The lineal descent of the people of the Five Nations shall run in the female line. Women shall be considered the progenitors of the Nation. They shall own the land and the soil. Men and women shall follow the status of the mother. (60-LXI,TLL)

45. The women heirs of the Confederate Lordship titles shall be called Royaneh (Noble) for all time to come. (61-LXI,TLL)

46. The women of the Forty Eight (now fifty) Royaneh families shall be the heirs of the Authorized Names for all time to come.

When an infant of the Five Nations is given an Authorized Name at the Midwinter Festival or at the Ripe Corn Festival, one in the cousinhood of which the infant is a member shall be appointed a speaker. He shall then announce to the opposite cousinhood the names of the father and the mother of the child together with the clan of the mother. Then the speaker shall announce the child's name twice. The uncle of the child shall then take the child in his arms and walking up and down the room shall sing: "My head is firm, I am of the Confederacy." As he sings the opposite cousinhood shall respond by chanting, "Hyenh, Hyenh, Hyenh, Hyenh," until the song is ended. (95-XII,EUC)

47. If the female heirs of a Confederate Lords title become extinct, the title right shall be given by the Lords of the Confederacy to the sister family whom they shall elect and that family shall hold the name and transmit it to their (female) heirs, but they shall not appoint any of their sons as a candidate for a title until all the eligible men of the former family shall have died or otherwise have become ineligible. (25-XXV,TLL)

48. If all the heirs of a Lordship title become extinct and all the families in the clan, then the title shall be given by the Lords of the Confederacy to the family in a sister clan whom they shall elect. (26-XXVI,TLL)

49. If any of the Royaneh women, heirs of a titleship, shall wilfully withhold a Lordship or other title and refuse to bestow it, or if such heirs abandon, forsake or despise their heritage, then shall such women be deemed buried and their family extinct. The titleship shall then revert to a sister family or clan upon application and complaint. The Lords of the Confederacy shall elect the family or clan which shall in future hold the title. (28-XXVIII,TLL)

50. The Royaneh women of the Confederacy heirs of the Lordship titles shall elect two women of their family as cooks for the Lord when the people shall assemble at his house for business or other purposes.

It is not good nor honorable for a Confederate Lord to allow his people whom he has called to go hungry. (62-LXII,TLL)

51. When a Lord holds a conference in his home, his wife, if she wishes, may prepare the food for the Union Lords who assemble with him. This is an honorable right which she may exercise and an expression of her esteem. (38-XXXVIII,TLL)

52. The Royaneh women, heirs of the Lordship titles, shall, should it be necessary, correct and admonish the holders of their titles. Those only who attend the Council may

do this and those who do not shall not object to what has been said nor strive to undo the action. (63-LXIII,TLL)

53. When the Royaneh women, holders of a Lordship title, select one of their sons as a candidate, they shall select one who is trustworthy, of good character, of honest disposition, one who manages his own affairs, supports his own family, if any, and who has proven a faithful man to his Nation. (64-LXIV,TLL)

54. When a Lordship title becomes vacant through death or other cause, the Royaneh women of the clan in which the title is hereditary shall hold a council and shall choose one from among their sons to fill the office made vacant. Such a candidate shall not be the father of any Confederate Lord. If the choice is unanimous the name is referred to the men relatives of the clan. If they should disapprove it shall be their duty to select a candidate from among their own number. If then the men and women are unable to decide which of the two candidates shall be named, then the matter shall be referred to the Confederate Lords in the Clan. They shall decide which candidate shall be named. If the men and women agree to a candidate his name shall be referred to the sister clans for confirmation. If the sister clans confirm the choice, they shall refer their action to their Confederate Lords who shall ratify the choice and present it to their cousin Lords, and if the cousin Lords confirm the name then the candidate shall be installed by the proper ceremony for the conferring of Lordship titles. (65-LXV,TLL)

OFFICIAL SYMBOLISM

55. A large bunch of shell strings, in the making of which the Five Nations Confederate Lords have equally contributed, shall symbolize the completeness of the union and certify the pledge of the nations represented by the Confederate Lords of the Mohawk, the Oneida, the Onondaga, the Cayuga and the Seneca, that all are united and formed into one body or union called the Union of the Great Law, which they have established.

A bunch of shell strings is to be the symbol of the council fire of the Five Nations Confederacy. And the Lord whom the Council of Fire Keepers shall appoint to speak for them in opening the council shall hold the strands of shells in his hands when speaking. When he finishes speaking he shall deposit the strings on an elevated place (or pole) so that all the assembled Lords and the people may see it and know that the council is open and in progress.

When the council adjourns the Lord who has been appointed by his comrade Lords to close it shall take the strands of shells in his hands and address the assembled Lords. Thus will the council adjourn until such a time and place as appointed by the council. Then shall the shell strings be placed in a place for safekeeping.

Every five years the Five Nations Confederate Lords and the people shall assemble together and shall ask one another if their minds are still in the same spirit of unity for the Great Binding Law and if any of the Five Nations shall not pledge continuance and steadfastness to the pledge of unity then the Great Binding Law shall dissolve. (14-XIV,TLL)

56. Five strings of shell tied together as one shall represent the Five Nations. Each string shall represent one territory and the whole a completely united territory known as the Five Nations Confederate Territory. (108-XXV,EUC)

57. Five arrows shall be bound together very strong and each arrow shall represent one nation. As the five arrows are strongly bound this shall symbolize the complete union of the nations. Thus are the Five Nations united completely and enfolded together, united into one head, one body and one mind. Therefore they shall labor, legislate and council together for the interest of future generations.

The Lords of the Confederacy shall eat together from one bowl the feast of cooked beaver's tail. While they are eating they are to use no sharp untensils for if they should they might accidentally cut one another and bloodshed would follow. All measures must be taken to prevent the spilling of blood in any way. (15-XV,TLL)

58. There are now the Five Nations Confederate Lords standing with joined hands in a circle. This signifies and provides that should any one of the Confederate Lords leave the council and this Confederacy his crown of deer's horns, the emblem of his Lordship title, together with his birthright, shall lodge on the arms of the Union Lords whose hands are so joined. He forfeits his title and the crown falls from his brow but it shall remain in the Confederacy.

A further meaning of this is that if any time any one of the Confederate Lords choose to submit to the law of a foreign people he is not longer in but out of the Confederacy, and persons of this class be called "They have alienated themselves." Likewise such persons who submit to laws of foreign nations shall forfeit all birthrights and claims on the Five Nations Confederacy and territory.

You, the Five Nations Confederate Lords, be firm to that if a tree falls upon your joined arms it shall not separate you or weaken your hold. So shall the strength of the union be preserved. (16-XIV,TLL)

59. A bunch of wampum shells on strings, three spans of the hand in length, the upper half of the bunch being white and the lower half black, and formed from equal contributions of the men of the Five Nations, shall be a token that the men have combined themselves into one head, one body and one thought, and it shall also symbolize their ratification of the peace pact of the Confederacy, whereby the Lords of the Five Nations have established the Great Peace.

The white portion of the shell strings represent the women and the black portion the men. The black portion, furthermore, is a token of power and authority vested in the men of the Five Nations.

The string of wampum vests the people with the right to correct their erring Lords. In case a part of all the Lords pursue a course not vouched for by the people and heed not the third warning of their women relatives, then the matter shall be taken to the General Council of the women of the Five Nations. If the Lords notified and warned three times fail to heed, then the case falls into the hands of the men of the Five Nations. The War Chiefs shall then, by right of such power and authority, enter the open council to warn the Lord or Lords to return from their wrong course. If the Lords heed the warning they shall say, "we will reply tomorrow." If then an answer is returned in favor of justice and in accord with this Great Law, then the Lords shall individually pledge themselves again by again furnishing the necessary shells for the pledge. Then shall the War Chief or Chiefs exhort the Lords urging them to be just and true.

Should it happen that the Lords refuse to heed the third warning, then two courses are open: either the men may decide in their council to depose the Lord or Lords or to club them to death with war clubs. Should they in their council decide to take the first course the War Chief shall address the Lord or Lords, saying: "Since you the Lords of the Five Nations have refused to return to the procedure of the Constitution, we now declare your seats vacant, we take off your horns, the token of your Lordship, and others shall be chosen and installed in your seats, therefore vacate your seats."

Should the men in their council adopt the second course, the War Chief shall order his men to enter the Council, to take positions beside the Lords, sitting between them wherever possible. When this is accomplished the War Chief holding in his outstretched hand a bunch of black wampum strings shall say to the erring Lords: "So now, Lords of the Five United Nations, harken to these last words from your men. You have not heeded the warnings of the women relatives, you have not heeded the warnings of the General Council of women and you have not heeded the warnings of the men of the nations, all urging you to return to the right course of action. Since you are determined to resist and to withhold justice from your people there is only once course for us to adopt." At this point the War Chief shall let drop the bunch of black wampum and the men shall spring to their feet and club the erring Lords to death. Any erring Lord may submit before the War Chief lets fall the black wampum. Then his execution is withheld.

The Black wampum here used symbolizes that the power to execute is buried but that it may be raised up again by the men. It is buried but when occasion arises, they may pull it up and derive their power and authority to act as here described. (SPW 81XII)

60. A broad dark belt of wampum of thirty-eight rows, having a white heart in the center, on either side of which are two white squares all connected with the heart by white rows of beads shall be the emblem of the unity of the Five Nations.[1]

The first of the squares on the left represents the Mohawk nation and its territory; the second square on the left and the one near the heart, represents the Oneida nation and its territory; the white heart in the middle represents the Onondaga nation and its territory, and it also means that the heart of the Five Nations is single in its loyalty to the Great Peace, that the Great Peace is lodged in the heart (meaning with Onondaga Confederate Lords), and that the Council Fire is to burn there for the Five Nations, and further, it means that the authority is given to advance the cause of peace whereby hostile nations out of the Confederacy shall cease warfare; the white square to the right of the heart represents the Cayuga nation and its territory and the fourth and last white square represents the Seneca nation and its territory.

White shall here symbolize that no evil or jealous thoughts shall creep into the minds of the Lords while in council under the Great Peace. White the emblem of peace, love, charity and equity surrounds and guards the Five Nations. (84-EUC,1)

61. Should a great calamity threaten the generations rising and living of the Five United Nations, then he who is able to climb to the top of the Tree of the Great Long Leaves may do so. When, then, he reaches the top of the Tree he shall look about in all directions, and, should he see that evil things indeed are approaching, then he shall call to the people of the Five United Nations assembled beneath the Tree of Great Long Leaves and say: "A calamity threatens your happiness."

Then shall the Lords convene in council and discuss the impending evil.

When all the truths relating to the trouble shall be fully known and found to be truths, then shall the people seek out a Tree of Ka-hon-ka-ah-go-nah,[2] and when they shall find it they shall assmeble their heads together and lodge for a time between its roots. Then, their labors being finished, they may hope for happiness for many days after. (II-85,EUC)

62. When the Confederate Council of the Five Nations declares for a reading of the belts of shell calling to mind these laws, they shall provide for the reader a specially made mat woven of the fibers of wild hemp. The mat shall not be used again, for such formality is called the honoring of the importance of the law. (XXXVI-36,TLL)

63. Should two sons of opposite sides of the council fire agree in a desire to hear the reciting of the laws of the Great Peace and so refresh their memories in the way ordained by the founder of the Confederacy, they shall notify Adodarho. He then shall consult with five of his coactive Lords and they in turn shall consult their eight brethren. Then should they decide to accede to the request of the two sons from opposite sides of the Council Fire, Adodarhoh shall send messengers to notify the Chief Lords of each of the Five Nations. Then they shall dispatch their War Chiefs to notify their brother and cousin Lords of the meeting and its time and place.

When all have come and have assembled, Adodarhoh, in conjunction with his cousin Lords, shall appoint one Lord who shall repeat the laws of the Great Peace. Then shall they announce who they have chosen to repeat the laws of the Great Peace to the two sons. Then shall the chosen one repeat the laws of the Great Peace. (LXIII-43,TLL)

64. At the ceremony of the installation of Lords if there is only one expert speaker and singer of the law and the Pacification Hymn to stand at the council fire, then when this speaker and singer has finished addressing one side of the fire he shall go to the

---

1. This is the "Hiawatha Belt" purchased by John Boyd Thatcher of Albany and now in the Congressional Library.

2. A great swamp Elm.

opposite side and reply to his own speech and song. He shall thus act for both sides of the fire until the entire ceremony has been completed. Such a speaker and singer shall be termed the "Two Faced" because he speaks and sings for both sides of the fire. (XLIX-49,TLL)

65. I Dekanawida, and the Union Lords, now uproot the tallest pine tree and into the cavity thereby made we cast all weapons of war. Into the depths of the earth, down into the deep underearth currents of water flowing to unknown regions we cast all the weapons of strife. We bury them from sight and we plant again the tree. Thus shall the Great Peace be established and hostilities shall no longer be known between the Five Nations but peace to the United People.

LAW OF ADOPTION

66. The father of a child of great comliness, learning, ability or specially loved because of some circumstance may, at the will of the child's clan, select a name from his own (the father's) clan and bestow it by ceremony, such as is provided. This naming shall be only temporary and shall be called, "A name hung about the neck." (XII-96,EUC)

67. Should any person, a member of the Five Nations' Confederacy, speciallv esteem a man or woman of another clan or of a foreign nation, he may choose a name and bestow it upon that person so esteemed. The naming shall be in accord with the ceremony of bestowing names. Such a name is only a temporary one and shall be called "A name hung about the neck." A short string of shells shall be delivered with the name as a record and a pledge. (XIV-97,EUC)

68. Should any member of the Five Nations, a family or person belonging to a foreign nation submit a proposal for adoption into a clan of one of the Five Nations, he or they shall furnish a string of shells, a span in length, as a pledge to the clan into which he or they wish to be adopted. The Lords of the nation shall then consider the proposal and submit a decision. (XXI-104-EUC)

69. Any member of the Five Nations who through esteem or other feeling wishes to adopt an individual, a family or number of families may offer adoption to him or them and if accepted the matter shall be brought to the attention of the Lords for confirmation and the Lords must confirm the adoption (XXII-105-EUC)

70. When the adoption of anyone shall have been confirmed by the Lords of the Nation, the Lords shall address the people of their nation and say: "Now you of our nation, be informed that such a person, such a family or such families have ceased forever to bear their birth nation's name and have buried it in the depths of the earth. Henceforth let no one of our nation ever mention the original name or nation of their birth. To do so will be to hasten the end of our peace. (XXIII-106-EUC)

LAWS OF EMIGRATION

71. When any person or family belonging to the Five Nations desires to abandon their birth nation and the territory of the Five Nations, they shall inform the Lords of their nation and the Confederate Council of the Five Nations shall take cognizance of it. (XXXIX-39-TLL)

72. When any person or any of the people of the Five Nations emigrate and reside in a region distant from the territory of the Five Nations Confederacy, the Lord of the Five Nations at will may send a messenger carrying a broad belt of black shells and when the messenger arrives he shall call the people together or address them personally displaying the belt of shells and they shall know that this is an order for them to return to their original homes and to their council fires. (XL-40,TLL)

RIGHTS OF FOREIGN NATIONS

73. The soil of the earth from one end of the land to the other is the property of the people who inhabit it. By birthright the Ongwehonweh (Original beings) are the owners of the soil which they own and occupy and none other may hold it. The same law has been held from the oldest times.

The Great Creator has made us of the one blood and of the same soil he made us and as only different tongues constitute different nations he established different hunting grounds and territories and made boundary lines between them. (LXIX-69,TLL)

74. When any alien nation or individual is admitted into the Five Nations the admission shall be understood only to be a temporary one. Should the person or nation create loss, do wrong or cause suffering of any kind to endanger the peace ot the Confederacy, the Confederate Lords shall order one of their war chiefs to reprimand him or them and if a similar offense is again committed the offending party or parties shall be expelled from the territory of the Five United Nations (XXVI-119,EUC)

75. When a member of an alien nation comes to the territory of the Five Nations and seeks refuge and permanent residence, the Lord of the Nations to which he comes shall extend hospitality and make him a member of the nation. Then shall he be accorded equal rights and privileges in all matters except as after mentioned. (XXXVII-120,EUC)

76. No body of alien people who have been adopted temporarily shall have a vote in the council of the Lords of the Confederacy, for only they who have been invested with Lordship titles may vote in the Council. Aliens have nothing by blood to make claim to a vote and should they have it, not knowing all the traditions of the Confederacy, might go against its Great Peace. In this manner the Great Peace would be endangered and perhaps be destroyed. (XXXVIII-121,EUC)

77. When the Lords of the Confederacy decide to admit a foreign nation and an adoption is made, the Lords shall inform the adopted nation that its admission is only temporary. They shall also say to the nation that it must never try to control, to interfere with or to injure the Five Nations nor disregard the Great Peace or any of its rules or customs. That in no way should they cause disturbance or injury. Then should the adopted nation disregard these injunctions, their adoption shall be annulled and they shall be expelled.

The expulsion shall be in the following manner: The council shall appoint one of their War Chiefs to convey the message of annulment and he shall say, "You (naming the nation) listen to me while I speak. I am here to inform you again of the will of the Five Nations' Council. It was clearly made known to you at a former time. Now the Lords of the Five Nations have decided to expel you and cast you out. We disown you now and annul your adoption. Therefore you must look for a path in which to go and lead away all your people. It was you, not we, who committed wrong and caused this sentence of annulment. So then go your way and depart from the territory of the Five Nations and from the Confederacy." (XXXIX-122,EUC)

78. Whenever a foreign nation enters the Confederacy or accepts the Great Peace, the Five Nations and the foreign nation shall enter into an agreement and compact by which the foreign nation shall endeavor to persuade other nations to accept the Great Peace. (XLVI-46,TLL)

RIGHTS AND POWERS OF WAR

79. Skanawiatih shall be vested with a double office, duty and with double authority. One-half of his being shall hold the Lordship title and the other half shall hold the title of War Chief. In the event of war he shall notify the five War Chiefs of the Confederacy

and command them to prepare for war and have their men ready at the appointed time and place for engagement with the enemy of the Great Peace. (I-70,SPW)

80. When the Confederate Council of the Five Nations has for its object the establishment of the Great Peace among the people of an outside nation and that nation refuses to accept the Great Peace, then by such refusal they bring a declaration of war upon themselves from the Five Nations. Then shall the Five Nations seek to establish the Great Peace by conquest of the rebellious nation. (II-71,SPW)

81. When the men of the Five Nations, now called forth to become warriors, are ready for battle with an obstinate opposing nation that has refused to accept the Great Peace then one of the Five War Chiefs shall be chosen by the warriors of the Five Nations to lead the army into battle. It shall be the duty of the War Chief so chosen to come before his warriors and address them. His aim shall be to impress upon them the necessity of good behavior and strict obedience to all the commands of the War Chiefs. He shall deliver an oration exhorting them with great zeal to be brave and courageous and never to be guilty of cowardice. At the conclusion of his oration he shall march forward and commence the War Song and he shall sing:

> Now I am greatly surprised
> And, therefore, I shall use it,-
> The power of my War Song.
> I am of the Five Nations
> And I shall make supplication
> To the Almighty Creator
> He has furnished this army.
> My warriors shall be mighty[1]
> In the strength of the Creator
> Between him and my song they are
> For it was he who gave the song
> This war song that I sing!
> (III-72,SPW)

82. When the warriors of the Five Nations are on an expedition against an enemy, the War Chief shall sing the War Song as he approaches the country of the enemy and not cease until his scouts have reported that the army is near the enemies' lines when the War Chief shall approach with great caution and prepare for the attack. (IV-73,SPW)

83. When peace shall have been established by the termination of the war against a foreign nation, then the War Chief shall cause all the weapons of war to be taken from the nation. Then shall the Great Peace be established and that nation shall observe all the rules of the Great Peace for all time to come. (V-74,SPW)

84. Whenever a foreign nation is conquered or has by their own will accepted the Great Peace their own system of internal government may continue, but they must cease all warfare against other nations. (VI-75,SPW)

85. Whenever a war against a foreign nation is pushed until that nation is about exterminated because of its refusal to accept the Great Peace and if that nation shall by its obstinacy become exterminated, all their rights, property and territory shall become the property of the Five Nations. (VII-76,SPW)

86. Whenever a foreign nation is conquered and the survivors are brought into the territory of the Five Nations' Confederacy and placed under the Great Peace the two shall be known as the Conqueror and the Conquered. A symbolic relationship shall be devised and be placed in some symbolic position. The conquered nation shall have no voice in the councils of the Confederacy in the body of the Lords. (VIII-77,SPW)

---

1. It will be recalled that when the Eriez demanded by what power the Five Nations demanded their surrender, the Iroquois replied "The Master of Life fights for us!"

87. When the War of the Five Nations on a foreign rebellious nation is ended, peace shall be restored to that nation by a withdrawal of all their weapons of war by the War Chief of the Five Nations. When all the terms of peace shall have been agreed upon a state of friendship shall be established. (IX-78,SPW)

88. When the proposition to establish the Great Peace is made to a foreign nation it shall be done in mutual council. The foreign nation is to be persuaded by reason and urged to come into the Great Peace. If the Five Nations fail to obtain the consent of the nation at the first council a second council shall be held and upon a second failure a third council shall be held and this third council shall end the peaceful methods of persuasion. At the third council the War Chief of the Five Nations shall address the Chief of the foreign nation and request him three times to accept the Great Peace. If refusal steadfastly follows the War Chief shall let the bunch of white lake shells drop from his outstretched hand to the ground and shall bound quickly forward and club the offending chief to death. War shall thereby be declared and the War Chief shall have his warriors at his back to meet any emergency. War must continue until the contest is won by the Five Nations. (X-79,SPW)

89. When the Lords of the Five Nations propose to meet in conference with a foreign nation with proposals for an acceptance of the Great Peace, a large band of warriors shall conceal themselves in a secure place safe from the espionage of the foreign nation but as near at hand as possible. Two warriors shall accompany the Union Lord who carries the proposals and these warriors shall be especially cunning. Should the Lord be attacked these warriors shall hasten back to the army of warriors with the news of the calamity which fell through the treachery of the foreign nation. (XI-80,SPW)

90. When the Five Nations' Council declares war any Lord of the Confederacy may enlist with the warriors by temporarily renouncing his sacred Lordship title which he holds through the election of his women relatives. The title then reverts to them and they may bestow it upon another temporarily until the war is over when the Lord, if living, may resume his title and seat in the Council. (XII-82,SPW)

91. A certain wampum belt of black beads shall be the emblem of the authority of the Five War Chiefs to take up the weapons of war and with their men to resist invasion. This shall be called a war in defense of the territory. (XIV-83,SPW)

TREASON OR SECESSION OF A NATION.

92. If a nation, part of a nation, or more than one nation within the Five Nations should in any way endeavor to destroy the Great Peace by neglect or violating its laws and resolve to dissolve the Confederacy such a nation or such nations shall be deemed guilty of treason and called enemies of the Confederacy and the Great Peace.

It shall then be the duty of the Lords of the Confederacy who remain faithful to resolve to warn the offending people. They shall be warned once and if a second warning is necessary they shall be driven from the territory of the Confederacy by the War Chiefs and his men. (III,86,EUC)

RIGHTS OF THE PEOPLE OF THE FIVE NATIONS

93. Whenever a specially important matter or a great emergency is presented before the Confederate Council and the nature of the mattter affects the entire body of Five Nations threatening their utter ruin, then the Lords of the Confederacy must submit the matter to the decision of their people and the decision of the people shall affect the decision of the Confederate Council. This decision shall be a confirmation of the voice of the people. (XV-84,SPW)

94. The men of every clan of the Five Nations shall have a Council Fire ever burning in readiness for a council of the clan. When it seems necessary for a council to be held to discuss the welfare of the clans, then the men may gather about the fire. This council shall have the same rights as the council of the women. (V-88,EUC)

95. The women of every clan of the Five Nations shall have a Council Fire ever burning in readiness for a council of the clan. When in their opinion it seems necessary for the interest of the people they shall hold a council and their decision and recommendation shall be introduced before the Council of Lords by the War Chief for its consideration. (VI-87,EUC)

96. All the Clan council fires of a nation or of the Five Nations may unite into one general council fire, or delegates from all the council fires may be appointed to unite in a general council for discussing the interests of the people. The people shall have the right to make appointments and to delegate their power to others of their number. When their council shall have come to a conclusion on any matter, their decision shall be reported to the Council of the Nation or to the Confederate Council (as the case may require) by the War Chief or the War Chiefs. (VI-89,EUC)

97. Before the real people united their nations, each nation had its council fires. Before the Great Peace their councils were held. The Five Council Fires shall continue to burn as before and they are not quenched. The Lords of each nation in future shall settle their nations' affairs at this council fire governed always by the laws and rules of the council of the Confederacy and by the Great Peace. (VII-90.EUC)

98. If either a nephew or a niece see an irregularity in the performance of the functions of the Great Peace and its laws, in the Confederate Council or in the conferring of Lordship titles in an improper way, through their War Chief they may demand that such actions become subject to correction and that the matter conform to the ways prescribed by the laws of the Great Peace. (LXVII-67,TLL)

RELIGIOUS CEREMONIES PROTECTED

99. The rites and festivals of each nation shall remain undisturbed and shall continue as before because they were given by the people of old times as useful and necessary for the good of men. (XVI-99,EUC)

100. It shall be the duty of the Lords of each brotherhood to confer at the approach of the time of the Midwinter Thanksgiving and to notify their people of the approaching festival. They shall hold a council over the matter and arrange its details and begin the Thanksgiving five days after the moon of Dis-ko-nah is new. The people shall assemble at the appointed place and the nephews shall notify the people of the time and place. From the beginning to the end the Lords shall preside over the Thanksgiving and address the people from time to time.(XVII-100,EUC)

101. It shall be the duty of the appointed managers of the Thanksgiving festivals to do all that is needful for carrying out the duties of the occasions.
    The recognized festivals of Thanksgiving shall be the Midwinter Thanksgiving, the Maple or Sugar-making Thanksgiving, the Raspberry Thanksgiving, the Strawberry Thanksgiving, the Corn-Planting Thanksgiving, the Corn Hoeing Thanksgiving, the Little Festival of Green Corn, the Great Festival of Ripe Corn and the complete Thanksgiving for the Harvest.
    Each nation's festivals shall be held in their Long Houses. (XVIII-101,EUC)

102. When the Thanksgiving for the Green Corn comes the special managers, both the men and women shall give it careful attention and do their duties properly. (XIX-102,EUC)

103. When the Ripe Corn Thanksgiving is celebrated the Lords of the Nation must give it the same attention as they give to the Midwinter Thanksgiving. (XX-103,EUC)

104. Whenever any man proves himself by his good life and his knowledge of good things, naturally fitted as a teacher of good things, he shall be recognized by the Lords as a teacher of peace and religion and the people shall hear him. (X-93,EUC)

THE INSTALLATION SONG

105. The song used in installing the new Lord of the Confederacy shall be sung by Adodarhoh and it shall be:

Haii, haii, Agwah wi-yoh
Haii, haii, A-kon-he-watha,
Haii, haii, Ska-we-ye-se-go-wah
Haii, haii, Yon-gwa-wih
Haii, haii, Ya-kon-he-wa-tha

Haii, haii, It is good indeed
Haii, haii, (That) a broom, —
Haii, haii, A great wing,
Haii, haii, It is given me
Haii, haii, For a sweeping instrument.
(LVIII-58,TLL)

106. Whenever a person properly entitled desires to learn the Pacification Song he is privileged to do so but he must prepare a feast at which his teachers may sit with him and sing. The feast is provided that no misfortune may befall them for singing the song on an occasion when no chief is installed. (XXIV-107,EUC)

PROTECTION OF THE HOUSE

107. A certain sign shall be known to all the people of the Five Nations which shall denote that the owner or occupant of a house is absent. A stick or pole in a slanting or leaning position shall indicate this and be the sign. Every person not entitled to enter the house by right of living within it upon seeing such a sign shall not approach the house either by day or by night but will keep as far away as his business will permit. (IX-92,EUC)

FUNERAL ADDRESSES

108. At the funeral of a Lord of the Confederacy, say: "Now we become reconciled as you start away. You were once a Lord of the Five Nations' Confederacy and the United People trusted you. Now we release you for it is true that it is no longer possible for us to walk about together on the earth. Now, therefore, we lay it (the body) here. Here we lay it away. Now then we say to you, 'Persevere onward to the place where the Creator dwells in peace. Let not the things of the earth hinder you, Let nothing that transpired while yet you lived hinder you. In hunting you once took delight; in the game of Lacrosse you once took delight and in the feasts and pleasant occasions your mind was amused, but now do not allow thought of these things to give you trouble. Let not your

relatives hinder you and also let not your friends and associates trouble your mind. Regard none of these things.'

"Now then, in turn, you here present who were related to this man and you who were his friends and associates, behold the path that is yours also! Soon we ourselves will be left in that place. For this reason hold yourselves in restraint as you go from place to place. In your actions and in your conversation do no idle thing. Speak not idle talk neither gossip. Be careful of this and speak not and do not give way to evil behavior. One year is the time that you must abstain from unseemly levity but if you can not do this for ceremony, ten days is the time to regard these things for respect."

109. At the funeral of a War Chief, say:
"Now we become reconciled as you start away. You were once a war chief of the Five Nations Confederacy and the United People trusted you as their guard from the enemy. (The remainder of the address is the same at the funeral of a Lord.) (XXVII-110,EUC)

110. At the funeral of a Warrior say:
"Now we become reconciled as you start away. Once you were a devoted provider and protector of your family and you were ever ready to take part in battles for the Five Nations' Confederacy. The United People trusted you. (The remainder is the same as the address at the funeral of a Lord.) (XXVII-111,EUC)

111. At the funeral of a young man, say:
"Now we become reconciled as you start away. In the beginning of your career you are taken away and the flower of your life is withered away. (The remainder is the same as the address at the funeral of a Lord.) (XXIX-112,EUC)

112. At the funeral of a chief woman say:
"Now we become reconciled as you start away. You were once a chiefwoman in the Five Nations' Confederacy. You once were a mother of the nations. Now we release you for it is true that it is no longer possible for us to walk about together on the earth. Now, therefore, we lay it (the body) here. Here we lay it away. Now then we say to you, 'persevere onward to the place where the Creator dwells in peace. Let not the things of the earth hinder you. Let nothing that transpired while you lived hinder you. Looking after your family was a sacred duty and you were faithful. You were one of the many joint heirs of the Lordship titles. Feastings were yours and you had pleasant occasions...'(The remainder is the same as the address at the funeral of a Lord.) (XXX-113,EUC)

113. At the funeral of a woman of the people say:
"Now we become reconciled as you start away. You were once a women in the flower of life and the bloom is now withered away. You once held a sacred position as a mother of the nation. (Etc.) Looking after your family was a sacred duty and you were faithful. Feastings... (etc.) (The remainder is the same as the address at the funeral of a Lord.) (XXXII-115,EUC)

114. At the funeral of an infant or young woman say:
"Now we become reconciled as you start away. You were a tender bud and gladdened our hearts for only a few days. Now the bloom has withered away... (etc.) Let none of the things that transpired on earth hinder you. Let nothing that happened while you lived hinder you. (The remainder is the same as the address at the funeral of a Lord.) (XXXII-115,EUC)

115. When an infant dies within three days mourning shall continue only five days. Then shall you gather the little boys and girls at the house of mourning and at the funeral feast a speaker shall address the children and bid them be happy once more, though by a death, gloom has been cast over them. Then shall the black clouds roll away and the sky shall show blue once more. Then shall the children be again in sunshine. (XXXIII-116,EUC)

116. When a dead person is brought to the burial place, the speaker on the opposite side of the Council Fire shall bid the bereaved family cheer their minds once again and rekindle their hearth fires in peace, to put their houses in order and once again be in brightness for darkness has covered them. He shall say that the black clouds shall roll away and that the bright blue sky is visible once more. Therefore shall they be in peace in the sunshine again. (XXXIV-117,EUC)

117. .Three strings of shell one span in length shall be employed in addressing the assemblage at the burial of the dead. The speaker shall say:

"Hearken you who are here this body is to be covered. Assemble in this place again ten days hence for it is the decree of the Creator that mourning shall cease when ten days have expired. Then shall a feast be made."

Then at the expiration of ten days the Speaker shall say: "Continue to listen you who are here. The ten days of mourning have expired and your minds must now be freed of sorrow as before the loss of the relative. The relatives have decided to make a little compensation to those who have assisted at the funeral. It is a mere expression of thanks. This is to the one who did the cooking while the body was lying in the house. Let her come forward and receive this gift and be dismissed from the task. In substance this shall be repeated for every one who assisted in any way until all have been remembered. (XXXV-118,EUC)

JOIN, or DIE.

In one of America's first editorial cartoons, Benjamin Franklin advocated colonial unity with the slogan "Join, or Die."

This drawing appeared in the *Pennsylvania Gazette* May 9, 1754, just before the Albany Conference with the Iroquois.

Franklin admitted that the Albany Plan of Union developed at the Conference was similar to and inspired by the League of the Iroquois.

Appendix B

THE ALBANY PLAN
OF UNION

July 10, 1754

Plan of a Proposed Union of the Several Colonies of Massachusetts bay, New Hampshire, Connecticut, Rhode Island, New York, New Jerseys, Pensilvania, Maryland, Virginia, North Carolina, and South Carolina, For their Mutual Defence and Security, and for Extending the British Settlements in North America.

That humble Application be made for an Act of the Parliament of Great Britain, by Virtue of which, one General Government may be formed in America, including all the said Colonies, within and under which Government, each colony may retain its present Constitution, except in the Particulars wherein a Change may be directed by the said Act, as hereafter follows:

That the said General Government be administered by a President General, to be appointed and supported by the Crown, and a Grand Council to be Chosen by the Representatives of the People of the Several Colonies, met in their respective Assemblies.

That within _ _ _ _ _ _ _ months after the passing of such Act, The House of Representatives in the Several Assemblies, that Happen to be Sitting within that time or that shall be Specially for that purpose Convened, may and Shall choose Members for the Grand Council in the following Proportions, that is to say:

Massachusetts Bay	7
New Hampshire	2
Connecticut	5
Rhode Island	2
New York	4
New Jersey	3
Pensilvania	6
Maryland	4
North Carolina	4
South Carolina	4
	48

Who shall meet for the first time at the City of Philadelphia, in Pensilvania, being called by the President General as soon as conveniently may be after his appointment.

That there shall be a New Election of Members for the Grand Council every three years; And on the Death or Resignation of any Member his Place Shall be Supplyed by a New Choice at the next Sitting of the Assembly of the Colony he represented.

That after the first three years, when the Proportion of Money arising out of each Colony to the General Treasury can be known, The Number of members to be Chosen, for each Colony shall from time to time in all ensuing Elections be regulated by that proportion (yet so as that the Number to be Chosen by any one Province be not more than Seven nor less than Two.)

That the Grand Council shall meet once in every year, and oftener if Occasion require, at such Time and place as they shall adjourn to at the last preceding meeting, or as they shall be called to meet at by the President General, on any Emergency, he having first obtained in Writing the Consent of seven of the Members to such call, and sent due and timely Notice to the whole.

That the Grand Council have Power to Chuse their Speaker, and shall neither be dissolved, prorogued nor Continue sitting longer than Six Weeks at one Time without their own Consent, or the Special Command of the Crown.

That the Members of the Grand Council shall be allowed for their service ten shillings Sterling per Diem, during their Session or Journey to and from the Place of the Meeting; Twenty miles to be reckoned a days Journey.

That the Assent of the President General be requisite, to all Acts of the Grand Council, and that it be His office and Duty to cause them to be carried into Execution.

That the President General with the Advice of the Grand Council, hold or Direct all Indian Treaties in which the General Interest or welfare of the Colony's may be Concerned; And make Peace or Declare War with the Indian Nations.

That they make such Laws as they Judge Necessary for regulating all Indian Trade. That they make all Purchases from Indians for the Crown, of Lands not within the Bounds of Particular Colonies, or that shall not be within their Bounds when some of them are reduced to more Convenient Dimensions. That they make New Settlements on such Purchases, by Granting Lands for regulating and Governing such new Settlements, till the Crown shall think fit to form them into Particular Governments.

That they raise and pay Soldiers, and build Forts for the Defence of any of the Colonies, and equip Vessels of Force to Guard the Coasts and Protect the Trade on the Ocean, Lakes, or Great Rivers; But they shall not impress Men in any Colonies, without the Consent of its legislature. That for these purposes they have Power to make Laws and lay and levy such General Duties, Imposts, or Taxes, as to them shall appear most equal and Just, Considering the Ability and other Circumstances of the Inhabitants in the Several Colonies, and such as may be Collected with the least inconvenience to the People, rather discouraging Luxury, than loading Industry with unnecessary Burthens. That they may appoint a General Treasurer and a Particular Treasurer in each Government, when necessary, and from time to time, may order the Sums in the Treasuries of each Government, into the General Treasury, or draw on them for Special payments as they find most Convenient; Yet no money to Issue, but by joint orders of the President General and Grand Council Except where sums have been appropriated to particular Purposes, and the President General is previously impowered by An Act to draw for such Sums.

Portrait of Tee Tee Need Ga Row, Old Hendrick. Painted in 1710 by Verelst when Hendrick was visiting Europe. This is said to be the earliest illustration of a wampum belt with tubular beads. Hendrick was named "Emperor of the Six Nations" by the British Queen.

Courtesy Smithsonian Institution.

Cornplanter, as seen by a painter of the times.

Joseph Brant, from a painting done in England.